ROUTLEDGE LIBRARY EDITIONS:
EARLY WESTERN RESPONSES
TO SOVIET RUSSIA

Volume 9

BOLSHEVIST RUSSIA

BOLSHEVIST RUSSIA

ANTON KARLGREN

Routledge
Taylor & Francis Group
LONDON AND NEW YORK

First published in Swedish under the title 'Bolstevikernas Ryssland'
First published in English in 1927 by George Allen & Unwin Ltd

This edition first published in 2018
by Routledge
2 Park Square, Milton Park, Abingdon, Oxon OX14 4RN

and by Routledge
711 Third Avenue, New York, NY 10017

Routledge is an imprint of the Taylor & Francis Group, an informa business

British Library Cataloguing in Publication Data
A catalogue record for this book is available from the British Library

ISBN: 978-1-138-04993-2 (Set)
ISBN: 978-1-315-11072-1 (Set) (ebk)
ISBN: 978-1-138-06995-4 (Volume 9) (hbk)
ISBN: 978-1-138-07010-3 (Volume 9) (pbk)
ISBN: 978-1-315-11517-7 (Volume 9) (ebk)

Publisher's Note
The publisher has gone to great lengths to ensure the quality of this reprint but points out that some imperfections in the original copies may be apparent.

BOLSHEVIST RUSSIA

BY

ANTON KARLGREN

Translated from the Swedish by

ANNA BARWELL

LONDON: GEORGE ALLEN & UNWIN LTD.
RUSKIN HOUSE, 40 MUSEUM STREET, W.C. 1

First published in Sweden under the title
BOLSTEVIKERNAS RYSSLAND

First published in English in 1927

Printed in Great Britain by
Unwin Brothers, Ltd., Woking

FOREWORD

THE present book, originally published in Swedish, deals with the social state of Russia as it now is, after eight years of Bolshevist rule and influence; in it I have traced its development up to the end of 1925.

I have always been interested in Russian social conditions—from 1904 to 1916 I visited the country every year and was, amongst other things, correspondent to the Swedish Press in the days of the first Imperial Duma (1906). Hence during the revolution years I have, on the one hand, endeavoured to utilize all opportunities that presented themselves to an outside observer wishing to form a correct judgment of Russian affairs—and here, I must own, I took less interest in the Bolshevist theoretical propagandist writings than in the Russian literature and newspapers which reflected these theories as translated into practice; on the other hand, for some months in 1924, I have studied conditions on the spot during a visit to Russia which tended considerably to modify my former conception of Soviet Russia and also, as I had hoped, gave me wider knowledge on which to form a judgment of its further development.

COPENHAGEN,
Spring, 1926.

CONTENTS

BOLSHEVIST RUSSIA

CHAPTER I

THE SUPREME POWER OF THE PROLETARIATE

"The supreme power of the proletariate!" Now, in the ninth year of Bolshevism, what reality lies behind these words expressing, as they do, the very key-note of the Bolshevist system?

"The supreme power of the proletariate"—what a perspective these words opened before the eyes of the Russian proletariate when they were first pronounced! It is true this enormous proletariate did not know much about Bolshevism, but they felt they did, since to have read Lenin was all that they needed for complete understanding of the matter. This was something for them—and with delight they began to build on the promises contained in the phrase itself. From the first, these words, in their direct simplicity, possessed a note of stimulation and flattery even in the ears of the Western proletariate, especially when accompanied by accounts of all the good things this "supreme power" was giving to the Russian proletariate.

Has this supreme power fulfilled the expectations of the Russian proletariate and the beliefs of that of the West?

* * *

"The supreme power of the proletariate"—from the very first, as we have said, the fact was quite clear to the Russian masses. What else could it mean but that, after the oppression of tsardom, they had now a perfectly free rein? Now, at last, they could stretch their limbs—and this they did with such good will that the cracking of their joints was felt throughout the whole social body. Away in the villages the peasants arranged matters according to their own fancy, until the whole land was but one gigantic pyre of their masters' property ; in factories and workshops the workers took all into their own hands and followed their own inclinations with such lack of restraint that very soon every machine throughout the whole of Russia was brought to a standstill. Order, discipline, every social obligation was thrown overboard. The Russian proletariate began, with full consciousness of their goal, to bring about that social state which, for centuries, had had the warmest place in their hearts—viz. anarchy. Centuries of tsardom had not exterminated the anarchical tendencies that are in the very blood of the Russian masses, and now the time had come when they could give full vent to such desires with no fear of consequences. "The supreme power of the proletariate" was an accomplished fact, and life was pure joy.

The time of real supreme power for the proletariate proved, however, quite short. So long as it was a question of the utter destruction of old Russia, this supreme power supplied the need of the moment—that was a part of the social programme of the Bolshevists which they could leave to the uncontrolled will of the proletariate with unbounded confidence, and one in which the people's supreme power satisfied even the most exorbitant demands. But when this task was accomplished and followed by the problem of building a new social structure, then came, too, the end of the supreme power of the proletariate, such as they had pictured it in their own minds.

And then the Bolshevists began, instead, to organize the supreme power of the proletariate in accordance with their own wishes. The untamed instincts of which the masses had given ample proof had certainly, during the earlier months of Bolshevism, been utilized as a valuable revolutionary instrument, but these instincts did not suffice as sole qualification for supreme power. The proletariate, as such, were not fitted to wield supreme power—above all, not the peasant class—and, by degrees, the vast body of peasantry was informed that when the supreme power of the proletariate was mentioned, they had not been included, for the term proletariate, in that connection, meant the proletariate of the industrial workers only. Nor was even the artisan class competent as a whole ; this overwhelming majority had also to be sifted ; only a small selection from the proletariate, the few élite who, after severe tests, desired membership of the Communist Party, formed an element capable of practical political work, and therefore the supreme power must be vested in this party alone. Those outside it were, it is true, not officially deprived of a share in supreme power, but they were placed, as it was so aptly termed, under the Party's guidance. "As vanguard and leader, the Communist Party must always march at the head of the artisan and peasant classes in general political questions, assuming the initiative and filling the rôle of founders and organizers of the whole of the practical work in the upbuilding of the revolutionary-proletarian social structure."

Thus the supreme ruler for a day was put into leading-strings, most certainly a necessary proceeding in itself, but involving a very precarious position for any dictator. But the question is now, how tightly drawn are these leading-strings ? Is the position of the proletariate under the "supreme power of the proletariate" always such as to give them a sense of participation in this power ?

* * *

Bolshevism itself now expends considerable effort in its endeavours to make the influence of the lower classes felt, not only in social work but in political activities as well, and their endeavours have been extraordinarily effective in the most varied directions. In comparison with the Western parliamentary system, which, now and again, calls upon the citizen to exercise his vote at the elections, but, in the intervals, cuts him off from all political influence, the Russian Soviet system gives the Russian proletariate a far more intimate and less intermittent influence in political matters—these Soviets play such an important part in the Bolshevist government that it might quite well be simply designated as Soviet rule. And, as a result of the numberless organizations dealing with social affairs, in which the proletariate are expected to take part—factory committees, special unions, insurance companies, co-operative societies, etc.—the people do indeed, to a great extent, have a share in the management of their life. We will first turn our attention to the Soviets. What is their value as instruments of the will of the proletariate ?

In one respect, the proletariate's influence upon these important organizations is undoubtedly secure. All but the purely proletarian element is excluded, not only from membership but also from power of election to the Soviets —thus excluding the remnant of the old bourgeoisie and members of the new trading class, produced by the so-called "new" political economy, and also that element between the artisan and peasant classes, which cannot be considered as genuine proletariate, and amongst these more particularly the "kulacks,"[1] a name given, as will be shown later, to all peasants who, in any way, have struggled up out of the average misery of country villages and thus become contemptible bourgeoisie. The Soviets belong to the proletariate and are chosen by their direct vote. They certainly occupy only the lowest place amongst the existing councils, yet they form the basis upon which the whole advisory system has been built.

The importance of the Soviets has, however, been not a little diminished by one or two circumstances. That only members of the proletariate can give or receive votes is, so far, well and good, but it is, to begin with, a drawback that the proletarian voters may not decide to which members of their class their votes are to be given.

"If they ordered us to elect a horse in the village Soviet we should be compelled to do it," a peasant said, some time ago, in a congress—an apt characterization of the freedom of choice allowed in these Soviet elections. The tactics employed are ten times worse than those of Stolypin himself, whose manipulations of the Duma elections filled the world with amazement at the Russian election methods ; never has the world known any voters subjected to such unscrupulous compulsion, to such an ignominious "whipping-up," as are the Russian proletariate.

[1] Kulack = close-fisted person.

It is the communistic "guidance" which here exercises one of its manifold functions. The Communist Party gave directions from headquarters, the local communistic organizations—either the Party unions or the Young People's Societies—carried them into effect, and thus, again and again, such conformation was given to the Soviets as the circumstances required. Situations have changed and modifications in election politics have been made with this end in view—some such alterations have been made quite openly, thus affording very interesting glimpses into the inner working of the method employed.

At first, and, indeed, for long after, the guiding principle was that the vast numbers not belonging to the Party must be forced as widely as possible to vote for Communists as their representatives in the Soviets. This was necessary for several reasons: on the one hand, they had to show the world what confidence the people felt in the Communists, and on the other, to guarantee the exclusion from the councils of all disturbing elements. And everything went without the slightest hitch; the little Communist Party obtained a representation almost comically out of all proportion to their insignificant numbers. Even when the peasants, away in the villages, hated the Communists, root and branch, the elections afforded an unchanging picture of their almost touching devotion to them.

So everything went excellently. Indeed, the only trouble was that it went too well. At last, there were so many Communists in the councils that, in the long run, it became impossible to keep up the fiction of universal confidence as the reason of the excessive communistic representation. In the autumn of 1923 the situation was indeed almost farcical. The communistic credit, even amongst the artisan classes, was extraordinarily low; a strike which broke out quite unexpectedly, combined with a considerable number of other vexatious incidents, had given clear evidence of widely-spread unrest amongst the urban proletariate. When the election for the Moscow Soviet took place about the same time, the result was a brilliant communistic success. The usual shriek of triumph—the people's confidence, the failure of anti-revolutionary plots, the evident improvement in the nation's political acumen, etc.—was heard, but the enthusiasm amongst the leaders was not very striking. "It seems to me," Stalin declared in a speech before the election was quite finished, "that one of the greatest defects in these elections is the return of too few non-Party representatives. They say it would not do to check the masses in their spontaneous choice of Communists, but I have very serious doubts about it." The matter was exceedingly simple; all that was necessary, he decided, was to check the continuance of the communistic majorities.

It was, however, not until the following year, 1924, that the lines so long followed in the conduct of the Soviet elections really seemed to threaten trouble. The elections of 1924, especially in the country districts, were in two respects most disturbing. One was that the communistic representation was enormously increased. To attempt to maintain the illusion that this was the result of communistic popularity in the country districts was simply hopeless, at a time when both the Press and political speeches were filled with discussion of the evident hostility to Bolshevism in the villages and of the best methods of dealing with it. The second, and chief, was that there had been such a fatal fall in the number of voters that, in great parts of the country, it looked like nothing but a boycott of the election. It was impossible to shut one's eyes to the fact that the peasant class now felt that they had had enough of the Soviet-election farce and would have no more to do with it. The position was awkward. The Soviets, that special Bolshevist invention, the only really effective organizations for the genuine rule of the people, had been discovered to be useless by the proletariate; Bolshevism's most precious gift to the proletariate was refused by them! Moreover, the situation was dangerous. If the proletariate had managed to find out the true worth of these councils, there was reason to fear they would also find some other way of making their voice heard.

If it was possible now to save the Soviets it must be by restoring, in some way, their ruined credit. Their reputation must be re-established as bodies created by the unfettered vote of the proletariate, and, to achieve this, it was necessary to discard entirely all former election tactics. So they openly acknowledged what, up till then, had been energetically denied—and this not least in the foreign Bolshevist Press—viz. the existence of a "whipping-up" method which had reduced proletarian control of the composition of the Soviets to a minimum. "For the last few years," Kalinin himself declared at the congress of the Soviet federation in the spring of 1925, "the elections of the Soviets have, in many ways, lost the character of a political campaign. Party-cells, the communistic Young People's Societies, the Party's Executive Committees, have secured the return of their candidates, not by winning a majority by means of argument, but by some other manipulation. All this has resulted in a removal of the masses from the Soviets, until the average peasant has got the idea that, no matter how great an interest he takes in the elections, the Party-cells or the communistic Young People's Societies will, in any case, manage to push in their own candidates."

It is evident that things must have gone far before the Soviet president himself was compelled to pronounce such a severe, even if cautiously expressed, judgment on the Soviets as they then were. At the same time newspapers and political speakers made the most incredible revelations of the compulsion and trickery employed by the Communists in their control of the elections. So much, then, is certain, as evidenced by numberless authorities from Kalinin down, that, up to the autumn elections of 1924, the share in supreme power that the participation in the Soviets was, in accordance with the political programme, to give to the Russian proletariate proved, in reality, quite illusive. Now if, on the one hand, this throws a not altogether favourable light upon Bolshevist politics, on the other hand, the candid way in which the whole matter was disclosed and disapproved is all the more striking; it shows without doubt the leaders' resolve to do away with the misrepresentation. A beginning should be made at once; elections where more than 65 per cent. of the voters had taken part in the boycott or those that had been marked by specially gross instances of communistic pressure, were declared null and void, and new elections, where the proletariate should be allowed to vote as they liked, and where they were expected, in return, really to exercise that right, were proclaimed in about one-third of the land.

But if anyone thinks that in these new elections a free vote was secured for the masses and that the result was the formation of Soviets that were something more than tools in the hands of those in power and were made up of such members as they chose, then he is mistaken. One impediment to the promised reform was found, first and foremost, in the Communists whose task it was to carry out the new principles amongst the masses. "It is no fault of the village Communist," one author in *Pravda* wrote after the election, "that after three years' service in the army and four years' rule in the village he cannot, in the space of twenty-four hours, change his methods of work amongst the peasants." If the Communist Party had, for years, required their representatives to superintend the "whipping-up" process, they could not expect to see them changed in the twinkling of an eye into discreet kid-gloved masters of the ceremonies at the civic festivals which the Soviet elections were to become, now that they had ceased to be circus performances. To begin with, the Communists, out in the country districts, did not understand one iota of the whole matter. It was said in *Pravda*: "The Communists are depressed, dispirited and perplexed." And could this be wondered at, when years of conscientious work were so totally undervalued? Here they had, in accordance with instructions received, stuffed the Soviets full of Communists—and now they were informed that there were far too many Communists in the Soviets! But then they accepted the Party views and reversed their work, in accordance with the new demands; unwilling peasants were dragged by the hair of their heads to the voting booths (in parenthesis it may be said that the Bolshevists dare not venture upon a secret vote system) and compelled to elect to the Soviets endless numbers of non-Party representatives, against which they set up a desperate resistance, but in vain.

Meantime, it was not only the subordinates amongst the Communist Party who, in this way, found it difficult to give up the conviction, gained by several years of practical experience, that the proletariate required absolute "guidance" in one direction or the other at Soviet elections. The idea never occurred even to the Party leaders—in spite of their declamations of a free choice—to allow the proletariate to go to vote without keeping a firm hold of their collars.

Behind the interpretation given by local communistic members to the new signals, the directng finger of those in power was very evident and all the more persistently used, since the result of this fresh election was a matter of the greatest importance. To begin with, it was absolutely necessary to stop the masses' boycott of the elections, and since it was more than doubtful that they would be tempted by promises of a free vote to take part in them, the Communists must be ordered to compel all peasants to vote, if they did not do so of their own accord; secondly, it was also necessary to force the proletariate to give a right vote. On the one hand, the excessive communistic over-representation, resulting from the election failures, must go, but, on the other, care must be taken not to run to the other extreme. If the peasants had really had a free vote, with the feeling against the Bolshevists that prevailed in the villages, not a single Communist would have been elected to a single Russian village Soviet. It was essential to find a happy medium and to compel the voters to follow it. The Communists must keep the position they had before the last election. That was the fixed standard. And note, the result was quite good. A satisfactory number of votes was recorded and the communistic percentage in the councils was reduced exactly to what it was before the last election. It was all an undoubted triumph for Bolshevist power of organization, but contributed very little, indeed, to increased freedom of choice for the proletariate.

It would be foolish, too, to believe that this freedom has anything to expect from the future. Even if the Bolshevist leaders' intentions in this direction were the very best, it would certainly prove difficult to induce subordinate Communists to carry them out. Not on account of any insubordination on their part—there is no lack of discipline in the Communist Party, as will be shown later—but on account of their inability. To work amongst the masses in any other way than with whip in hand is a matter they simply do not understand; the habit of ruling by force has become second nature to them. Moreover, those at the head of the Party find it impossible not to lend their expert guidance to secure a successful issue for the elections. Experience has taught them the best component parts for the Soviets, and this knowledge has been gained at too great a cost not to be utilized in the future. A sufficient quantity of non-Communists to enable the Party to point to them in answer to shameless accusations of undue pressure at the elections, and a large enough number of Communists to ensure suitable handling of the non-Party members in the councils, so that the Soviets may remain the easily handled political tools which they are intended to be—this is the recipe. The Bolshevists have too much at stake to neglect any means of keeping the mixture in right proportions.

Under such circumstances, it is easy to see the utter insignificance into which the Soviets—the proletariate's only means of power—have fallen. The non-Party proletarian representatives may vary a little in number, but, in any case, they are never more than the Communists can easily keep in check. The councils are dominated by the Communists; that is made certain, and the non-Party members are condemned to be mere figure-heads. Either they follow the communistic lead—for much of the importance laid upon the existence in the council of several non-Party members lies in the fact that a certain proportion of the proletariate are thus brought under communistic influence—or, if they should happen to show any inclination to independence, suitable measures can be taken to cure such tendencies. Something else too must be noted. The Communists attach decided importance to the leading positions in the Soviet system and, without further ado, claim for themselves the presidency of the village Soviets with membership of the executive committees, chosen by the Soviet congresses, and also the presidency of these executive committees. And these means alone are enough to secure their dominating influence. For these people's organizations are so constituted that all power is practically vested in the president and the individual members have no real weight. In fact, things have gone so far in this direction that it has become impossible to maintain that correct outward appearance to which the Bolshevists, in their freedom from prejudice, attach so much importance. In the country congresses, during the spring, Kalinin himself was obliged to admit the evidence of " a decrease in the Soviets' rôle as organs of the real power of the people and the substitution instead of the presidents of the executive committees." " The Soviets and their congresses " have, he declares, been " degraded into institutions for the registration of ready-made resolutions," a development which has " alienated the masses from these councils and thereby destroyed the real value of the Soviet forms of power."

Kalinin is right. Their value is not great, at any rate for the lower strata of the proletariate. First, entrance into the Soviets was denied except to a small number under the strict control of the Communists; then even the small number, to whom entrance was permitted, were refused every possibility of making their voice heard. Under such conditions the political influence that can be exercised by the proletariate endowed with " supreme power " is, undeniably, exceedingly circumscribed.

* * *

Exactly the same picture meets our eyes when we pass from the Soviets to consider the manifold organizations of various types, by means of which the proletariate themselves are supposed to control their lives in different social fields. Their name is legion; in the most varied directions opportunity is apparently provided for the proletariate to take part in the great work of the collective social life. Yet in every case, 99 per cent. of this opportunity is empty show only; that same communistic " guidance " makes the proletariate's own participation a pure illusion. It is the Communists who determine the component parts of the different organizations and they, too, who exercise complete control of them; the non-Party members are only allowed in as dumb actors, supernumeraries which the other side cannot dispense with for the sake of outward effect. Very little intercourse with the Russian working-class is sufficient to show how completely the lower strata of the proletariate is pushed on one side. They are put out of the game, and this so completely that even they themselves scarcely reflect that things might have been otherwise. Any discontent they may have is rather because they are compelled to take part in a vast number of deliberations where they feel entirely superfluous and of no account.

Some election—for a factory committee, a thrift society, no matter what—is to take place in a factory. The procedure is always exactly the same. First, the matter goes to the "Party-cells," little groups of members of the Communist Party amongst the workers, and there the list of candidates is drawn up—the method I will give later. Then follows the general election-meeting, where the forms of procedure are simple in the extreme. The meeting is informed that the chairman has received from the Party-cells a list containing the following names—who votes against them? Dead silence reigns in the room; to demand discussion would be a bold proceeding, to put up any opposition foolishness. The president's tap is heard—the proposed candidates are unanimously elected.

Digressions from this programme may occur—some members bent on self-destruction do exist.

"In a factory in the Don district," *Pravda* writes, "an election was held of members for an insurance union and a revision committee. Immediately the meeting was opened, a list was read from the Communist-cell with the question: Who votes against them? The Communists observed their Party discipline and were silent, so were the non-Communists for fear of reprisals. But then an ordinary non-Party workman got up and said: 'Elections like this are no good. Tell us how many are to be elected and for what, and we will name the candidates ourselves and vote.'

"The cell-secretary and the chairman of the factory committee, who had not expected such an occurrence, began to defend the list and the old election method. The workman, seeing the futility of discussion with them, spoke for the last time: 'I see I am quite superfluous and will leave the meeting, since I do not intend to vote to order.' In an instant the speaker of the factory committee mounted the platform with a resolution to exclude the objector from union membership and to discharge him from his place."

"The Communists know their power so well," writes another contributor to *Pravda,* "that after the question of the candidates has been settled in the Party-cell, they do not even trouble to go to the general election-meeting. This is," he adds, "a characteristic feature of a large number of elections. Many Communists argue thus: Why should I go there, when everything has been discussed already in the Party-meeting?" "The Communists boast openly," is the confirmation of a third writer, "that at the elections they can secure the appointment of any candidate they wish."

It is superfluous to quote further; not only *Pravda,* but every Russian paper continually gives fresh side-lights of this nature—side-lights that illustrate, in the most dramatic way, the astounding indifference with which non-Party voters are, daily and hourly, pushed to one side. It certainly can be said that the present candour of the Russian Communist Press may be interpreted as a symptom of a desire to modify the existing methods. But even if that is so—and it is indeed none too soon to begin to think of fulfilling, in this respect, the promises made eight years ago to the proletariate—yet the same difficulty exists here as we have shown in the election of the Soviets. It is no easy matter to induce the ordinary Communists to give up the idea which they have formed in the last eight years of their social task and the right method of performing it. And to relinquish forcible methods, to give the proletariate a free hand and to allow them to fill the various organs of the social fabric with anti-Bolshevist elements, is what simple self-preservation deters the Bolshevist rule from entertaining for a moment. The training must continue;

the utmost to be expected is that possibly the trainers may not flourish their whips in quite such a defiant manner.

* * *

The supreme power of the proletariate under communistic guidance means, then, first and foremost, that the non-Party proletariate are completely shut out from all participation in political or social work. But, at the same time, it means something more—that the proletariate are placed under Communist guardianship in all they do or allow to be done.

It is the fore-mentioned Party-cells that carry out this oversight. In every factory, in every corporation, in every village where there are Communists, these form a centre; the work of these "cells" is the responsibility of maintaining a healthy revolutionary feeling in their surroundings. They are the agitators and spies in one, whom the proletariate always have in their midst and who possess convenient points of vantage for close observation of all that occurs in the proletarian class; the least trace of political opposition, the slightest tendency to independent thought, can instantly be followed up and crushed. But it is not only sins of commission against Communist orders that are penalized, but there is expected even from those outside the Party—at any rate from the artisans—if not the Communist creed, at least a certain proletarian attitude, shown by observance of a series of formalities, the neglect of which is looked upon as a serious sin of omission, viz. presence at numberless meetings and gatherings, provided for the workers' communistic education, participation in the demonstrations and manifestations arranged on every imaginable pretext, and agreement in the speeches and resolutions by which the proletariate at various times give their support to the existing Government.

All this, indeed, had at one time the charm of novelty, but now, in most cases, the working-man is utterly sick and tired of it; since these proletarian duties all demand some time, their fulfilment is considered a most disagreeable addition to the eight hours' working-day. But there is no escape. When the artisan cannot save himself by some acceptable excuse—like a schoolboy he has become incredibly expert in inventing such—he has to show himself in the demonstration or take his place at the meeting. In every street demonstration, marching forward under its waving banners, amongst those taking part, there are always some to be seen who can scarcely drag themselves along—e.g. women in the last months of pregnancy. At first one is struck by the loyalty of these revolutionaries, until, by degrees, it is understood—the very first artisan one talks to will prove the reality of this—that the citizens are simply forced out under the demonstration banners. Patient and compliant, although disturbed in mind, the working-classes sit, evening after evening, at discussions and lectures of a political nature or at dissertations of general culture with a communistic bias; they listen with resignation to the never-ceasing flow of communistic eloquence and congratulate themselves when they hear at last the compulsory resolution: "After hearing comrade Ivanov's lecture the meeting passes a resolution declaring its approval of the Party's policy and its prudent course of action."

The sooner they can utter this amen to the sermon that has so sorely tried their patience, the better; it doesn't, after all, matter so very much to what they give their approval, as long as they are quick about it. "After hearing comrade X's lecture on Copernicus," thus, according to *Pravda*, one such resolution ran, "the meeting passed a resolution approving his action."

Such, then, are the broad outlines of the people's part in the supreme power of the proletariate. Comparison with former times shows, it is true, that they have changed their place in the political drama. From the topmost gallery, where brutal chuckers-out, in bygone days, tried in vain to silence their whistling chorus, they have been allowed on to the stage. But the part allotted to them there is that of a totally insignificant supernumerary, and it has to be played under very strict supervision, which tolerates no discordant notes, no slackness in the chorus of hurrahs.

* * *

But, it may be said, even if the Government which is called the supreme power of the proletariate does not give to the majority of the lower classes any share of power, but, on the contrary, forces them under a very oppressive rule, yet, in any case, the existing Russian dictatorship is of such a nature that the proletariate can—certainly only in a somewhat modified sense—call it their own. The proletariate were formerly ruled by a bureaucracy, separated from them by an insurmountable Chinese wall; whilst now the present Russian Government is the rule of peasants and artisans carried out by men who still belong to the proletarian ranks and are bound to the masses by all the ties of a mutual community of interests. And if the first class sacrificed the masses to their own unbridled caprice and their unbounded tyranny, yet these others, their comrades—*tovaristji*—even if their methods are rough, have no other aim than to serve the interests of the masses, who often do not understand what is best for them.

As far as that goes, it must be granted that no methods have been neglected to impress upon artisans and peasants that now they are ruled by their peers, by those who are bone of their bone, flesh of their flesh. Again and again, day after day, week after week, year in, year out, this is preached by word, by writing, by pictures; any number of stage-management tricks serve outwardly to raise this truth above all argument. No one need come and say that the power does not lie in hands still hard from handling hammer or reaping-hook; look how, at the very top of the Soviet power, there stands a Russian peasant in his rough homespun, a peasant who still goes—as is constantly shown by fresh photographs in the papers, specially provided for the delectation of the peasants—for his holidays, rake in hand, side by side with the peasants in his village at home (in parenthesis it may be said that old Kalinin would feel very ill at ease in this occupation). The whole of his working life he has spent as an artisan and has only kept his peasant name, thanks to the fact that in Russia of former times the peasants who emigrated to the town or factory were always looked upon as still belonging to the village commune.

But this is all play-acting. Even if those in highest authority lay stress on presenting a genuine peasant appearance, and if Party members, as a general rule, observe a certain proletarian touch in some few matters of etiquette —there is no lack of this in many details of dress, e.g. in a real revolutionary boycott of stiff collars—there is still a gulf fixed between the proletariate and their new masters. Even apart from the fact that a large proportion of the proletariate's Communist authorities never handled either artisan or peasant tools, and that great numbers, who did, have long since thrown them aside, even apart from this, it is nevertheless true that the Communists, whether they still work with machine and plough or not, are becoming more and more differentiated from the masses. Their official dignity as the élite and leaders of the proletariate puts them in a class apart, and gives them a special position which they themselves are not among the least eager to maintain. Already the newly-acquired Party ticket makes the holder, at the very least, into a corporal with all a corporal's sense of infinite superiority to the "rankers," and every promotion in Communist service increases the distance between them. The tendency is clear and the result already evident: a new upper-class is growing out of the Communist rank and file, quite as widely separated from the proletariate as was ever the old ruling-class, now exterminated in Russia.

That such a new upper-class is being differentiated from the proletariate is apparent at almost every step in the new conditions of the new Russia. One would need to be blind indeed not to notice how these young men, in leather jackets and spurs—the Communist uniform—take the upper hand and how the other ranks of the people give way in the sense of their inferiority in comparison with these swashbucklers. An indescribable air of romance surrounds even the ordinary Communist, and higher up, amongst the bureaucracy of the innumerable Communist official activities, we come face to face with a society whose feeling of class superiority knows no bounds and owns no restraint.

And as the last remnants of the old upper-class are being

destroyed, this new social élite, with a bold confidence evident to the eyes of all, takes possession of the comfortable position of superiors. A traveller, coming to Russia fresh from all he has heard of the new proletarian society, entirely without class distinctions, does not believe his eyes at first. Is this really proletarian Russia? Indeed, he feels tempted to forget that there exists anything called the great Russian revolution—what lies before his eyes is purely and simply the old genuine pre-revolutionary Russian system of social distinctions. Aboard a Volga steamer then and now—how well one recognizes the *milieu.* The steamer's name has been changed from the *Prince Nikolai* to the *Third International,* it is true, but in every other respect! . . . The same stinking chaos down in the third and fourth class—since there far away towards Asia they have not troubled about that thoroughgoing reform which in other places does away with class distinctions even in the matter of means of transit. Here Russian peasants and artisans are packed together in repulsive quarters below deck, so housed that if they had been beasts instead of human beings, it would have been called cruelty to animals in Western Europe. And then, up in the first-class saloons, just as before, a chosen few, enjoying the same luxury and comfort as in olden times—a luxury not very unlike that afforded by the first-class of American steamboats. Down in those lower regions they chew their black bread with a raw cucumber as their only relish, whilst, up above, the company eat up the steamer's fine four-course dinner, beginning their meal with bowls full of fresh Volga caviare and leaving behind them on deck whole batteries of empty champagne bottles. The proletariate and the bourgeoisie! The matter cannot be put more simply or clearly in a Bolshevist propaganda placard. It is all exactly as it was in old Russia, the only difference being that the types in Turgenev's upper-class romances and Tchekov's middle-class novels are replaced by heroes of the new day—young, arrogant, self-confident gentlemen in leather jackets and spurs, and young, shingled and rouged ladies whose dress is marked by the same provocative carelessness as their general bearing—all of them holiday-making officials from Moscow. The peasant down there may well be pardoned if he cannot appreciate the difference to any great extent.

The Communist belongs to the upper-class. If anyone should chance to believe that the rule exercised by these *tovaristji* over the Russian proletariate is rather that of a comrade than of the officials of tsardom and that therefore, in spite of all its severity, the people find it easier to bear, then he is mistaken. The Communists approach all the rest of society with this assumption of superiority in its worst form. In a disconcertingly short time they have adopted all the most arrogant bearing of the dethroned ruling-class, which their want of good manners and culture makes all the more irritating and offensive.

The confident arrogance with which these grand gentlemen treat the plebeians—i.e. the general public—is perfectly indescribable. One afternoon I was sitting at work in a little branch library in Moscow. There were about twenty of us, sober-minded folk, bending in silence over our books; an amiable old lady in charge of the lending department moved about on tiptoe, providing each reader with the literature he needed. Then, in came the Communist with clinking spurs—I may say I have seen many hundreds of Communists with spurs but never one on horseback—he stamped into the hall and shut the door with such a bang that the books jumped on their shelves. His cap, cocked at an angle of 60 degrees, he calmly kept on his head and his lighted cigarette in the corner of his mouth. Without vouchsafing the slightest gesture of greeting to the lady-in-charge, he ordered some book in a loud tone. And in the same loud tone he continued his discussion with her, only raising his voice still more, in answer to her discreet whispers; to her timid reminder that smoking was forbidden in the library, he responded by contemptuously throwing his lighted cigarette on the floor. Then he threw himself on a chair and the book came out; in five minutes he had finished with it, and, tossing it in an elegant curve on to the superintendent's desk, he marched off again without the slightest attempt at any leave-taking.

The old lady was, it is true, a bourgeois and we others

also of contemptible bourgeois class; that the young man, under such circumstances, should treat us cavalierly was, perhaps, not only comprehensible, but even praiseworthy. But even in their relations with the so-called ruling proletariate their tone and manner are the same.

During my Russian journey, my first Communist acquaintance was a young man who was returning from some official journey abroad in the same train that was carrying me through Finland. He was, so it seemed, a pleasant, reasonable young fellow, honestly convinced of Communist truths and very eloquent in their praise. We crossed the frontier and had to change into a train for Leningrad. For some reason that day there were no "soft carriages" (i.e. second-class compartments), but the train consisted of coaches of the kind popularly christened "Maxim Gorky," third-class carriages whose interiors recall, in certain particulars, the night-quarters described by that great author. The Communist was a little ashamed of Soviet Russia's coaches before the new foreign arrivals and was anxious to neutralize our first somewhat unfavourable impression of Russian modes of transit. After having reproved—in the choicest language—the poor innocent conductor who stood at the salute to receive the outpouring of his vials of wrath, he issued a strict order not to allow any other passengers into our compartment. At any rate we were not to be overcrowded. At every station the train was besieged by hosts of fresh passengers, most of them peasants, taking their produce into the city; in spite of the guard's most earnest efforts, now and again he could not prevent a passenger from making an attempt to enter our carriage. But the bold intruders went out faster than they came in; terror-stricken, gasping for breath, utterly overwhelmed by the Communist's blast of fiery invective, they hid in fear amongst the crowd. In the other carriages the overcrowding grew more and more incredible, with people hanging on the footboards like bees on the footboard of a hive. We tried to convince the Communist of our willingness to share with others our superfluous room, but all in vain. So in solitary state the Communist and we others—five or six persons in all—continued our journey to Leningrad, where we got out almost paralysed by this first experience of the tone of the social intercourse between proletarian comrades.

But this astonishment soon wears off, for like experiences are to be met with every day and every hour, in the new Russia. At the railway booking-office—this is a scene of which I have often been a witness—there stands a patiently waiting queue, since the places on the train are limited and to secure a seat one has to be on the spot hours beforehand. At last the office is opened and the issue of tickets begins. Then come the leather jackets, a company of young hooligans round about the twenties. Without the slightest hesitation, up they march to the ticket office, without a word roughly knock aside those who have been waiting there for hours, and demand their tickets. No one ventures upon any resistance; those who have been knocked to one side accept it as the most natural thing in the world, and one's neighbour in the queue quite calmly gives the explanation : " Communists."

But this arrogant bearing is demonstrated in quite a special way amongst the Communist Government bureaucracy. Long hours of waiting in various Russian official centres have given me opportunities of seeing them in the exercise of their office. It is certainly true that the old Russian bureaucracy could rouse people to the greatest indignation, but what was it compared with the new ? I could never, in all my life, have conceived the like of their arrogance towards the poor public. It amounted to the crassest general abuse of one after another of the poor, humble creatures who, with evident terror, ventured to disturb these great ladies and gentlemen. It is but just to name the ladies first, for undoubtedly they carried off the prize for arrogance. (Personally I have no complaints to make ; as a foreigner I generally met with the sweetest of receptions. And I can well understand that members of all kinds of official delegations to Russia have found the Communists most delightful people. It is the same with them as it was with the old bureaucracy ; no more charming people can be found, provided one has not to deal with them in their official capacity.)

"We are a frightened people. Here comes a Communist, shouting and stamping, and if we say a word, he stares us in the face and roars till we regret we ever opened our lips." These are the words of a Russian peasant; the quotation comes from a source from which I shall draw more than once in the following pages, viz. a reliable Russian Communist who was commissioned by his Party to make investigations in the country districts, and, as a result, wrote a couple of very enlightening books entitled, *The Village as it Is* (1923) and *Our Village* (1924). Such testimony as this concerning the behaviour of the Communists to the general public is by no means rare and has become much more frequent, especially lately. That the average Communist attitude to the proletariate is not that of an older comrade ready to guide and help, but rather that of a superior, ordering, domineering, terrifying, is a certain fact to which the leaders can no longer shut their eyes nor to its attendant dangers. This domineering method is the subject of general debate, and meetings of different kinds pass resolutions against it. It is worthy of all recognition that now—rather late in the day perhaps—notice is being taken of that feature in the Russian Communist of the present day which strikes the proletariate as most characteristic of the type; optimists may believe too in the ultimate success of the efforts to correct it. Here, we can only state with certainty that the revolution to free the Russian people from the brutal oppression of a ruling class is, so far, still incomplete. The Bolshevists have not accomplished it, at least not yet.

But it is not only by arrogance and brutality that the new upper-class estrange the masses; now, as in the times of the old bureaucracy, power also brings with it its absolute abuse.

In many cases, it must certainly be granted that the abuse is actuated by the most worthy motives. The duty of the Communists is, of course, to act as the people's guardians and to be responsible for the promotion of their interests, even when protectors and protected hold opposite views as to these interests. Thus, their tender consideration for the people's welfare leads them to action that their wards cannot but consider as the purest, most unfeigned tyranny, quite equal to the bureaucracy of tsardom. And something worse as well—that is, the new powers-that-be give evidence in their demonstrations of authority of a wealth of invention and imagination of which the old stiff-kneed *tjinovniks* were incapable. To what lengths the Communist enthusiasm for the moment leads thousands and tens of thousands of Russian social reformers is often literally fabulous. At the Communist Federative Assembly in the spring of 1925, one of the chief speakers declared that " cases occur which might be considered pure fiction, if fresh occurrences did not give daily confirmation of their truth."

Here and there, examples are quoted of the decrees drawn up by local authorities which seem to be of such a fictitious character, decrees by means of which these authorities—according to *Pravda*—" endeavour to control every step the people take," and in respect of which they "show a wealth of resource which sometimes exceeds the boldest flights of fancy." In this respect gubernia,[1] district and volost committees vie with one another, and it is difficult to decide whose decrees are the most illegal. Here a volost committee in the Vologda gubernia issues a decree—partly in the interests of hygiene, partly to do away with stupid old bourgeois habits—forbidding the shaking of hands; any transgression of the prohibition is punishable with a fine of 25 roubles. Here another volost committee in the same gubernia forbids the inhabitants to keep dirty linen in their rooms; the penalty for transgression is the same and the supervision, necessary to secure observance of the order is placed in the hands of the military. Here a writer from the gubernia of Jekaterinoslav gives instances of the " tricks "—this is the technical term for administrative abuse of power—by which the local authorities in this part of Russia train the proletariate into worthy citizens of the Soviet State: " On the initiative of the village council which is fighting for the realization of the new social order," he writes, " a meeting in the village of Sofievka adopted, word for word, the following resolution:

[1] Gubernia = province.

Young people are forbidden to smoke and to use bad language in the streets; and the local authorities are to see that this resolution is observed." And in the village of Rozjdestvenska, the speaker of the village Soviet simply brought about a state of siege by issuing a decree as follows: "Young people are forbidden to walk on weekdays after 11 p.m. Walks are only allowed on Sundays and festivals and then not later than 8 p.m." "Such tricks," the writer continues, "we could recount by the dozen."

The Communists in the Viatka gubernia tried other means in the education of the people entrusted to their care. A village Soviet there issued the following order to a neighbouring authority: "The Soviet in Rybakov orders you at once to send all illiterates to school for instruction. Should they refuse to go, they are to be taken there under convoy. If this order is not obeyed, you will be brought to court for disobedience to authority." In Volynien their methods were still more radical; to further the work amongst illiterates, a justice made an example of peasants, who had been irregular in the enforced attendance at the courses of instruction, by condemning four of them to three months' penal servitude and a State fine of three roubles. "You see," was his comment on his sentence, "the way is not to talk, but to act; peasants like being ruled with a rod of iron." A village Soviet in the Kiev gubernia chooses an apparently different way to the same goal by decreeing that no girls who cannot read are allowed to marry, with the result that the instruction courses are literally besieged by young ladies.

Or take a trick—this time a really star turn—from one of Central Russia's gubernias, that of Ryasan. The doctor of a hospital, one fine day, gets a communication from the volost watch-committee ordering him "to pay a visit of inspection of the young women in the village of Aristovo for the purpose of notifying the names of those who are pregnant." The doctor has to obey, makes his inspection, and hands in to the health authorities in the town of Ryasan the following official document: "You are herewith notified that in pursuance of an order from the head of the volost watch-committee I examined to-day in the village of Aristovo 13 unmarried women for the purpose of notifying the names of those who were pregnant. None such were found at the examination. The inhabitants showed signs of hostility to the inspection. Signed . . ." Or here is another variation in this work for the welfare of the public. The local authorities' financial resources are somewhat scanty—any attempt to increase their finances and thus make it possible to advance a little more quickly in their communistic work cannot surely be anything but praiseworthy. And so, from the Government of Jekaterinoslav, mentioned above, comes a report of "an extensive use on the part of the local authority of their right to impose administrative fines up to 25 roubles. This right is exercised in place after place to fill the local coffers. Fines are imposed right and left, never less than 25 roubles, without any regard to extenuating circumstances or to the economic position of the offender. Cases have occurred where one or two fines of 25 roubles have ruined a poor peasant household." Also reports come from other parts of the wholesale imposition of fines; especially towards the end of the year, when funds are sometimes low, this hail of penal fines is sent down upon the just and unjust. As instances, a correspondent from the Ekaterinoslav gubernia tells how two peasants were punished, one because on some unsuitable occasion he uttered a sound, the other because he had allowed himself to sneeze in some official quarters.

These are a few instances out of many, all quoted from *Pravda* in the spring and summer of 1925. The majority of the numberless administrative excesses that occur, daily and hourly, and which people, especially away in the villages, will tell by the hour together—excesses that certainly are not always mitigated by a certain comic touch like some of those quoted above—such excesses never appear in the columns of the Russian newspapers. It is easy to forgive the proletariate, the object of an educational activity carried on by such means, if they overlook the good intention behind it all and only see in it evidence of a pure and simple despotism in face of which, like the good village Aristovo, they "show signs of hostility."

But the Communists' abuse of power is not only of the kind referred to above, nor is it always the result of a certainly somewhat original idea of their duty to the masses placed under their guidance. To a very great extent, it is actuated by far less ideal motives, such as the desire to profit by their privileged position and to utilize its abundant opportunities for their own pleasure and advantage. Their power has gone to the head of these newly-baked upper-classes; the temptations it brings with it have proved too strong, and so all honesty goes to the wall.

The power is theirs—should they not, before all else, take economic advantage of it? Dishonourable dealing, barefaced robbery belong to the order of things in Soviet institutions of different kinds; fresh examples are continually being brought to light, the whole forming a faithful continuation, only on still bolder lines, of the traditions of the old Russian bureaucracy.

Great numbers of thefts have, so Kursky, the People's Commissary for Justice, states in the summer of 1925, assumed an epidemic character. From State institutions they have spread to social organizations, branch unions, factory committees, Co-operative Societies. By the side of this, a system of corruption flourishes as never before, more or less hidden, it is true, in the central management, but openly and with no attempt at disguise in its offshoots. Out in the country particularly, this system has become one of the main pillars in the relations between the ruling-class and the masses. Nor to a certain extent do people complain about it: the peasant recognizes that he would never be able to defend himself under the innumerable, continually changing laws and regulations of Bolshevist rule if he had not the help of bribes to smooth his way. But the local Soviet authorities have such an insatiable appetite that the peasants cannot, after all, help a feeling of reaction. "I used to come to the *ispravnik*"—the police commissioner in the time of the empire—a peasant said to me, "with a score of eggs, but the *tovaristji* take both eggs and hen as well." Every village relates the most drastic instances from its own experience; not even the Bolshevist Press can quite shut their eyes to the terrible revival of a system of bribery. But at headquarters they declare they are unable to take any effective measures against it ; the administrative workers in the villages are too badly paid, and as long as there are no means of improving their position they will continue to take bribes, however much we moralize. But this is only a detail in the system of tyranny and lawlessness which the communistic rule has established throughout the land. As a privileged upper-class, they feel they can allow themselves whatever they like, from a life of unbridled self-indulgence, in which *samogonka* (home-distilled spirit) and sexual debauchery play the chief part, up to the establishment of a literal reign of terror over the masses, accompanied by distinctly criminal actions.

I quote at random a few examples from communistic sources, in which, of course, it must be observed that only the less guilty cases are published.

Here is a description out of *Pravda* from the town of Cherson, in South Russia, a town where, according to the newspaper, " as a general rule the Party's prestige and the principles of revolutionary legality are interpreted in the way peculiar to Cherson."

" Last year," so the tale runs, " the Cherson authorities ordered a day for ' the red barracks ' ; whether the red barracks got any benefit from this day is unknown and very doubtful. But the day became almost a matter of history. They hired the steamer *Karl Marx* and arranged a pleasant excursion up the Dnieper. As soon as they landed at a delightful place, noted for its wine, the Cherson authorities dispersed, some to the wine-cellars, some in other directions. Some bathed, others went for a walk, here and there couples settled down amongst the bushes. A man of the civic guard, passing by, came upon such a couple, engaged in the transgression of one of the ten commandments, and made some such remark as ' God bless you ' or ' A pleasant time.' Up sprang the gentleman and struck the soldier in the face. He had his answer ready and banged his fist on the ' winged Cupid's ' mouth, never suspecting that he was striking a Party man, a certain Borisov from the Commissariat for Foreign Trade. His opponent shrieked for help, and all the Chersonites came running up, amongst them Sidorov, secretary of the Party committee, Ditmar, the chief of the civic guard, as well as others. The united Communist force thrashed the soldier and then decided to drown him in the Dnieper. So they took him up and threw him into the water, but he managed somehow to get to land. Then they beat him to a jelly again and shut him up in the hold of the steamer. The 'red-barracks day' came to an end and was followed by an ordinary Soviet working-day. What was to be done with the soldier they had half-killed? How could they best uphold the Soviet's prestige? The Cherson authorities had the happy thought of putting him in a madhouse, where he would find it hard to make complaints and seek redress. No sooner said than done. Meantime they plastered up the guard's wounds in the madhouse, but the doctors refused to keep him any longer, since there was evidently nothing wrong with the man. So the worthy Chersonites stuffed a few hundred roubles into his hand, managed to get leave for him, and sent him off somewhere on condition he didn't come back to Cherson—or it would go ill with him!"

The affair, however, got known, thanks to the information of a fellow-soldier, and was brought to court.

"The affair is now dragging on," *Pravda* writes in the spring of 1925, "since last summer. Every sparrow on the Cherson roofs chatters about the notable red-barracks day, and all the inhabitants see how the wild scandal-makers get off scot-free, see them in posts of honour, hear their fiery Communist speeches on special 'days' and 'weeks.' Does this tend to fill the people with confidence in Soviet rule? Scarcely, to any great degree."

Or look at this, a little supplement to this portrait of the fighters in the South Russian town—a picture of the Communist element in a little Samara village. There are not a great number of Communists there, but, at any rate, three. The name of the first is Anseny Shapkin, familiarly called Arsenka. His task is not one of the easiest, viz. to carry on a campaign against home-distilling, and he fights in the most determined manner, using all his strength even till he becomes unconscious. In principle, his tactics are sound; to root out the evil one must study it closely, and that he does, bending down over the transparent liquid. In the first distiller's he pours out the brew, at the next he tastes a little, at the third he sits down—and towards evening he is seen, unable to utter a word.

Once a few peasants tried to complain of him. He was summoned and examined—after that they left him in peace.

But he can speak. At the village meetings he will pour forth for three hours. "Stop and take your breath," the peasants say; "after all, we don't understand anything."

But Arsenka is not to be stopped. His drunken eloquence knows no end. He has not prepared it beforehand, for his only help is a wall-calendar.

"Why should I read newspapers and pamphlets?" Anseny asks. "A wall-calendar is quite enough for a man with brains; there he will find on Tuesday a quotation from Marx, on Wednesday another from Lenin. Cannot anybody with political insight get a speech of several hours out of that?"

Number two is comrade Michaelov, called "The Cat," chairman of the peasants' thrift society.

Money is sent for the help of widows and orphans, and widows come, begging for help. The Cat looks at them critically and then says: "It can't be done."

"Why can't it be done? I have four children, fatherless and naked."

The woman cries, but the Cat does not yield. Afterwards it becomes evident that no women are put on his list but those with good looks, black eyes, and rosy cheeks. But even to be on his list does not mean getting help; for that they have to visit him at night. The ugly women boil with rage, and not all the good-looking ones swallow the bait.

And then number three, Viryepaev. He, too, has his little hobby, which is shooting. As soon as he has drunk a little too much, he goes about shooting—up in the air, right, left.

"The peasants," so *Pravda's* description ends, "shake

their heads in disapproval with a murmured: 'Communists.'"

A small sample of Communist exploits—a motley collection of bribery and debauchery of different kinds gathered from one single little country corner—is given by Jakovlev in his book, *The Village as it is Now*:

"To Kargin, the former chairman of the volost acting-committee," so runs the terse record, "a number of the peasants used to come with milk, fowls, eggs; those who did this got, in some way incomprehensible to peasants, a reduction of their taxes; those who did not got none, even though they were entitled to it. We heard about this from many dozens of peasants in different villages." The secretary of the volost committee and the commandant used to sit in a room drinking home-distilled. The finance inspector, catching sight of this, said: "I must interfere for the sake of principle." He went into the room to draw up his report, but, of course, they persuaded him to sit down and drink with them. The same finance inspector secured a tax reduction for his father, although no regulation gave him any claim to it; his uncle got timber at a reduced price to build a cottage, then sold the same wood at its full price and bought a cow. We were told of this in at least five villages. The civic guard in one village were given a confiscated horse; the civic guard commandant sold it for his own pocket to a local dealer. A demobilized Red army man, meeting a drunken member of the guard, lost his temper and began to rate him, but all the answer he got was: "We belong to the authorities; we have a right to drink." Another peasant said: "We had here a civic guard man, a certain Diatlov; he took a fancy to a woman and said to her: 'I will help you to get your taxes reduced, if you will only do what I want.' When she refused, he tried to shoot her. The volost civic guard here, in the course of a year, have had six commandants, three of whom have had to be dismissed for drunkenness and crime." Last winter Zinoviev, in a speech concerning the state of affairs in a small village where there had been one of the increasingly numerous murders by village representatives of the Soviet, said: "Here we see, unveiled, a most unheard-of picture; a number of purely criminal elements have attached themselves to Communist cells and know how to terrorize a whole village and thus to compromise terribly the Soviet rule." And all this has happened only 50 versts from the great manufacturing centre of Nikolajev.

Almost every day we read in the papers of such terrorists. Here a correspondent from the Samara gubernia to *Pravda* complains—in the paper's smallest type, it is true—about a couple of Communists, whose names he gives, "who not only tyrannize over the village, but are guilty of entirely criminal actions; they flogged a peasant to death, but went unpunished." Another account tells of the chairman of a village Soviet in the Government of Jekaterinoslav who was actually arrested "charged with vile misconduct, cruel oppression of the peasants and violation of forty (!) women." "Exceptional cases!" someone may say. "The existence amongst such an enormous body as the Russian Communist Party of a few black sheep, who now and again are found out and had up for legal penalties, is no proof of the spirit of the Party as a whole." But then these are *not* the exceptions; the exceptions are the respectable members who work conscientiously for unselfish ends. Of course, there are these as well—quite a number, too, I believe; personally I met several, not least often in the villages, whose work, as far as I could form an idea, in the country districts filled me with the greatest respect. But that the great majority, in an amazingly short time, have developed into lawless despots is a fact that permits of no doubt whatever.

Simply listen to the people themselves. We can understand that the absolute solidarity of opinion which we find existing amongst them as regards the Communists is not built upon isolated cases of abuse of power here or instances of tyranny there. The lower ranks of the working-classes—those for whom there is no prospect of ever entering the Communist Party and, more especially, the vast body of the peasants—look upon the Communists, in whom, according to the Party programme, the proletariate should see the givers of all good gifts, as people from whom everything bad may be expected. "The Communists—they are thieves and bribe-beggars." "What sort of Communist is he ?" the peasants in a village that I visited said of one of their neighbours who belonged to the Communist Party—" what sort of Communist is he ? Why, he is an honest man ! " The Communist is an evil-liver, a drunkard and fighter who terrorizes whole villages unpunished ; the Communist is misfortune personified. Here is a single slight episode that throws a real lightning flash upon the relations existing between the common people and the Communists. The Soviet investigator, Jakovlev, tells how, accompanied by several other Communists, who were taking part in his examination of conditions in country districts, he came to a little village and there summoned a number of peasants who, it was believed, might be able to throw some light on a certain question. The conversation began, but had not lasted long when a knock came on the door of the room where they were gathered.

This proved to be a party of women who had come to inquire : " Is it your honours' pleasure that the trial of the arrested men shall take place at once, or can it wait till later on ? " The village public, who cannot believe that a visit from a handful of Communists can pass without some gross tyranny—such is a little picture of everyday life from Bolshevist Russia which tells us better than the lengthy reports of many special commissioners what manner of masters the people have got under the supreme power of the proletariate, guided by the Communists.

And if it is thought that the lower classes' opinion of the Communists is influenced by the Russian national suspicion and spiteful stupidity with regard even to those who mean nothing but good by them, evidence that cannot be challenged, as to the degeneracy of the Communist rule, is to be found in the utterances of the leading Russian statesmen themselves "There is no doubt," Lenin wrote towards the end of his life, " that we live in a sea of lawlessness and that the local influence constitutes one of the greatest, if not *the* greatest, hindrances to the establishment of law and order." These words of Lenin's were quoted at the Communist Federal Congress last spring and, at the same time, it was stated that " almost nothing " had been done since they were uttered to remedy the wrong state of affairs. " Some representatives of the Government," stated the opener of the great debate on the revolutionary law and order, " hold the conviction—and not without reason—that whatever they may do, they will escape unpunished." And Kalinin himself compared present conditions with those in pre-revolution days ; he pointed out that " in old Russia there existed absolutely no legal rights for the masses, but immunity from punishment for the nobility and—above all—for the capitalists, corruption amongst officials and complete administrative tyranny in the attitude of the local authorities to those who were their subordinates. So things continued, not for years nor tens of years, but for centuries. From such soil—exploitation on the part of the strong, complete deprivation of legal rights for the weak—sprang and grew the national idea of justice. It is self-evident, then, that respect for law and justice did not and could not take root in the hearts of the people. Law was law, but life went its own way. It would be too self-satisfied and wrong to imagine that in this respect we have travelled far from pre-revolution times."

When Kalinin in this manner represents the excesses of the communistic administration as the unfortunate result of the old tsarist system, he is certainly right to a certain degree, yet to a certain degree also they are, of course, the inevitable consequences of Bolshevism's own method of putting some hundreds of thousands of raw young men, full of crude ideas, in possession of powers for which they are in no way fitted. But let that be as it may ; the real point of interest is that in the eighth year of the proletariate's supreme power, the head of the Government is forced to get up and confess that the position of the people has not been perceptibly improved in the one respect of the proletariate's absence of legal rights, and that in the tyranny of those in power Communism has but upheld the worst traditions of tsardom.

* * *

The first reservation—and this one of certain importance—that must be made in speaking of the introduction in Russia of the supreme power of the proletariate is therefore this: the share of the supreme power given to the vast masses of the proletariate is not what they expected to get and what the term itself must inevitably suggest to them, in spite of any later interpretations which Bolshevist theories may have chosen to give the words; their share, in fact, is not as much as would cover a sixpence.

But, it may be said, even if this is so, in any case there lies behind the phrase a sufficiently deep and significant reality. Even if the masses, as a whole, have no direct share in the supreme power—such an idea, of course, never entered into the Bolshevist programme—and if they were misled by the words into such belief it was their own fault; they must have read Lenin. So this Government, which put the power into the hands of the élite of the proletariate as their real and true representatives, must, of course, be such a proletariate's dictatorship as to satisfy all reasonable claims. Let us, then, accept this reasoning and leave the proletariate themselves to consider the problem why the proletariate's dictatorship should mean for them an oppressive rule of the worst kind. Let us only, to begin with, make sure of two not entirely unimportant facts.

To begin with, can the so-called élite of the proletariate, the Communist Party, be considered as such a perfect proxy for the proletariate? And secondly, when we come to the point, is it so absolutely certain that this representative of the proletariate possesses real supreme power?

First and foremost we must agree on one point: when Bolshevism now permits a certain number of the proletariate, clad in communistic wedding-garments, to enter the banqueting-room and to enjoy the fruits of power, without letting the smallest crumb fall from the table for him who is sitting outside the door, this arrangement can be considered as a feast for the proletariate, only under the one condition that the circle of invited guests is not too small. If the Government is to be a People's Dictatorship, then the proportion of proletariate, chosen as worthy to take part in it, must not be too microscopic. The final result must, after all, be a popular Government, extending into the ocean depths of national life, not only a thin layer of froth, floating on the top.

Even the most casual glance at the membership numbers in the Communist Party shows clearly the striking lack of proportion between the entire Russian proletariate and their numbers in the Communist Party. Of the 130,000,000 comprising the Russian people, about 15,000,000 are artisans, about 100,000,000 peasants; the Communist Party at the beginning of 1926, even if we include the so-called "candidates"—that is, people on the threshold of the Party, who comprised about half the grand total—something over 1,000,000 members; thus the Communists do not form more than one of the more than a 100,000,000 comprising the proletariate.

Nor is this all. Judging from the numbers given, the Communists would number 1 per cent. of the Russian proletariate. As a matter of fact, they are not much more than half that; for the truth is that a certain clique, numerically exceedingly small in comparison with the vast proletarian total—who have received the designation of "Russia's only real and genuine proletariate"—consists, as to half its number, of elements not in the least proletarian. From the statistics concerning the composition of the Communist Party, made in January, 1925, and published in *Pravda* in May—a similar statement of Party figures in January, 1926, is not yet available—very interesting deductions are apparent; to begin with, that of the somewhat more than 741,000 Party members only 429,000 belonged to the category of artisans, 154,000 to that of peasants. The remaining 158,000 members came, therefore, from other social categories. And secondly, it was granted that even of those included in the categories of artisans and peasants, certainly not all were genuinely proletarian. Among the 429,000 artisans were included all those who had ever been—even if only at a very remote period of their lives—artisans; real artisans ("machine-hands," as the phrase goes) numbered only 302,000, or 40 per cent. of the Party numbers. And in the same way, the category of peasants included people who had long since ceased to belong to that class. Of the 154,000 peasants in the Party the majority were employed by the Communists in the villages: civil guard, co-operative officials, tax-collectors, foresters, etc.; only one-third of the so-called peasants, at the most 50,000 men, were real peasant proletariate—" the men behind the plough."

302,000 actual artisans, 50,000 real peasants—this was, therefore, in the beginning of 1925, the proletariate admixture in the 741,000 members of the Communist Party; even if we assume that of the quarter million new members added in 1925, the majority were genuine artisans or peasants, still the general proletariate does not now form more than half the Party and not more than one two-hundredth of the whole of the proletariate. Only one in every two hundred of the proletarian class has a share in the supreme power of the proletariate—it would not be strange if the proletariate should feel itself a little neglected.

The matter is undeniably somewhat bitter if, like the Bolshevists, we deny to the peasant class all right to be called proletariate and look upon their 100,000,000 only as a tail to the 15,000,000 artisan proletariate. Then there is no need to emphasize the grotesque disproportion of the peasant class representatives in the Communist Party: 50,000 peasants of Russia's 100,000,000, that is, one Communist in every 2,000 peasants, or, according to a calculation in *Izvestia,* on an average one Communist in every Russian village. We can, instead, point out that amongst the real proletariate—the artisan class—the Communists reach a considerably higher percentage. Especially if the category of Russian artisans only includes those who are actually trade union men—the number of these was at the beginning of 1926 nearly 8,000,000—and if the artisans in the party are reckoned at half a million, it may be stated that every fifteenth man amongst the artisans is a Party member. The Bolshevists themselves think these figures magnificent; an outsider perhaps is not quite so much impressed by them.

But, says the Soviet enthusiast, granted that the proletariate, considered as a whole, is somewhat sparsely represented in the Communist Party—the real proletarian organization—yet this is a defect in the supreme power of the proletariate which is gradually being remedied. The Party indeed grows quickly. When the Communists came into power they numbered, at most, 35,000—these were the Party figures at the end of 1917; the number of Communists at the actual moment of the Revolution is not known. Now the number of genuine proletarian members, if we confine ourselves to these only, is more than half a million. With every year the disproportion diminishes between the number of the proletariate with a share of the supreme power and that of those excluded from it. With every increase in the Communist education of the proletariate, greater numbers pass from the latter class into the former.

But should anyone, judging from the Party increase up to the present, look forward to the day when either the whole or a great majority of the Russian proletariate will, through membership in the Communist Party, have a share in the supreme power of the people, he is entirely out of his reckoning. The Party increases plainly enough, but it always contains a minority—a very small minority—of the Russian proletariate.

To begin with, it is by no means certain that the Russian Communist Party can reckon on a similar great proletarian influx. It is useless to deny that the records of the Party recruiting have not been quite so satisfactory as might appear from a cursory examination. Even if the Party has been overwhelmed—as we shall soon show—by aspirants from certain quarters, yet the recruiting shows one distinctly weak point: however little importance the Bolshevists may attach to the influence of the peasant class, they cannot, in any case, notice without anxiety their obstinate refusal to allow themselves to be drawn into the Party. It is a bad symptom that, in spite of more than eight years' intensive propaganda, Communists—if we exclude the special officials in the villages—are still very hard to find in Russian country districts. *Izvestia* speaks with evident annoyance of " this endless non-communistic sea which is scarcely touched, and that only on the very surface, by the Party influence." And not least serious is the fact that the light breeze that has caused this insignificant rippling of the vast face of the water is beginning to fail even in this. The peasant attitude to Communism and the Communists is such that, far from being able to enlist vast numbers of fresh peasant representatives, the Party has to make great efforts to maintain the peasant membership at its present numbers. Not a few peasants, who entered the Party in the first year of the Revolution, now find it best to leave it again, being unable to endure the atmosphere of ill-will which is growing in the villages towards the Communists. A first stage in the break with the Party is the familiar occurrence—I met several instances in the villages I visited—that the peasants, who still practically belong to the Party, are ashamed of this, keep the fact as quiet as possible, and look upon any reminder of it as an insult. As a rule, this is followed by stage number two; they no longer fulfil their Party duties and have to be crossed off the rolls. In village after village I was shown such ex-Communists; whenever they were worthy and respected peasants, people considered their action only natural and quite to be expected. The extent to which such desertion has grown is made evident, amongst other facts, in Jakovlev's investigations. He found in a large village eleven Communists. "These Communists," he states, "are the result of an unbroken reduction in a membership which in 1918 numbered hundreds. And the limit is reached when this fatal desertion fever also infects the ranks of the darlings of Bolshevism, the soldiers of the Red Army, who during their military service had a communistic training which no others enjoyed; even these, after returning to the villages, fall victims to the anti-Bolshevist opinions prevalent there." In five villages alone Jakovlev found, during his investigations, twenty to twenty-five such Red soldiers who had left the Party ranks. The result of all this is, that the inclusion of new members, which the Party is, at the present, making in the country districts, to a great extent only suffices to fill the places of those who leave its ranks.

To a certain degree this may, however, be changed. A

more active propaganda movement—as lately as the autumn of 1925 several thousand artisans were taken from their employment centres and sent to the country districts to carry on propaganda work—may bear fruit, and gradually the idea may perhaps dawn on the peasants, as it has already on other classes, that, quite apart from any liking for Communism, membership of the Party may offer great practical advantages. The first and foremost reason why the vast masses of the proletariate are always to be found outside the Party is another matter; the Communist Party itself, when it has accepted as many representatives of the general public as suit its convenience, without more ado slams the door in their face. For this organ of the supreme power of the proletariate is not at all calculated to receive more than a strictly limited number of them. It is a particularly exclusive corporation, which controls the admission of new members as strictly as the most aristocratic club in Western Europe. In opposition to ordinary political parties, whose chief endeavour is to increase their numbers as much as possible, the Russian Communist Party, even though it sometimes seeks development in certain directions (as, for instance, upon occasions, amongst the ranks of the peasants), deliberately keeps down the numbers of its membership.

This is but a persistent continuation of the Party's tradition in their first eight years. To understand the Russian Communist Party, its organization and ideology, it is, above all, necessary to bear in mind how it arose and under what conditions it has developed. When the Russian Social Democratic Party in the beginning of 1900 split and divided into a majority of Russian Bolshevists and a minority of Menshevists, one of the disputed points that led to the break was how a revolutionary party should be organized in Russia at that time. The Bolshevist leader, Lenin, insisted that such a party must find its strength, not in quantity, but in quality. It would not do to get a great army which, owing to its size, would be both unreliable and difficult to handle, but a small, exceedingly well-sifted troop, small enough for the leaders to be able to have an eye on every man's entire reliability and to keep most absolute control of their companies. Only such an organization could be used for the conspiracy work which lay before the Party then, maybe, for ten more years.

The same lines of action for recruiting which were adopted by the leaders themselves, and which proved to be the strength of the Party in its years of secret work against tsardom, are still in force, even now, when it has moved up from its subterranean work to exercise the government from the Moscow Kremlin. The Party continues not to grow too large, chiefly that it may not lose its singleness of aim. The fear, felt by members of an illegal conspiracy, of admitting into their body not entirely reliable elements, persists in the care by which they try to protect their party from the entrance of individuals who do not, heart and soul, share the Communist convictions. This care had, moreover, been amply justified, for as soon as the Communist power seemed fairly secure, all kinds of adventurers and fortune-seekers poured into it—also those on guard scarcely kept their eyes open wide enough, since, in spite of them, such an element crept in colossal numbers into the rank-and-file of the Party. But secondly, the Party's growth must be limited for the added reason that too large an organization would be too awkward to manage; now that the Party's growth is so infinitely great and more involved than before, it is doubly important that their instruments should be easily handled. In addition to these two reasons for the limitation of Party recruiting, there is, it must be confessed, a third, which did not become evident until the Party had come into power, but which is now, at any rate for a number of the Party members, perhaps the most weighty of all, namely, that the privileges conferred by membership, whether of a purely material nature or as regards higher social position, must not be divided amongst too many if they are to remain of any value.

In accordance with these views, to begin with, the conditions of entry have been made so strict that they alone are a sufficient guarantee against too great an increase. A recommendation from a definite number of Party members, who have themselves been a certain time in the Party—

the number of guarantors and their qualifications depend on the candidate's social standing—a long probation period, during which the would-be member has to do definite work in the Party service and thus give proof of his zeal and fitness, and, lastly, an exceedingly severe examination in the so-called communistic catechism—that is, in the communistic teachings and the Party history; such are the more important points in the entrance examination. By sometimes raising, sometimes lowering, the standard, complete control is exercised over fresh entries into the Party. Occasionally, moreover, for a time, a complete stop is put to the admission of new members, either of those from a particular social category or in general, during which—we will come back to this later—a more or less radical sifting-out takes place in the Party itself.

But, it may be asked, if this is correct, if the Communist Party really wished to remain a close ruling caste, strictly fenced off from the rest of society and from the proletariate, whose representative it is said to be, why this extension of the Party boundaries which has, in fact, occurred and which, in the course of eight years, has increased the Party figures from 35,000 to 1,000,000? Does not this large increase actually prove that the Party is endeavouring to shake off its exclusive character and really wishes to become an organization of the Russian proletariate?

In dealing with this point, we must, first and foremost, note that a certain quite considerable extension beyond the numbers which the Party reached at the Revolution had, from the first moment, been considered by the Party leaders as an inevitable and self-evident matter. A proletarian dictatorship, consisting of 35,000 men, of whom a large number were not members of the proletariate, ruling over 115,000,000 was, after all, something too absurd; however they might twist and turn the phrase "supreme power of the proletariate," yet they could not venture to present to Russia itself or to the rest of the world a Government directed by a handful of people, a bare three-thousandth of the Russian proletariate, as the realization of their supreme power. And, what was more important, even if the Lilliputian force did succeed by a *coup de main* in achieving supreme power, thanks to its having found a few magic words to which the Russian mass—who had not the faintest idea of what Communism was—listened with rapture—namely, immediate peace and an immediate general distribution of land amongst the peasants—yet it could never be expected, unless several cubits were added to its stature, to be sufficiently strong to keep a giant in leading-strings. The Party, therefore, must pass on to fresh recruiting; the question was only how far it should go in this direction.

Here, pros and cons have to be weighed; on one side the same old reasons against the Party increase, on the other the necessity of making the Party big enough to avoid the appearance of being a too bare-faced ruling clique and to insure a firm enough grip on the proletarian collar. It has not been so easy to strike the happy medium. It is instructive to study the different phases in the Party policy on this point.

At first, whilst it was still uncertain if the Bolshevists would be able to keep in power, there was no eager crowd at their doors; the idea that their real home was inside remained, at that time, completely latent amongst the Russian proletariate. The Party had not to worry, in the least, how they would be able to keep undesirables at a distance. Those who came were received with open arms; it was all the easier to do this, since at that time the chances of Bolshevism were still so uncertain that it would occur to none but those who really held the Communist faith, and were prepared to endure everything for it, to cast in their lot with them.

The situation changed after a couple of years; the Bolshevist position seemed secure, and suddenly vast numbers of their countrymen, both in and out of the proletarian ranks, were filled with the warmest feelings towards Communism and with an irresistible desire to join the Party. For a moment, the Communists were a little staggered by all this sudden demonstration of affection; they accepted it as genuine, and, touched by it, clasped all and sundry to their tender bosom. In the course of two years some 100,000 new members were accepted.

But, even whilst proudly calling attention, both at home and abroad, to the swelling Party ranks, the leaders began to feel anxious. The consequences of giving up their former strict recruiting methods began to be visible. First and foremost, varying numbers of a very undesirable element had found entrance into the Party; on one hand, long lines of fortune-hunters and adventurers—the majority from non-proletarian classes—on the other a great number of purely criminal types, whose lawless excesses in the name of Communism were a byword throughout the land. And yet more: the Party, lately an easily managed, pliable tool in the hands of the Communist leaders, had changed into a cumbrous machine whose wheels and cogs were no longer under their complete control. Continual friction between the Party leaders and the staff of Communist officials first gave food for thought; the circumstance that Lenin, when it was a question of changing Russia's whole economic policy and of introducing the so-called "new economic policy" should not have been able—as might have been expected—to effect this by merely pressing a button, but, instead, had to fight down a very serious opposition, brought matters to a head. Thus, in 1921, 200,000 members were turned out of the Party, and during the whole of 1922 a placard was nailed to the entrance door with the inscription: "All further admission suspended."

But in thus attempting to strengthen the Party by its inner consolidation they went too far. Certainly, it was indeed, according to Lenin, more important for the Party to be pure than to be great, but still it must not be so small that it was lost amongst the mass. The sorting-out and total closing of doors for a whole year, afterwards followed by excessive care in the admission of new members, so reduced the Party's numbers that it was not large enough to carry out satisfactorily its office as corporal amongst the masses. The influence of the communistic "cells" was too inefficient to restrain that discontent amongst the artisans which during 1923 began to find expression of a more and more blameworthy nature. (It is useless even to speak of the discontent amongst the peasants, for that the Communists during their whole career have never been able to control.) And what is even more astounding, the contact of the Communists with the masses had diminished to such a degree that they did not even try to control the voices which were making themselves heard amongst them. To quote Stalin: "The wave of strikes and unrest which in August, 1923, rolled over parts of the Republic, in union with the question of artisan wages," surprised the rulers when they were quite unprepared; the Communist oversight over the workers had failed.

"We must wake up and strengthen organizations that were sitting asleep when the summer disturbances and strikes came," Zinoviev declared. What this "waking-up" really meant, we need not explain, since we can understand it without any great strain of imagination. But it became increasingly plain that one means of achieving the essential waking-up must be a fresh increase in the communistic numbers. If some 100,000 more artisans were taken into the Party a double advantage would ensue—the discontent amongst them would be neutralized and rendered harmless, also their strength would be gained for the control and oversight of those remaining outside the Party.

It was certainly not without some pain and reluctance that the Communists decided to open once more their gates, but lately so carefully closed. A great Party discussion arose, to a certain degree carried on in the public Press, as to how far it was possible to avoid this admittance of great numbers of the proletariate, for which many Communists showed decided reluctance. "Our ranks are not fitted," a writer in *Pravda* declared, "to admit so many new recruits." But no escape was possible; on different occasions the resolution was passed that 200,000 fresh members must be admitted.

Even if the newcomers were looked upon almost as troublesome intruders—which was also evidenced in the cavalier treatment meted out to them after their admittance and still prevailing—the Party decided to adopt an outward attitude of delight.

Lenin died—and his death inspired the Party with a happy thought. In the twinkling of an eye it was seen that when the Party admitted vast numbers of new members they did so, not for any tactical considerations, forced upon them by the critical situation; the matter was quite otherwise. The whole Russian proletariate, understanding what Russia had lost by Lenin's death, had placed themselves in unheard-of numbers at the Party's disposition to help to fill up the great gap he had left. And the Party, touched by their fine initiative, naturally could not then do other than gladly accept this mighty help. Lenin was dead, but the proletariate closed up their ranks as never before around his work, and the new accession to the Party strength was honoured with the name of "Lenin's levy." In spite of the devious paths followed by the Party's new recruiting policy and the petty tricks with which an attempt was made to cover its real character, the evident tendency can be clearly seen; the Party shall be just as large as is requisite to keep the masses firmly in check, but not a particle larger. It is plain that a distinct increase of its present strength is still necessary, a little more is still required before the artisan class reaches the numbers which, after the experiment described above, is regarded as requisite here and there, for the moment; one Communist to every ten outsiders seems to be the standard now considered fitting. And as regards the peasant class, the Party is making every effort to gain in strength. If the Bolshevists thus continually manage to point out their swelling numbers, and the credulous see in them a never-failing fresh proof of the Party's efforts to become something more than a minority clique keeping aloof from the masses, yet, in spite of all this, there was never the slightest intention of placing the Communist Party on a really broad basis and of developing it into the Russian proletariate's own organization. If the supreme power of the proletariate was now exercised by a small ruling caste, it was no transition-stage; it was destined to remain, for such was the will of the Bolshevists.

One additional fact must be mentioned here. So far, in the account of the small size and exclusive nature of the Communist Party, regard has only been had to the chief strength, that of the Party itself. There are also, however, two auxiliary companies—branches, or, rather, training-schools for the Party; first, the Communist Young People's Unions, the "Komsomols" (the word is formed from the initials in the Russian name), secondly, the so-called Pioneer Unions, a sort of communistic boy-scouts' club. If these are included—and the Bolshevists do not fail to do so when counting up their Party resources—the picture given above is seen to be somewhat modified. It has just been stated that the Communist Party is amazingly small in comparison with the whole proletariate, but if the Komsomols and Pioneers are reckoned in as well, the meagre Party total is, without doubt, considerably improved. The Komsomol membership at the beginning of 1926 was 1,700,000, whilst the Pioneers are about 1,800,000. In this way the total Communist figures are nearly 5,000,000, which sounds indeed very good—even although, in any case, they do not form 5 per cent. of the Russian proletariate. And further, the Party's low numbers are partly due, as was pointed out above, to the fact that one of the classes whom the Bolshevists endeavour to draw into the Party—even if only to a certain limited extent—namely, the peasant class, so far have turned a deaf ear to the charmer. As regards the communistic young people's and small children's unions, however, no tendency to such a boycott is to be noticed. Forty-five per cent. of the Komsomol members belong to Russian villages, which means that over 13 per cent. of the 25,000,000 of young people, notified as belonging to villages, are members of a communistic organization; in the same way, in every hundred peasant children between the ages of 7 and 13, 13 are Pioneers. It seems, then, evident that, even if the adult peasant population are not yet won over to Bolshevism, the ice in the villages is nevertheless broken. And finally, if we have just made it evident that the prevailing principle of the Communist Party's recruiting policy is—certainly with the extension necessary to insure the Party's hold on the masses—to preserve the Party's character of a small ruling caste, we yet notice, with regard to the young people's organizations, the policy of the open door. No impediments are put in the way of their growth, although it proceeds with great rapidity; time and again proposals to check what many consider the too hasty development of the Komsomols have been negatived. All this seems to mean that the Party's present exclusive character should be understood as a passing phase, rendered necessary by the present adult generation's lack of communistic training; when these constantly growing hosts of young people, in their time, enter the Party ranks it will—so some think—gradually assume a much more universal character.

A closer inspection, however, shows this argument to be unsound.

It is not worth while wasting many words over the method of counting children down to seven years of age among the active Communist forces, in order to make the Party more important and to give the impression that its power is built on a broader basis. It is true that in modern Russia, as a rule, tender age is no impediment to the exercise of authority. Many of those placed in quite responsible posts have, as the Russian peasants say, their mothers' milk still wet upon their lips. Still no one surely would venture to believe that seven-year-olds would be entrusted with any considerable share of the supreme power of the proletariate. The Party duties that are given to the little Pioneers, for example, to be on show on different festive occasions and at exhibitions—as, for instance, at the reception of foreign delegates (intent on studying conditions)—may afford complete satisfaction to them and their mothers and also to the guests thus welcomed, and in this way they may have a psychological importance, but to reckon them in with the active Communist Party is about as reasonable as it would be in Western Europe to reckon the boy-scouts—the organization copied by the Russian Pioneers—as part of the regular army. As regards the Komsomols, their members are, undoubtedly, fully convinced of their ability to rule Russia, and do indeed often organize their own dictatorship in the villages, but they are, as a rule, emphatically snubbed by the Party members except when, as sometimes happens, the control over what occurs in isolated country districts is so slight that the Komsomols have in the course of years got quite a free hand. The Party itself will look after the supreme power of the proletariate.

The character of a ruling clique which the Communist Government has, at present, is therefore not in the least affected by the existence of the Young People's organizations. They have, as indeed is but reasonable, nothing to do with the exercise of power. And the growth of these organizations holds just as little promise of such a development of the Party as to alter entirely its character in the future. To begin with, the fact that peasant young people join the Komsomols and Pioneer Unions more readily than the adult peasants do the Communist Party is no proof whatever that the next generation of peasants will renounce their opposition to Bolshevism. When the village young people give in their names to one of these unions, this in no way means that they are subscribing to Communism; for Communism and Communist convictions are one thing, whilst the Communist Young People's Unions are another, and the last has little to do with the first. The communistic varnish on the village Komsomols and Pioneer Unions is uncommonly thin. There are indeed thousands of things in the new Russian social fabric which, even though remaining at bottom fairly unchanged, still have a different label stuck upon them; institutions and State officials who oppress the peasants as shamelessly as did those under the old régime have been given names which are certainly a little difficult for worthy tongues to pronounce, but which appeal to the imagination; even the old village street, which is still more tumbledown than before, is now called Karl Marx Street. Then why not organize the social life of the village under an abracadabran but fine-sounding name, especially an organism flying, for appearance' sake, the communistic flag, with an incredible gain in resources and freedom of action? The Young People's Unions are, to a great extent, nothing more than organizations for counteracting the monotony in country districts—organizations that certainly have, at the same time, the official duty of imparting communistic instruction and education; but what is given in this way is entirely swamped by a recreative programme, filled with old and new delights. Nor is this all: if the Pioneers' so-called communistic activity is still of a fairly innocent kind, the Komsomols, especially away in the villages, owing to the nature of the element which has assumed the lead in them and the sort of amusements carried on there, have become nothing but organizations for "hooliganism," rowdyism, and unruly gangs in the Russian country districts.

Hooliganism is an old Russian feature which, for many years now, has been a source of anxiety to society in general. It was especially in the great upset in the rural districts, as a result of the revolution years of 1905 and 1906 and following the demobilization after the Japanese War, that the young people's wildness gave cause for uneasiness; during the years between the revolutions, volumes were written about it and the best methods of checking it. The Great War, for a time, freed the villages from the wildest spirits. The bitterness of mobilization was very considerably assuaged, at any rate to begin with, by the fact that it gave the villages time to breathe after the hooligan terrorism. But now this hooliganism has again appeared, in a legalized form and therefore one more difficult to deal with. It is now the young hot-heads who set the tone in the Komsomols, and they are guaranteed complete freedom of action in such activities. The sober-minded inhabitants are completely powerless before them; to interfere with a Komsomol is legally notified as an anti-revolutionary offence. They have to be given a free hand, and the Komsomols make use of this to arrange orgies in the name of the Revolution and to commit rowdy exploits that make the hair stand on end even on the moujiks' shaggy heads.

As soon as we come to the villages we notice at once what a perfect pest the Komsomols are. I stayed some days in a Russian village where there was a particularly energetic Komsomol, and I must say I could never have dreamt of such rowdyism. The whole village was completely terrorized by these young idlers, 18 to 20 years of age, surrounded by a delighted circle of girls about the same age. In the priest's house down in the middle of the village—they had commandeered the house and driven off the priest—evening after evening, as night fell, the Komsomol began its daily activity, and from the moment the "International" was played—soon followed by inarticulate screams—life in the rest of the village entirely disappeared; to go outside the house was to imperil one's life. Later in the evening and throughout the night, the village street, to which the Komsomol soon transferred its activity, resounded with noises of a horrible nature; the inhabitants lay trembling in their huts behind bolted doors, shuddering for fear of the young ruffians' fresh exploits.

Wherever I went later, the villages were full of tales of Komsomol excesses, some of them exploits in the Communist service—as, for instance, a special outburst of anti-religious propaganda carried on by incredibly rough means—some only aimless demonstrations of general wildness, finding expression in all kinds of unbridled action up to criminal violence of the most repulsive nature. The Komsomols' reputation is generally known and acknowledged throughout all Russia; even the Party itself cannot close its eyes to the serious nature of the whole movement. It is admitted that the communistic training given in the Komsomols leaves much to be desired; it is not at all what the young members want. At meetings of the Komsomol-cells, where, for instance, the international situation is being discussed—so Bucharin in a speech made January, 1926, reports discoveries that he has made—the members either sit asleep or pelt each other with their caps. "What good is it for me to be a Komsomol member? It teaches me nothing; I would rather learn something useful." Such, according to the same author, is the opinion held by the more serious-minded village youths concerning the Komsomols. And, to continue according to Bucharin, this is confirmed by the fact that 100,000 of their members have not mastered the arts of reading and writing, that 80 to 90 per cent. of them are political illiterates, and that, according to the computation of a conference held to consider the question of the Komsomols, 25 to 30 per cent. of their members use alcohol in excess. And a still more striking characteristic of the Komsomols is the sexual licence rife amongst them; this gave rise, in the spring of 1925, to a very anxious newspaper debate which gave the most incredible accounts of the inner life of the "cells." From the Komsomols moral infection spreads to the Pioneer Unions. A Party report in December, 1925, states that here and there cases are noticed of sexual excesses amongst the Pioneers (six- to ten-year-olds). Time after time there is a difference of opinion in the Party as to the Komsomols; at various councils, resolutions are passed condemning their wild behaviour, their arrogant attitude to the general public, their wild actions at repressing religion, the only effect of which is to increase the peasants' dislike of Bolshevism; time after time, different Party members and speakers have dwelt on the necessity of putting the Komsomols under such control as will compel them to abstain from conduct compromising to the Party.

The enormous increase in the Komsomols—as an addition to the picture of their great increase we must, however, give the fact that if, for example, during eight months in 1925, 560,000 new members joined the Komsomols, 110,000 of the better elements left their ranks—if we bear in mind the elements that take part in this increase and their aims in so doing, cannot be taken as an omen for the coming accession to the Party of the peasants, who, up till now, have been so slow to respond to invitation. Any increase in the Komsomols, far from being a sign that the peasants are becoming less opposed to membership in the Party, is a guarantee of increased hostility on their part. The closer their acquaintance with the Komsomols—next to the *Tjeka* and its successor, the G.P.U., the most repulsive outcome of Bolshevism—the more certain the continued existence and increase in all decent, nice-minded peasants of their horror of Bolshevism.

For it is, of course, the peasants they wish to get at, but, on the other hand, the idea of admitting the Komsomols into the Party would not be entertained for a single moment. When we see Pioneers and Komsomol members reckoned in the Party statistics as Communists, even though only two different species of small Communists, we naturally think that the Russian citizen who has gone through these training-schools for the Party will, when he reaches years of discretion, be automatically passed on into the Party ranks. But this is not at all the case. The conditions of entry are exactly the same for a Komsomol member as for any other other citizen whatever, or, rather, they are still stricter, for in addition to all required from non-Communists—viz. recommendation, probation, examination, etc.—Komsomol members also need a good character from their Komsomols. We can easily understand the Party's extreme caution in the admittance of these newcomers when we have seen what kind of institutions the Komsomols are, but, on the other hand, all this shows how groundless are the conclusions as to the future of the Party which some are inclined to draw from the freedom with which Young People's Unions are allowed to develop. They may increase as much as ever they like; the Party still maintains its character of a select society which the proletariate is only allowed to enter in small contingents, and these strictly controlled as to their component parts.

* * *

But as we accepted before the Bolshevist point of view that the supreme power of the proletariate must be considered as realized when the power—from which the masses themselves are entirely shut out—is laid in the hands of the proletariate's representatives, so now we will pass over the very disturbing fact in the actual working, viz. that the representatives consist of a numerically very small clique—only half of whom are proletarian—which some of the proletariate disclaim and which in turn holds itself aloof from them. Let us assume that, in any case, the realization of the people's dictatorship is all right—with the proviso, of course, that this proletarian élite, such as it now is, does indeed, in actual fact, possess power. This is the one thing to be determined. We thus come to the second of the questions asked above with regard to the Communist Party: Is it indeed absolutely certain that we have found the real ruling factors in the land?

That the Communists, even in quite humble positions, have considerable power over the rest of society has already been shown. In company with the proletariate's "guides," they have, as was pointed out, achieved extreme command over the masses—a command whose fairly wide limits they, thanks to weak control, exceed in most bare-faced demonstrations of authority. The Communists are in full possession of the same kind of tyrannical power that a corporal enjoys over a company of recruits put under his control. There is no failure in that respect.

But no matter how tyrannical a corporal is, no matter how peremptory in the exercise of his prerogative as leader, his power yet has clearly defined limits which, beyond a certain point, make it fairly illusive. It is the same with the Communists. The share in the supreme power enjoyed by the great majority of the proletariate is very much like the part a corporal takes in the control of the army, for the Party displays, not only in its recruiting policy, but also as regards the position of individual members, specific features, which distinguish it from Western European parties of every description. In this respect the Party still bears the same stamp as in the period of its existence as a conspiracy, working by underground methods. Then it was necessary, as Lenin emphasized at the formation of the Party, that they should possess such an organization that an all-powerful central control could "reach the farthest man in the Party"; then, too, the threads of the warp—to avoid any risk of entanglement—must all be held in one sole sovereign hand. And just as, speaking generally, all the conspiracy technique and psychology were taken with them when the former illegal conspirators assumed the position of the rulers of Russia, so too the Party is still characterized by the same unbounded autocracy on the part of its leaders, the same self-surrender—induced by suitable measures—on the part of individual members.

If any Communist who, after many efforts, has at last succeeded in entering the Party is naïve enough to harbour the hope that now he will find scope for his political personality, he soon finds out his mistake. He feels, on the contrary, somewhat cramped when he is pushed down, as Zinoviev expresses it, "to be boiled in the pot of Party discipline." And when he has become properly tender, there is not so much of the dictator left in him.

The very first thing to be boiled out is any presumptuous

pretension to put in his word in the shaping of the Party policy. Everything that has to do with that, every detail in the Party's progress and tactics, is decided in the supreme headquarters. He has not been given a place in the organization to have any opinion about it, still less to express one, and, least of all, to try to get others to listen to that opinion. In this respect the general body of the Party are quite ignored. It is true that in various congresses, where even the humblest ranks are represented, the Party passes resolutions dealing with its policy, but, as a matter of fact, the resolutions are passed and fixed in detail long before the opening of the congress; it has never yet happened that a congress has been able to alter a single letter in the ready-made Party resolutions. Opposition—and that too of a very decided character—has indeed occurred as lately as in a Party congress held December, 1925, but it has always been mercilessly crushed as criminal insubordination. The opposer is considered and treated, not only as a perverted sinner, but also as an arch and dangerous traitor who must be rendered harmless, if he does not escape by falling down to kiss the Party rod. The best-known instance—mentioned above—is when Lenin, in 1921, without having consulted even the innermost Party circle, carried through the remarkable resolution which, at one stroke, reversed the whole of the Bolshevist economic policy. Then, indeed, it happened that large sections of the Party could not refrain from reminding him of their existence by venturing to voice an opposite opinion. But, in spite of all, the matter was carried through, with the result already given, viz. a clearance amongst the rebellious element which made a reduction of 200,000 in the Party membership. Under such conditions, the political life in which the Party members are invited to take part is, to say the least, somewhat one-sided. It is true, political activity is demanded from them, but activity which consists only of a prompt and willing acceptance of the Party leaders' resolutions and of docile submission to the policy directed from headquarters. Political meetings are held, by the thousand, among the lower branches of the Party, but the only aim of these meetings is to emphasize the excellence and infallibility of the Party policy; resolutions without end are passed, but only such as express nothing but deep and unmodified approval of the official lines of action.

It cannot indeed be denied that the audience sometimes find all this a little unsatisfactory. "Of what does the ordinary member's share in the life of the Party consist?" asks a writer in *Pravda*. And the answer is: first, and often last as well, in attendance at the meetings. There he has to sit, listen to the speeches, in accordance with which resolutions have already been made, and if, contrary to expectation, someone gets up and he does not follow the lines laid down or speaks in a spirit of opposition, he is severely called to order with emphasis on his want of discipline and self-control, and his ignorance of political principles.

Silence in the ranks is therefore the Communist's first duty, and the only sound to be heard from these Party ranks is the mechanical repetition in chorus of the orders given. But then comes—and this is the actual share taken by the great body of the Communists in their Party's policy—the duty of putting these orders into practice and of working, heart and soul, for a policy in the determination of which they have had no share. Such and such lines of action are laid down, and the Communist, from his particular place in the Party service, must blindly follow them. His business is, by the daily and hourly propaganda work that forms the alpha and omega of his existence, to force the vast numbers outside the Party to the conviction—even though he may by no means always hold it himself—that the Bolshevist policy, as determined in the Party headquarters, is in every detail, no matter how it changes, excellence personified.

Right turn, left turn—he must heed the words of command. One day the Party wishes to have a firm Communist majority in the Soviets, and the Party officials must keep a keen eye on them to prevent the entrance of undesirable non-Communists; next day the Party finds there are decidedly too few non-Party members in the Soviets, and the Party officials—even though they may feel rather bewildered—must, so to speak, drive outsiders into the Soviets at the point of the bayonet. One day the Party pursues its original economic policy, and the members work with the sweat of their brow to get the Russian proletariate to understand that free trading is a repulsive capitalistic abomination; then the Party, with an entire change of front, adopts its new economic policy, and the members—though all their being may rise in opposition—must impress upon the somewhat startled minds of the proletariate that free trading is exactly what will save Russia.

But the Communist demand for blind submission goes much farther than this. It is not only the leaders' policy in general that they must accept and work for, but they must take up arms against the masses in defence of the Bolshevist social order, as it now exists, even with all its weaknesses and drawbacks.

"Every Communist considers it his duty," a correspondent wrote, some time since, in *Pravda*, "to justify, in the workers' eyes, every injustice, even of the worst type." Another correspondent speaks with real indignation of a number of Party members who, when illegal conditions were disclosed in a factory, sided with some non-Party workmen in the criticism of the Communists who had charge of the factory. "We can pardon uneducated non-Party men if they put their fingers on the wrong conditions described and ask: 'Why isn't so-and-so done?' but the matter assumes quite another complexion when a Communist stands up next and begins to criticize."

In questions dealing with things such as poor wages, the forced reduction of piece-work prices, slack payment on the part of employers, it is perhaps not so much to be wondered at that the Communist workers are compelled to uphold, in opposition to their non-Party fellow-workmen, what, in other countries, would be called the employers' point of view; but when matters go so far that Party members in the labour disputes, that fairly often occur on these questions, are forced by threats of expulsion from the Party—such cases happened as lately as the spring of 1925—to act as strike-breakers, this indeed bears eloquent testimony to the humiliating slavery of Party service, that is, in other words, of participation in the supreme power of the proletariate. It is a service that requires the renunciation of one's own will, thoughts and instincts, demanding as it does, not the work of men, but the mechanical action of automata. "It sometimes happens that I do not subject myself to discipline; when it is a question of trifles I rely upon my own judgment." This answer, as *Izvestia* reports, was given by a "Lenin's levy" member during an examination of the new member's soundness of view. What a disturbing answer! "He divides," is the horror-stricken exclamation of *Izvestia*, "affairs and things into important and unimportant, and, with regard to the latter, relies upon his own judgment. He does not understand how inevitably such an independent member breaks away from the Party; he does not grasp the danger of dividing affairs and things into important and non-important; he does not reflect how inimical to the Party such action is; he does not consult the Party-cells, but comes to a decision himself." One can understand the necessity of a proper Press to break so thoroughly the bones of everyone with anything like a backbone. But the disciplinary apparatus is perfect, a drill unequalled in any Prussian barracks. The whole Party is built up on purely military principles, and automatic obedience to his superior officer is the first lesson drummed, by suitable means, into the new recruit. And superior officers do not show themselves too nice-fingered in the process. When the ordinary Communist trains the non-Party public by the methods already shown, he is only avenging himself for the training of which he is the continual object, just as, under the old régime, everyone acted lord and master over his inferior.

No false steps in the careful march! A factory committee had to be chosen, *Pravda* reports. In the meeting of the Communist-cell, where the list of candidates is drawn up—its acceptance as a whole by the workers is, as already shown, a pure formality—one of the Communists, cotnrary to all customs, ventured to object to one name that the cell-secretary intended to carry through at all costs. At the voting, 26 votes were recorded for, 38 against the disputed candidate; the secretary, however, declared him elected with 36 votes to 25. Comrade Sarmanova, a member from pre-revolution times, declared that the meeting was not rightly conducted and the counting of the votes was also wrong. But the cell-secretary ordered her to be silent "in the name of Party discipline." All who ventured to take part in her protest were afterwards summoned, one by one, to the Party office, where they received a thorough dressing-down. When *Pravda* describes this little inner scene in the communistic barracks, the paper naturally attempts to make it appear an exception—it is only to be expected that it, and similar happenings, should sometimes occur—but all Russia knows that such is the general state of affairs, such and a hundred times worse; extreme cases, of course, do not get into the papers.

Arrogance often becomes bullying; even here *Pravda* confines itself to the more innocent and trifling cases, when it relates how cell-secretaries use Party comrades as their private errand-boys. An artisan on piece-work may have to employ several hours of his best working-time at a sign from his mighty chief, who "in the name of Party discipline" orders him to run with some unimportant letter to the other end of the town. Nor can any down-trodden recruit tremble before his military tormentor as the Communist does before his superior in position. I repeatedly saw most curious cases in different offices of the capital; ordinary communistic employees, who at one moment were raging like roaring lions at the poor public, stood the next like trembling lambs before a superior who had occasion to speak to them. I recollect amongst others a braggart of a brutal type in a Leningrad office. He was just busy roaring abuse at a queue of timid citizens, collected before his table, when a young lady with a cigarette in her mouth, evidently his immediate superior officer, flew into the room. She threw a paper down before his nose and gave him, in the hearing of all, a terrible setting-to-rights; he had dated a paper wrongly—July instead of August. Out poured the stream of rebuke, and there the sinner stood at attention, completely paralysed by fear, his forehead covered with sweat—an almost pathetic figure. "I have repeatedly," writes a correspondent to *Pravda*, "observed how those speaking through the telephone to some influential person in a responsible position stand up, bow and assume an amiable smile." "Some workers," he adds, "only use the word 'comrade' when they speak to a social inferior. Involuntarily they address every superior by his Christian name and patronymic. These superiors have grown so accustomed to this that, if anyone says 'comrade' to them, they do not know at once if they are being addressed or not." This system of overbearing tyranny, which keeps subordinates "on the mat" and sometimes changes them into perfect lackeys, receives its final touch—again an inheritance from the Party's earliest years—in a well-organized system of spying, which keeps a watch over their neighbours' non-penal communistic behaviour. Even during the Party's "subterranean period" its members could not have shown more anxiety in regard to any treacherous tendencies in their fellow-conspirators than do Party comrades now, in their zeal for each other's soundness in communistic principles. This arises partly from a desire to keep the Party free from any falling off in principles, but partly, too, from considerably less ideal reasons; the discovery of any weakness in a comrade may mean personal advancement. They spy—the superior on the subordinate, but quite as often the subordinate on the superior, even though at the same time he may be lying prone before him; they collect scandal and gossip and lay snares and pitfalls. The "barrack" air, of itself already heavy enough, becomes filled with poisonous vapours.

And when a slip is discovered, punishment follows. In more venial cases, it is no more than a commandeering for Party work in some isolated country corner—that is, deportation. But generally it consists of expulsion from the Party—complete political death. Very little more is needed to end a Communist's proud career. Not only opposition and heretical opinions are punished, but also want of energy and lack of offensive in propaganda work, or ignorance of the Party catechism, discovered at the regularly recurring examinations which bathe grown men in the cold sweat of a schoolboy's nervous fear. Sometimes expulsion is dealt out for such reasons as seem to lift the whole matter into the realms of imagination. A woman member from pre-revolution times, well known for her energetic work in a Red Army hospital, was, so *Izvestia* recounts, expelled from the Party because, on her return after a short holiday to her army post, she left her young child in its father's charge—the father, as it happened, was a priest. This is but one little example of the mechanical working of the expulsion machine: sometimes going at a slightly more moderate pace, but sometimes possessed with a veritable lust of blood, it rushes on, putting a definite end—although they have already been fairly well checked—to thousands of dictators' dreams.

The Communist Party is called the proletariate's advance-guard, and its picture, as a whole, shows it to be an attacking party, marching in the van of the revolution. It is an attacking party whose good conduct is well provided for, and whose arduous service is rewarded by the right of marauding—one of the pleasures of campaigning and a recompense for many trials. But, in return, automatic discipline is demanded in the military service; without using any personal judgment, without allowing their spirit of attack to flag for a moment, the Communists must march forward into the great battle whose strategy they have no voice in determining. And to complete the likeness to a modern battle-field, their own Party squirts—a whole arsenal of Party compulsion methods—are directed on their backs to stimulate their zeal in attack. This is the Communist Party. But where is the supreme power? To find this we must, after peeling off 99 per cent. of the Russian proletariate as entirely superfluous, do the same with practically all the Communist Party, for nothing of supreme power is to be seen here either. Narrower and narrower grows the circle where we may look for the real centre of power, and not until we come to the innermost circle of the Party government do we reach our goal. There we have, at long last, the real dictators. Instead of the people's power upheld by the wide ranks of Russia's masses, a most pronounced oligarchy ; instead of millions who have become masters in their own home, a handful of people who have managed to create and now manœuvre the most efficient machinery for the subjection of these masses that the world has ever seen! Supreme power of the proletariate carried out with a proletariate minority as tool—that is what goes by the name of "the supreme power of the proletariate."

CHAPTER II

THE BOLSHEVISTS AS SOCIAL BUILDERS

THE idea that the Russian proletariate can now, as master in his own house, regulate his life according to his own judgment may, as has been shown in the foregoing chapter, be dismissed as entirely incorrect. The order existing in the Russian home is established without the proletariate—except as a pure matter of form—being asked for or allowed to express their views on the matter.

This, however, is by no means to say that such order may not be the very best imaginable. Certainly, as a rule, people are accustomed to consider it an indispensable condition of the success of their home that they should have some little voice in its making and shaping. But when, as in the case of Russia, we have to do with people who are somewhat difficult inmates and who, if they followed their own fancy, would turn everything upside down and smash all the furniture to atoms, then it may need someone else to take the arrangement of the matter under their control, especially when experts are at hand, who know, in every detail, what an ideal home should be.

Let us, then, see how far the Bolshevists have been successful with their patent designs in equipping the old tumbledown Russian mansion and turning it into an ideal home for workers. But, first, let us glance at the Bolshevists themselves, in their rôle of organizers and leaders in the great work.

* * *

That the Bolshevists, apart from anything else that may be said about them, are really capable and energetic, with the best qualifications for their great task, that they, more than any imaginable competitors, are the men to shape a new and habitable Russia, is an opinion that may be quite widely held even in quarters where there is, in other respects, no love to spare for Bolshevism.

For my own part, I had scarcely any doubt at all in the matter before I went to Russia. That the Bolshevists were stern, hard masters did not affect the question; when anyone has seen Russia during tsardom's misrule and the misery of the war, he understands fairly well that silk gloves are quite unsuitable for those who are to put things right there. I had also no doubt but that Bolshevism, even if it was a hard school for Russia, was, at the same time, a very healthy one. I expected to find the country far on in constructive work for a rich future, carried on with a zest and energy that gave promise of the conquest of the great difficulties still existing. I felt sure of finding a Russia certainly very far from economic recovery after the years of war and revolution, yet, in any case, showing unmistakable signs of convalescence. And I was quite specially prepared to find a country making quick advances along the lines of higher civilization. Had not the Bolshevists' interest in this become a dogma in the West?

And to begin with, I thought that most of what I heard and saw confirmed my ideas. The slight defects in the outer aspect of the social fabric that I, like all other travellers, viewed at first with amazement, were, after all, easy to ignore; no one can reasonably expect a building, in the midst of extensive repairs, to present a clean and elegant façade. The chief point was that every step I took seemed to justify me in bearing witness to the new breath of life and the quickening of pulse that the Bolshevist efforts had brought about in the sluggish Russia of former times. I wandered about in central Moscow with a sense of scarcely knowing where I was. It is true, the exterior was much the same—a few red flags here and there, communistic mottoes over a few doors, great trappings of welcome to various strangers who had come to visit congresses on a few walls, and a few terrible modelled portraits of leading Bolshevists, in set flower-beds of the parks, did not appreciably affect the general impression. And yet, what a change! In earlier days the Kremlin slumbered in mediæval quiet, and beneath the walls of Kitaigorod—the Chinese town—life flowed on in Oriental ease. Now I had a deep sense of the new strength radiating from the heart of Russia, of the electrical impulses that filled the air and swept over the land.

It was no longer Russia, but a bit of the most up-to-date America. It struck me from the very first that I had recognized the same general feeling, lived in the same atmosphere once before, in America during the months of 1918, when the nation pulled itself together for its great decisive entrance into the World War. In both cases everything around one was regulated for and stamped by the activities of the great work of organization. These activities, perhaps rather unnecessarily bustling, with over-emphasis on the note of pathos and a trifle too much boastfulness and self-satisfaction in display, were, in each case, in their own way, the biggest thing in the world, and, above all, full of a contagious youthful enthusiasm and an imposing manly determination of aim—a work really great in its nature and executed on great lines. And the same tearing haste in the pace of the work! As I worked my way through the nervous hum of the gigantic ant-hill that forms the Soviet offices in the centre of Moscow, I felt transported to the enormous new war-offices in Washington, where the errand-boys, tuned up to the general feverish speed, flew on their roller skates through the endless corridors. For these offices are an enormous bourgeoisie palace that the Information Department has commandeered —a palace whose kitchen hall would house all the northern ecclesiastical bodies and have room to spare. What a non-Russian evidence of haste! Armies of short-haired Soviet young ladies were tapping for dear life on thousands of typewriters; young officials, in leather jackets and spurs, were flying round with heavy portfolios; and higher functionaries dashed up to the entrance in their motor-cars, only to disappear, in a few minutes, at the same breakneck speed. What a work it must be!

And afterwards, when I began to look round, I found, at first, pretty much what I expected. I met a number of more or less advanced representatives of the new system who impressed me most favourably—cultured men and women, full of zeal and enthusiasm for a cause for which they evidently, without a thought of self, offered their strength to the uttermost, and inspired by an imperturbable optimism, which at times, indeed, gave the impression of firm religious faith. Under the guidance of a small office—bearing the name of the Information Bureau for Foreigners, whose courteous helpfulness I cannot sufficiently praise—I visited a number of institutions that seemed to bear irrefutable witness to the Soviet Government's fund of initiative and creative power in the most diverse directions. There were model schools of varying types, where interested pedagogues explained to the visitor new and daring educational principles that apparently proved completely successful, when translated into practice; museums and exhibitions of different kinds, exceedingly well arranged and cleverly adapted for the general public, for whom they were specially intended; marvellously equipped homes for the reception of the vast numbers of little orphans that war and revolution have tossed in the cities' gutters; the institution for the benefit of the so-called "science-workers," named from the Russian initial letters the *Tsekubu,* a bourgeois palace of the excessively luxurious type, now converted into a meeting-place for Moscow's "science-workers," etc., with restaurant, debating-halls, library, club-rooms, etc. And whilst seeing all this, I received from the same office little typed information-sheets, evidently written by experts in different departments, explaining the achievements or plans in various directions, economical or cultural, and bearing witness to the Soviet Government's unwearying, progressive zeal for the development of a new Russia.

Thus I could, on the spot, verify what I had read in many descriptions of Russia. I could not do otherwise than share the enthusiasm with which these model institutions were described by travellers who had studied the new Russia. It was evident, I may add, that there would be many more such descriptions, for everywhere the doors were crowded with travellers, intent on observation, from all the ends of the world. These were receiving the same guidance as I was, and for their service commentators, speaking all languages, were forthcoming. At one of the Children's Homes I had the company of an American who had really come over to study Russian modern drama and art, but who had been, gently but firmly, compelled, to his own despair, to sacrifice a morning to the philanthropic institutions. It was, of course, all right—this sample of the Soviet Government's powers of performance spoke an eloquent language which could not fail to carry conviction.

That would have been all right—if I had not simultaneously discovered, as soon as I fell to work by myself with the above-mentioned kindly guidance, that the harmony of the total impression began to be somewhat disturbed. I found how very soon the echoes of the hammers in the new social fabric died away, how the quick life-pulse slowed down as soon as the Russian centre was left behind; I found that the fresh breezes waving the red flag on the very top of the Moscow Kremlin came, as a matter of fact, from a rather noisy but not very effective wind-machine which could not, to any appreciable extent, infuse life into the heavy Russian atmosphere. The Bolshevist power of organization did not seem nearly so impressive and the Russian organizing machinery ceased to remind me of America.

* * *

Bold and purposeful power of action certainly was once the distinguishing feature of Bolshevism and its surest guarantee of progress. It, more than anything else, put the power into Bolshevist hands in 1917. In a Russia whose leaders themselves did not know their own mind, and veiled their weakness in empty phrases and old wives' tales, in a Russia that tended more and more to become nothing but floating chaos, the one fixed point to be seen was the little Bolshevist clique, with its firm, unceasing efforts to reach the goal upon which it had fixed its eyes, viz. the achievement of supreme power. Russia had only very hazy ideas as to what Bolshevist aims really were. But one thing it thought was clear, that they were real men possessing grit and capability, people who in the wide world—whither years of exile had carried them—had laid aside Russian unpracticality, with the Russian habit of unending talk, and had, in their stead, learnt decision of purpose and of action. This impressed their countrymen and inspired them with confidence. And when Lenin gave the signal, Russia followed him, first and foremost, because he and his Party stood out as the strong men of whom the country was in need. But in the years that have passed this healthy power of action has been most seriously crippled. As long as the original plan of battle lasted, they still kept their confident spirit of offensive; the strongholds of the old capitalist order were taken with irresistible speed and boldness of attack. But when they did not thus gain a decisive victory, but, for years afterwards, had to maintain a war of defence—whose end even yet it is impossible to foresee—and, step by step, had to win space for the new social fabric which they had planned, then their legs grew stiff in the trenches. No masterly writing of reports—and surely no fighting forces have ever possessed such clever reporters—no demonstrations to foreign war-correspondents of carefully chosen, well-prepared sections of the front, can disguise the fact that the Bolshevist power of attack is by no means what it once was. In the guidance of Russia's administrative economic and cultural life the Bolshevist system undoubtedly shows many very serious weaknesses.

To begin with, it has, quite naturally, become evident that the forces at the Bolshevist disposal are very ill-qualified for the task. It is certainly true that the leaders themselves, even though originally they were nothing more than very unpractical theorists, have, more or less, risen to the position, even when confronted with the practical task of ruling Russia. But, after all, they are but a handful; the tools to their hands in carrying out their ideas and plans are, as a rule, extremely poorly qualified. Without any disparagement of the Russian working-class, it may still be stated that, where it was necessary to stamp out of the general mass the officials required to form an effective social machine, the result did not prove very striking. The standard of requirements for the new social workers had to be fixed very low—so low that sometimes, even with regard to especially important posts, it had to enter into the ranks of illiteracy.

At first the condition of things was simply preposterous. There are innumerable tales of the complete inefficiency that marked many of those placed even in very responsible posts; tales of the chief of police in one of the larger South Russian towns who, not being able to write, affixed his mark to official documents; of the bank-manager who considered it essential, when he took up his post, to call together the bank personnel to refute the report that he was ignorant of the meaning of debit and credit; of the Red director who studied any reports he received by, now and again, turning the whole paper upside down; of the member who could not read in Russia's highest Educational Council. These are but a few examples out of many—much of what is told is, of course, invention, but infinitely more is undeniably true.

Time has, however, certainly brought about some improvement. The most impossible element has been removed or degraded, whilst others have, by degrees, grown equal to their duties. It is not to be denied that many of the artisans, taken from their machines and placed, in great numbers, high up in leading positions, have shown themselves endowed with outstanding, in isolated cases, even with brilliant, qualifications. And, in addition, the competent members of the middle-class, formerly the object of such contempt and suspicion, have, to an ever-increasing extent, found recognition again—in certain cases so much so, indeed, that some of them, who have succeeded in worming their way into the Communist Party, have there won so large a share of all the more important work that the proletarian elements, undeniably with some justification, feel themselves pushed on one side; certain other members of the middle-class, with specialized training or knowledge, are not only invited but half compelled to place themselves at the disposal of the Bolshevists. Yet, without doubt, their hands are still to a great degree tied by the distrust and ill-will with which they are regarded by the proletariate.

But in spite of all this, it cannot be disputed that the standard of the Bolshevist bureaucracy, in offices and institutions of all kinds, is very low. We cannot, indeed, say much in praise of tsaristic bureaucracy in its decadence, but, rotten as it was, it undoubtedly possessed a certain measure of routine and capability. But the Bolshevist bureaucracy hides, behind a mask of hurry and bustle, terrible helplessness and incapacity, when faced with even the simplest tasks. The very slightest experience of their administrative or economic machinery is enough to give ample proof of these young men and women's uncertainty in dealing with business matters of the most trifling character. Complaints are heard on all hands, from people who have to rely upon them, especially from the peasants who are accustomed in all life's happenings to get help, in every detail, from their superiors; also from those, a little higher up on the bureaucratic scale, who are in despair over their subordinates' uselessness. Of this we find a symptom in the continual change of staff in Soviet institutions, where the officials are rolled about ceaselessly from post to post in a hopeless attempt to get the places filled in something like a satisfactory manner.

This weakness in the individual cogs of the system is partly responsible for another fault in the machine, i.e. its enormous size, which makes it so slow to move and so difficult to handle. The authorities have attempted to make up in quantity for lack of official quality. Work which a competent person could manage alone has been divided amongst several, e.g. ignorant heads have been provided with capable experts to help them, etc. All this has caused a very serious increase in the size of the machine. Two other circumstances, characteristic of Bolshevism, have also contributed largely to the same result. As the Communist Party is now constituted, the various Soviet institutions form the social flesh-pots round which communistic members crowd in great numbers. A higher position in the Soviet activities is purely pay and reward for Party service; the pleasant feeling of power and the no less pleasant material advantages, both direct and, above all, indirect, that such a position brings with it, are for many what makes this Party service endurable. With increase in the Party comes, of course, equal increase in the numbers desiring positions in offices and institutions, and to meet such demands there must be a continual supply of fresh possibilities. And again, a general feeling of suspicion amongst the Party members and the consequent extensive system of spying from above down and from below up is, as we have already shown, a distinguishing feature of the Communist Party. Party tactics demand ever-increasing suspicion and an ever-increasing watchfulness over those of the non-Party public whose work they require. All this is a control which requires, for effective working, a widespread organization that results in cumbrous additions to the machinery.

So the country swarms now with mighty organs of a thousand kinds, all with the same incredible increase in equipment. An outsider cannot count up the Soviet offices that fill central Moscow, requiring so much space that they are responsible, to a considerable degree, for the terrible shortage of housing accommodation existing in the city. Not even the most initiated of the Soviet rulers would venture to enumerate the commissions and committees working for all possible—and impossible—objects. In Moscow alone, according to *Pravda's* computation, the Communist cells in the factories tell off the members to sixty-one different commissions. Several different authorities, as a rule, work side by side—and often at cross-purposes with each other—in the same undertaking. A little time ago, when it was decided to try to raise the labour output, not only one or two, but sixteen commissions were simultaneously formed; the State Bank in the town of Rostov was, so *Pravda* says, for six months the object of the work of six revision committees of different kinds; such small examples could be multiplied indefinitely. And the number of officials in all these Soviet organs is overpowering. A reduction is sometimes made, when this number threatens to burst all bounds. In 1924 the official staff of the People's Commissariat was reduced by 110,000 members, but the absurd amount of overstaffing is evident when such a reduction is in any way possible.

But in a short time it increases again. The army of officials under tsardom was modest compared with that under Bolshevism. Jakovlev gives a few figures from a little out-of-the-way country place. In the office of the district police there were five to seven officials in the time of the tsar, in the Bolshevist civic guard there are thirteen ; in the veterinary and first-aid office there used to be two officials, the Bolshevists have seven ; in the *semstvo's* agricultural bureau in Imperial days there were sixteen persons, in the corresponding institution the Bolshevists have fifty-six, and so on.

To get a machine of these abnormal proportions to work properly without a hitch is, of course, difficult, and becomes all the more impossible when there is no possible escape from the bureaucratic hand that takes hold of cogs and wheels and makes it impossible for them to move. The danger that threatens every great—and unnecessarily great—working organization, the danger of hardening of the arteries, when quick vital circulation is replaced by one of paper only, has been all the more inevitable for Russia, owing to the existence of a number of circumstances directly calculated to produce such a result. The whole character of Bolshevist State-machinery presupposes that the details of its working are controlled from above. This is rendered necessary chiefly by the incapacity that distinguishes the great majority of Bolshevist officials. It would be dangerous to let them have a free hand ; in cases where it has been unavoidable the consequences have been, as already shown, of the most fantastic character. Moreover, the higher official's supreme command and the subordinate's complete reliance upon it are quite simply one of the leading principles of the Bolshevist system. This system is indeed built upon an iron discipline, which aims at crushing individuality and turns the separate Party members into soulless automata. In the working of the Bolshevist State-machinery this is shown by the exceedingly strict limitation of the individual official's freedom of action. He is not allowed, nor does he venture, to use his own judgment or act on his own responsibility, even in trifles ; he must act in accordance with instruction and superior orders. And owing to the vast size of the Bolshevist machine, this guidance can take but one form, viz. that of circulars, instructions, explanations, etc., from above, met by reports, questions, considerations, etc., from below—and thus they land in the midst of the most unadulterated bureaucracy. "We are overwhelmed with circulars and instructions, but have no pleasure in them." This, according to *Pravda*, is a common complaint of the Communist cells in country places. "When the cell-meeting was ended," another correspondent writes to a paper, "the secretary took out a little paper, 2½ metres long and ½ metre wide (exact measurements). This proved to be an inquiry that must be filled up and sent to the Volost Committee. If all the cell-members were stacked, one above another, and all the circulars, inquiries and communications put in a common heap, the paper collection would certainly be the higher."

"Guidance from higher circles," writes another, "is chiefly in the nature of papers and circulars. The gubernia committees generally send out to subordinate bodies one or two circulars every day, and consider that, by so doing, they have fulfilled all their duties to the local authorities. These papers, like the numerous resolutions passed at meetings, conferences, and congresses, contain many of the usual phrases, but very little that is of any practical use. Our Party and Soviet organizations have to learn that our new policy cannot be successfully carried out along the lines of papers and circulars; local authorities must have real, direct, and practical guidance." "Circulars are almost a national misfortune; once for all, the writing of circulars, no matter by whom, should be forbidden" is another utterance.

A *Pravda* article goes on: "Lately it has become customary for gubernia and district officials to make visits of inspection in the villages. This is, of course, a good thing. But the whole matter is so arranged that the local officials get no help from these visits and no practical guidance in the carrying out of the new working principles. The inspectors collect notices, make notes and tabulate, but the local officers get no help worth mentioning from them; and *Pravda* reproduces a local newspaper's description of the procedure in these inspections of the lowest Soviet and

Party organizations. " Such a representative comes to the village Soviet, takes paper and ink from his portfolio and asks for the decree book. He looks how many decrees there are and calculates whether there are more or less than the number prescribed in the work schedule. If there are fewer, he begins to reprove the Soviet for poor work. He forgets that sometimes there may be many decrees but only a few that are actually put into practice. It never happens that a gubernia representative goes round to the school, the mill, the co-operative society, etc., to see their condition and what work is being carried on in them and judge the Soviet's work accordingly; no, everything depends on the number of decrees. With that he begins and with that he ends."

The counter-protest that, in this respect, local authorities save their paper, is now, we must own, in the majority of cases entirely without foundation. For even if the lower Soviet officials are fairly weak in other respects, they have, at any rate, learnt this one thing: they too know all about writing, or, if their own penmanship is not very strong, they get the writing done. From the village cell-secretaries up through all the ranks, this writing is the chief occupation of the Soviet officials. If the first years of Bolshevism saw streams of blood, now streams of ink are to be seen instead; after their machine-guns, men threw themselves down to the typewriters and on them gave full vent to their revolutionary zeal. The practical work is mostly scanty, but the mountains of reports grow ever higher; indecision in the simplest of practical questions is great indeed, but one or more papers are firmly drawn up for wider circulation in the bureaucratic machinery; no one ventures—nor is he allowed—to form a judgment in any matter, great or small; they dispose of the matter in a paper of the regulation kind.

* * *

The Bolshevist energy and power of action have become entangled in a machine of this kind, faulty in construction and impossible in its working. When we now see it at work, guiding and directing Russian life in various directions, we find but little of that which was, in earlier times, the source of Bolshevist strength.

Once the Bolshevists stepped forward to cut with one stroke of their steady hands the Russian Gordian knot; now even the simplest things turn, in their fumbling fingers, into tangled skeins. In an incredible way, they have managed to confuse and complicate everything belonging to their domain. Nothing is so simple as not to require for its settlement a long journey into the bureaucratic labyrinth, no trifle so unimportant as not to need a multitude of writings. For every peasant who does not pay taxes, so Jakovlev relates from one of the provinces that he visited, nineteen papers are drawn up, and these travel round from authority to authority in fifteen different stages. He reproduces in detail the papers' passage amongst all these officials, and calculates that, when the circuit is finished, they have traversed, on their journey by messenger from place to place, a distance of 250 versts. Kalinin himself tells, in a public speech, how sometimes petitioners come direct to him to ask for help in the clearing-up of a matter which has been muddled by the administration in its usual incorrigible way. "These people," he adds, "never have less than half a hundred papers per head from different authorities."

As a slight illustration of how the system works, I will relate a little experience of my own. When leaving Russia, I wished to obtain permission to take with me, first a number of books bought in Russia, mainly Soviet propaganda, and secondly, a couple of small specimens of native hand-work. The matter was not questionable in any way; according to the relative regulation, both articles could be taken out of the country, free of duty; in both cases, too, they were things that the Russians would be glad to have distributed in other countries. The first act was played in Moscow, where the introductory ceremonies, as regarded the books, were kindly performed for me by the Information Office for Foreigners, so that I do not know how much writing it required. The second act followed in Leningrad. It was found that here the business had to pass through five different offices. In one, an examination had to be made to prove the books were not such treasures that they must not be exported; in another an examination to find out whether the native specimens (some wooden articles for a writing-table) had too artistic a value for the Soviet to part with them; the third—a branch of G.P.U.—had to see that the books were not of such a nature that their export was unfitting, from a political point of view; the fourth, to decide that none of the things were dutiable; the fifth—the Commissariat for Foreign Trade—certainly declared that the question was not, in the very least, any concern of theirs, but the other four firmly refused to deal with the matter, unless the Commissariat expressed their opinion. After extensive negotiations I managed to get—for the edification of the other four—a numbered, registered, and stamped declaration—signed too with four names—stating that the Commissariat, although not really concerned with the matter, kindly permitted the export. The business required, on my part, energetic work for three and a half days, during which time I flew like a shuttle, to and fro, between the institutions situated in different parts of the city. The time was, after all, a record only made possible by my action in going, contrary to all rules, straight to the person in the position of authority; when I began, there was every prospect of the business taking at least three weeks, because every institution, whilst declaring its own willingness to do its utmost, assured me that the others, especially G.P.U., were the most impossible people in the world. Before the final settlement, the documents concerned with the business had grown to a dossier of twenty-eight sheets (the original book-list took two), and the matter had been handled by eighteen persons, amongst whom I do not include all those who had turned their attention to it only in a more cursory way. In parenthesis I may say that during the proceedings, on five different occasions, I had been asked for a stamp-duty of two roubles, and after all this, at the frontier, the matter was again the object of real consideration and—again a parenthesis—I was made to pay three roubles for a charity stamp—for the benefit of poor children—that was stuck on the box of books.

" We are smothered in paper " is a complaint universally heard. The public's daily life becomes more complicated then ever before by its dependence on this paper dominion. Write a paper ! is the solution in all life's problems. Fill up an inquiry form ! is the cry in all dealings with the State mechanism, these forms that the Russian citizen fills up on the most trifling occasion and that put questions about every subject on earth ! According to Bucharin, there is but one question lacking, viz. have we been arrested under the Soviet power ? or, if not, for what other reason ? This is a cry that re-echoes through the land. An article in *Pravda* makes the disrespectful assertion that the yearly output of inquiry-forms would circle the earth three times and the State finances would be absolutely exhausted if they had to pay for the printing of these forms at five kopeks a printed sheet.

The Bolshevists were once men of action, who knew what they wanted and quickly brought it to pass ; now all Russia complains of the stagnation that is the result of a marching order, according to which the simplest, most trivial matters have to be tossed endlessly to and fro by the bureaucratic system of investigation. Two peasants dispute about a piece of ground ; the matter takes an average of two or three months to pass all the officials concerned—according to Jakovlev's reckoning for those parts of the country that he visited—and, during this period, the ground lies uncultivated, a distinctly serious matter in Russia, where such disputes belong to the order of the day in every village. In this respect, the whole of the Russian administration of justice, that source of Bolshevist pride, is especially impossible. Even the simplest cases, pending in the first year of Bolshevist rule, are still awaiting judgment ; often they get lost once or twice by their dispatch from one official to another, and the plaintiff has, if he wishes, to begin all over again.

The Bolshevists were once men with a practical outlook and a sense of reality, not troubling over what roads they passed or what forms they trod underfoot in the effort to reach their goal. But now the system that they have created has stiffened into unmitigated formalism. No old tsaristic *tjinovnik* could have marched more stiffly according to rule, even though it ended in absurdity, than does the Bolshevist bureaucracy; no one can more royally surmount the pressure of circumstances when they come into collision with the fixed standards. The programme put before Bolshevist officials must be carried out to the very last item; no omissions are to be allowed from considerations of sound sense or reasonableness, as clear as day. Jakovlev tells how the Finance Commissariat issued an order that all taxes were to be paid by February 15th and a fine imposed for any delay. But before the order could be registered, copied in all the intermediate offices and sent out to the villages that he was visiting, February 20th had come. The local authorities, without hesitation, put the direction in their respective pigeon-holes and dutifully set about demanding both tax and fine. What is written is written! The judges, appointed from the proletarian ranks to the people's law courts, are, indeed, in accordance with principles solemnly proclaimed, to judge as their revolutionary conscience dictates, but, in practice, their judgments are framed in literal obedience to Soviet laws and ordinances, and these often, indeed, not clearly formulated and badly expressed. Such judgments are the subject of universal complaint and—especially in the villages—are condemned, for not only an ordinary sense of justice, but even the revolutionary conscience, rises in horror against them.

Formalism is everywhere rampant. In theory, the poor peasant has a right to a number of privileges; he may have reduction of taxes, free building-timber, wood, etc. But he comes to the authorities with complaints of his need and gets in answer: "Write a requisition and leave it properly stamped." "I went to the Volost Committee," said a peasant to Jakovlev, "and said: 'My cottage has fallen down.' 'Bring a gold rouble for the stamp,' was the reply. And with that I had to be content."

"In front of me," Zinoviev said a short time ago, "lies a communication from the province of Tver. It is a little picture from life. A woman-worker, away in a village, could not get three roubles from her employer, who refused to pay. She summoned him, and legal proceedings took some weeks; then she got a judgment for the three roubles. But when she wanted to have them and applied to the proper office she received a most interesting reply. I have this document in my hand and give it *in extenso:*

To the citizen Maria Ivanova Paramonova, in the village of Pistyalkino.

With reference to your letter, which reached me September 18th last, I beg to inform you that the public auction of Citizen Ivan Aleksejev Tomilin's property, distrained for the payment of your claim, in pursuance of the decree of the Public Court in the third section of the Kasjin district, pronounced the 2nd of June, 1924, under the No. 1144, can be advertised as soon as you have paid 35 roubles 35 kopeks for the announcement in the newspapers and other expenses connected with the sale.

Signed . . . .

Thus the revolutionary spirit of fresh life and energy that once characterized the Bolshevists is now replaced by the hard, unbending mind of bureaucracy.

Bolshevism, that combination of strength and hope, has become a dry, pale-faced, impersonal officialism, weighed down with all the inherited sins of a degenerate bureaucracy. Russia expected to find in the Bolshevists men who could restore the ruined land, but they have found, instead, rattling typewriters, pouring out a flood of papers on great and small matters—principally the latter—in which all fine ideas and reformation plans are drowned and perish. "Let us," said one of the speakers at a Congress, according to a report in *Izvestia,* "take, for instance, the Headquarters for Communal Management. With what is this institution busy? It is busy with plans for great garden cities, with plans for various castles which we do not build." (A voice from the audience, "It builds castles in the air.") "Yes, it builds castles in the air. It has tens of engineers, many hundreds of officials, yet round about in the country we have schools lying in ruins, with no glass in their windows, etc."

And such building of castles in the air we find on all hands (the Bolshevist architects are past-masters in this); and also in one other thing, viz. constructing pretty little plaster models, specimens of what the new Russia is to look like, charming little models, over which foreigners are in ecstasies. Castles in the air and plaster models—unfortunately neither of them are of any use as dwellings. When it is a question of setting about more solid social fabrics, the results achieved are sadly disproportionate to all the busy hammering and bustle on the building-site.

CHAPTER III

THE AMAZING INDUSTRIAL ADVANCE

We will now pass from the general characteristics of the Bolshevists, as builders of the Russian social order, to a somewhat closer examination of the several fields of their activity. We will first turn to the economic question and deal specially with three divisions of it, viz. the industrial system, trade, and agriculture. What progress can the Bolshevist policy record in these ?

The answer is : It has failed, and that in double measure. First, in so far as that their attempt in these fields to carry out the ideas of the Bolshevist programme, as originally sketched, proved a general fiasco at an early stage ; secondly, in so far that, after they had hit upon a new economic policy, which threw a good many of Bolshevism's leading principles on to the dust-heap, and after making a compromise with the capitalist economy which had till then been condemned, the result, even if not so wretched as it had lately been, was, after all, far from brilliant.

* * *

With regard to Russian industry as a whole—for we will first pause to consider this, the child of the Bolshevists' special care but also their chief source of anxiety—the first Bolshevist attempt to apply to it undiluted Bolshevist theories had a quick and decided result, namely this, that, practically speaking, industry ceased to exist. In accordance with the Communist programme, the State assumed control of the industry of the whole country ; sixty all-Russian management boards, "*glavki,*" belonging to a Supreme Economic Council, should each direct their own branch of industry from the central headquarters. The system, according to which every industrial undertaking in its smallest detail—the getting of raw materials, provision of fuel, the fixing of wages, etc.—was made dependent on a distant bureaucratic organization of phenomenal dimensions, of phenomenal ignorance and unsuitability as well, within a few months brought Russian industry to complete ruin. Certainly, it must be allowed that conditions were so unfavourable that any industrial control whatever would have been in great difficulties; the civil war was going on, there was shortage of raw material and fuel, a certain number of industrial workers were fighting in the Red Army and others had fled in crowds from the hunger of the cities away into the villages. But these difficulties are not, in themselves, a sufficient explanation of the catastrophic decrease of industry, particularly as this decrease steadily continued, even when both external and internal warfare had practically ceased. It became more and more evident, even to the Bolshevist Government itself, that the whole system was impossible. Now they only speak in a half-shamefaced manner of this so-called "War-Communism," which yet exactly followed the lines traced out beforehand by Bolshevist theories. It was, so they say, the outcome of the moment's need and never aimed at anything more than the saving, during a critical moment, of those remnants of industry that still survived, as a basis of future development; they do not, however, attempt to deny that this industrial policy, even when considered from this point of view, was a failure. "It was apparent," so runs the official statement in a book, *Soviet Culture*, published in 1924, "that these *glavki* were not equal to their task. Among the multitude of industrial undertakings those most indispensable to the State were singled out and placed in a specially favoured position as regarded the consideration of their needs. But even these undertakings did not get all they required, and it is useless even to speak of the great numbers of other factories—their output continued in its fatal decrease. It became clear that the State could not manage its industry by means of central control. The system of these management boards, this centralization, ended in utter failure.

Communist eyes were opened to this at the time when they perceived that the Bolshevist economic policy, faithfully followed from the first, was untenable. And when the Bolshevists, in 1921, were compelled, in a way that shall be described later in more detail, to introduce the so-called "new economic policy," this policy included also a reversal of the industrial system. By sacrificing some of the theories which had been held sacred before and by approximating to those capitalistic lines that, at first, they could not sufficiently condemn, they tried to set stricken industry on its feet again.

The innovations of the new policy were two in number, of which the first was the least important, viz. opening industry to private enterprise. This proved of little consequence, because only slight concession was made. Even if they understood that they had in this the only really effective way of industrial recovery, they could not make up their minds to go the whole way—the capitulation was, after all, too costly. The branches of industry where private industrial enterprise was permitted were so few in number, the terms granted to it were so impossible, that individual initiative wisely held aloof. At the present moment only 5 per cent. of industrial concerns are in private hands, workshops, on an average, not employing more than twenty or so workers.

The second innovation was that, although the State still continued to own industry, in principle it withdrew from direct management and only reserved the right of control. The management of industry was given over to a number of Trusts, each of which was to be responsible for business activity in its industrial district, and thus, to a certain degree, freedom of action and independence of the State was recognized—but to a certain degree only. Thus, a theoretical decentralization took the place of the earlier strict centralization; Bolshevism's economic patent was abolished in favour of an economic order that, by its terminology alone, gives proof of being copied from the despised capitalistic world.

* * *

What has been the result? An amazing success, if we may believe the official Bolshevist assurances. The system had not been working long before it was clear that the right road had been taken; with each year, the song of triumph reached a higher note. That the progress, so far as it was really achieved, had been made along a road which does not coincide with the narrow path of the pure teaching of Bolshevist theology is, of course, certainly true. Now and again voices were raised to point this out; as lately as the Party Congress in December, 1925, Party opposition—at first quite sharp—openly declared that Russian "State-capitalism," in this point, had uncommonly little to do with Socialism, but, instead, had a very suspicious odour of ordinary capitalism. But this opposition had its lips closed; such things were not to be said. From the Bolshevist orthodox point of view the system may have its defects, but people have long since become accustomed to take such defects very lightly. The chief point was that this road had been instrumental in bringing about industry's "amazing" advance, as they never wearied of calling it.

It is also doubtless true that the Bolshevist statistics can show industrial upward gradients that at first sight seem calculated to justify the shout of triumph. Since 1921 every Russian industry shows a colossal increase. A number of industries, indeed, display an advance of many hundred per cent. Every year industry, as a whole, has moved to a stage higher by an average 50 per cent. than that of the preceding year.

"The rate of development is such that no other country has ever known its like, not even at any previous period," was stated by Rykov as early as 1924; and Kalinin supported him by saying: "We make quicker progress than any of the Western European bourgeois countries whatever. If we continue to develop at the same rate, I hope that in the next few years, we shall not only catch up but leave behind Western Europe." Similar songs of victory, since then, belong to the order of the day.

In this connection it must be said that conclusions drawn from statistics beginning in 1921 and giving the percentage of Russian industrial increase from that time, are not worth very much. 1921 was the year when the combined forces of civil upheaval and Bolshevist industrial theories had succeeded in bringing about the almost total ruin of the whole of the Russian industrial system; in any case, the upward curve need not be so very remarkable to appear brilliant in comparison with that year, when figures had fallen almost to zero.

When Rykov and Kalinin made the speeches last quoted, they could, for instance, point out that the iron industry was four times greater than in 1921—a statement which would have been more impressive had it not been for the fact that the output, which in 1921 had fallen to 2 per cent. of pre-revolution days, had now reached the amount of 8 per cent. If only Bolshevism had continued its original industrial policy for a few more months it would have been possible to report an increase, not only of some hundred, but of some thousand or possibly even million per cent. If, as Rykov asserts, no other European country has seen the counterpart of Russian industry's swift increase, this by no means implies that its present level has reached a giddy height, but only that no industry has ever been at such a low point as it was in Russia during the earliest years of Bolshevist power.

Comparisons with 1921, however flattering to the present industrial position, do not therefore stand for very much. The Bolshevists have firmer ground under their feet, when, as undeniably generally happens, present industrial figures are compared with those of pre-war time. Even here it must be said that the starting-point is exceedingly favourable for the Bolshevists. Russian industry, indeed, under tsardom, certainly did not stand at a very high level. The Bolshevists themselves have not been, by any means, the least active in continually proclaiming that Russian industry then lagged behind. Djersjinsky, the present supreme head of Bolshevist industry, still speaks contemptuously of "the beggarly standards in the semi-slavery of tsaristic Russia." Even if the Bolshevists could have shown figures that plainly outdistanced those of poor tsardom, these, therefore, would scarcely have justified any exultant ecstasy.

But what do we find? Only that the Bolshevists have

beaten tsardom in such branches of industry as were then practically non-existent—e.g. the electrical industry—but otherwise, along the whole line, they are still behind their despised predecessors. The latest yearly report—October, 1924, to September, 1925—proudly produced by the Bolshevists, states that the sum-total of Bolshevist industrial output amounts to about 70 per cent. of that under the old régime.

The spectator of the "amazing" Bolshevist advance in the industrial race-course has sufficient grounds, without need of any nearer scrutiny, to consider it fairly modest, to say the least of it, and barely justifying the competitor's boastful attitude. It is no such brilliant running that after eight years' training—the last few under quite favourable conditions—has not managed to overtake old stiff-legged tsardom. But the disillusion grows still greater if we examine the published result somewhat critically. First of all, it must be said that we have not any exact guarantee that the Bolshevist estimate of the running is really reliable. In saying this, I am thinking less of the emphatic complaints, continually made by competent judges, of the lack of truth in Bolshevist statistics in general. It is certainly true that these remarks seem, *à priori*, fairly plausible. We have, indeed, seen so many instances of the Bolshevist unscrupulous attitude with regard to all usual moral ideas, that it is not difficult to understand why in such an important matter as inspiring their own country as well as foreigners with belief in Russia's industrial revival, they should allow themselves the fairly innocent trick of some juggling with statistical figures. Besides, we so often hear Bolshevist assurances that every branch of science is useless unless it promotes Bolshevist aims—I will return to this later on—that we should feel astonished if they allowed the science of statistics to escape without giving its contribution as well. And it is certainly true, too, that when, as simple laymen, we try to grasp the import of all the statistics scattered broadcast by newspapers and speakers, we are continually stumbling against such contradictory figures that we cannot reconcile them, even with the best will in the world. But this last fact may be due to the critic's lack of statistical training; the general suspicions may be base and unworthy, so that, to avoid doing any injustice to the Bolshevists, let their statistics be considered as trustworthy as divine truth.

But, on the other hand, there is another objection to Soviet statistics which can the less easily be ignored, since it is very emphatically made by critics in Soviet-land itself. When Trotsky again entered the political arena—this time as an economic expert—in the summer of 1925, he had the courage to declare plainly, in his speech, that the practice of comparison with the pre-war standard ought to be discontinued as worthless, since, as he pointed out, " within the range of this comparison, no account at all is taken of the quality of production." The standard is quite simply the quantity of goods produced, and their value is calculated according to the price-lists of 1913—and then the statistics are complete. A pood of manufactured goods is now, without further ado, calculated as of the same value as the same amount in 1913, although the pood is now immeasurably inferior in quality.

That the quality is now really much inferior is openly acknowledged on other occasions. Nearly every copy of the newspapers publishes lamentations over the bad workmanship of the Soviet goods. Trotsky relates how, after having aired the matter, thus confuting the doctrine so long maintained in the Soviet Government that " to protest against the poor quality of Soviet wares was much the same as striking a blow at the very foundations of the Soviet régime," he was completely overwhelmed by complaints from different parts of the country—complaints that were often accompanied by specimens of inferior goods. " The Russian consumer," he declares, " is no longer such a helpless, deaf, blind, toothless creature " as to be content that the Trusts, " trading on their monopolist position, increase production, without any regard whatever to the quality." Here the peasants send him a sample of bone-dust which, in their own words, " is no good as manure, but only to begrime the fields " ; here comes a complaint from Moscow itself, that a customer buying a pair of shoes can never be sure that the right shoe is the same number as the left. A speaker at one of the discussions—now becoming more and more frequent—concerning the poor quality of manufactured goods asserts that " whenever a peasant has to buy a scythe or reaping-hook he looks at it and says: 'This one here is just a Soviet scythe; bring me another.' "

Such grievances are confirmed by a number of official investigations that result in the most remarkable discoveries. Here—to take a couple drawn from February, 1926—it is stated that a tobacco factory in Leningrad itself sends out a cigarette " extra " which is " quite unfit for use " ; here, that a South Russian factory manufactures pencils, 5 per cent. of which contain no black-lead and are only " polished wooden pegs with a hole in them."

It is self-evident that statistics which only take into account the quantity of manufactured goods and shut their eyes to the quality are but a poor test of the real industrial advance. Trotsky takes a practical example and tells how someone gave him at a conference a red and blue pencil. It was certainly marked " superior quality," but was found to be completely worthless ; it was a pencil manufactured by a Russian Trust but with an English mark, a trick that Trotsky, whilst giving a number of similar cases, unhesitatingly declares to be an attempt to deceive the public. When one has to deal with goods of this sort, statistics, in Trotsky's opinion, should take into account their real value when compared with goods in the world's markets. " If our red pencil, with its deceitful foreign mark, is twice as dear as the foreign one, if, owing to its brittle nature, it only lasts one-third the time, if it writes three times as badly, then it is eight times worse than the foreign pencil, and ought therefore to figure in statistics at this decreased value." If, therefore, the result, as given by the Bolshevists as 70 per cent. of the prewar production, requires a considerable levelling down—it is not exactly necessary to reduce it so far as to one-eighteenth—it must also be remembered, at the same time, that this result has been achieved under such circumstances and by such methods that it is still more evident there is very little cause for jubilation in the whole matter. If we consider the factors that have combined to produce the advance, such as it is, we certainly do not gain an impression of any great life-force inherent in industry itself.

To begin with, Russian industry, at its start in 1921, had the advantage of a handicap very greatly in its favour, and one which, during the last few years, must have lightened its task to a very high degree. In spite of the confusion prevailing in the Russian industrial world, there was yet much amongst the ruins worth keeping. There were factories—to be sure, many had come to rack and ruin, but there were still enough left to provide amply for a long time for the Bolshevist industrial needs; many were also very much knocked about, but not to such an extent that it was impossible by utilizing several such battered remains to construct from them one or two quite useful works, provided with all necessary industrial equipment. Bolshevist industry got all this as a free gift, and during the following years not a kopeck had to be written off for construction expenses. And up till now there has been no necessity to think of any new costly buildings, for the old have been sufficient. Kalinin, as lately as the end of 1924, affirmed that not a single factory had been erected in the last few years. Nor was this all; a part of the industrial capital was still left and even a quite substantial supply of finished products which the stoppage, in the preceding years, of all means of transport had saved from dispersal to the four quarters of the globe—this, too, industry took as fair game.

In making any evaluation of the results achieved up to the present, we must, of course, take into account the fact that the Bolshevist industry has enjoyed an advantage such as no other has ever possessed. But, in addition to this, the advance has been favoured by another circumstance of an even more extraordinary nature, viz. its stride has never been hampered by the necessity of making the industry an economic success. Naturally there has been a desire to balance the credit and debit accounts, but this desire has not been by any means overwhelming; the chief thing has been to get industry working; the State has been unfailingly willing to pay for the losses. The maintenance of industry, even when working at a loss, has, namely, been an interest of prime importance to the Bolshevist Government; even if Russia can exist without industry, Bolshevism cannot exist without an artisan class.

During the years immediately following 1921, an endeavour was still made to carry on industry, in accordance with business principles, to enlarge the manufacturing programme and, at the same time, to make the manufactures self-supporting. This resulted in double failure. For one thing, the movement was accompanied by terrific loss. During the year 1922–3 alone the State had to pay, in nothing but subsidies, a round sum of 150 million roubles, of which industry, in the receipts it handed to the Government, was able to repay barely a third. For another, it became apparent that although the prices received were not sufficient to allow industry to meet its obligations, they were yet high enough to prevent people from buying its goods. In the autumn of 1923 Russian industry was in the midst of a critical position; manufactured goods filled the stores with no possibility of finding a sale; the whole industrial life was face to face with a compulsory stoppage. Industry had then achieved a production of something over 30 per cent. of pre-revolution times and seemed, with this, to have reached the limit of its amazing advance.

Thus the Bolshevists had stuck fast; so they determined to try to get their craft afloat again by throwing overboard every consideration of industry's economic result, a resolve which was partly forced upon them by the threatening dissatisfaction of the public—more especially of the peasantry—with the fearful prices then reigning. An economic revelation came to their aid, namely, that to consider that the price of any goods must be in reasonable proportion to their cost of manufacture was nothing more than an absurd prejudice of capitalistic economy.

"It became clear to us," so Djersjinsky writes, "that the prices of our industrial products must be lowered. And then we followed this up by the conviction that the cost of production must not always be the determining factor in the price."

If industry had been brought to a standstill because

the Russian public could not buy goods at the prices with which the Soviet had tried to get a profit, then it was possible to set it going once more—another example of Columbus and the egg—by selling goods at prices which the public could pay, no matter if this was clearly at a loss. Thus from the autumn of 1923 there began a series of price-reductions, by means of which the prices in the metal industry were forced down gradually by about 20 per cent., in the textile industry by 40 per cent., and so on, in a similar way.

This step was undeniably a great success, and the result expected was achieved. It is true the public did not get in their purchases anything like the full benefit of the wide range of price-reductions; the retail trade—as will be shown later—could not be induced to make such reductions as would correspond to the Party's lowered prices. But by repeated use of what Djersjinsky, the head of the Supreme Economic Council, called "the axe-method," it was found possible, at last, to bring down prices more or less to a level that fairly suited the new price-regulator, the light purse of the Russian citizen. Manufactured goods found a sale again and the half-stopped factory wheels could be set in motion once more. Under such conditions, during the year from October, 1923, to September, 1924, industry rose to 40 per cent. of pre-war production, and in the following year, from October, 1924, to September, 1925, touched the 70 per cent. to which we have already somewhat demurred.

But this is only one side of this policy of price-reduction; the economic consequences are not quite so bright a picture. The Bolshevists, it is true, when they adopted the "axe-method," declared their faith in its pedagogical mission. If industry was compelled to sell its goods below cost price, this would spur it on in an effort to bring down the cost of manufacture. According to Djersjinsky, the method would be a mighty lever, a powerful means of raising the work-coefficient, of forcing the factories really to work. To bring about such progress as would diminish the loss in manufacture, the State began, at the same time, a great campaign, which shall be discussed later on. In certain branches of industry it has also been found possible so to reduce the costs of manufacture that the undertaking is now financially sound ; in such cases, this has happened because the industry secured protection from loss by all sorts of tricks. In the speech which we have already quoted, Trotsky states : " We have seen how 'price-reduction' has been facilitated by putting forty matches instead of fifty, how 50 per cent. of shoddy has been mixed with the wool, or how materials have been 'eased' at the cost of quality ; such instances have occurred and still do occur. It is clear," he adds, " that such cases can in no way be reckoned as price-reduction." But the greater number of industries have not, even by means of such tricks, succeeded in bringing down their cost of production to a low enough level. The margin has been too greatly increased. The cotton Trust in Tver was ordered to sell unbleached cotton material at a price of 62.37 roubles per pood, whilst the cost of production was over 72 roubles ; the price of linen yarn was fixed at the price of 28.73 roubles per pood, whilst the cost price in February, 1924, amounted to 36.17 roubles ; the price of print was put at 86.30 roubles with a production cost of 97.49, etc. A Soviet economist writes in a book, published at Moscow in 1924 : " In most cases and in the most important industries the reduction of prices could not be accompanied by a corresponding fall in the cost of manufacture and was therefore a source of loss to the industry."

And then the State has to pay for the loss. It is impossible to give any certain figures of what industry has lately cost the Government. To maintain the illusion that the industrial finances are improving every year, and to give some semblance of foundation for such bold assertions as that industry, taken all in all, is, at the moment, making profits, the State now gives, in direct subsidies, no greater sums than can be shown in Government statistics to be less than the contributions received by Government from industry. If during the year 1923–4 Government gifts to industry still amounted to 12 millions more than they received in industrial contributions, yet in the year 1924–5 industry, according to State statistics, gave the Government 33 millions more than it received. Instead of larger subsidies, the State manages to finance industry in less noticeable ways, principally by extended bank credits—in October, 1924, the industrial indebtedness in the banks was 466 millions, in October, 1925, 926 millions, credits which, in great measure, were nothing but pure and simple poor-relief. With regard to individual industries, a figure creeps out here and there. The all-important metal industry, on which a whole number of others are absolutely dependent, had in 1924, according to Djersjinsky's information, a credit column of 11 millions and a debit of 31 millions—a loss, therefore, of 20 million roubles.

Djersjinsky certainly declares that such figures almost make him weep, but, otherwise, the Government assumes an attitude of forced pleasure at the successful results of the new price-reduction policy. They cannot congratulate themselves enough on having adopted "a policy that would seem incredible for a 'bourgeois' State" (Djersjinsky); they feel that in it they have got "a lever that will lift our industry to an unforeseen height." An outsider finds it a little difficult to understand why there should be anything so revolutionary and new in the discovery that a producer can get a market for his goods if he is willing to sell at a loss, or why it should be a sign of some higher national economic wisdom to arrange the industrial life of any country on that principle. Judged from a non-communistic standpoint, the advance of Russian industry, achieved by such methods, most certainly appears open to reasonable doubt. In backward Western Europe any undertaking that endeavoured to keep going by such desperate means could scarcely—no matter how fine its statistics—escape being considered as fairly rotten. The question may well be asked whether Russian industry deserves any other verdict.

In the Federal Soviet Congress in the spring of 1925 a speaker, taking part in the discussion on Russian industry, said that in his "capacity as peasant" he was anxious to hear why the State-aided industry should always work at a loss and how long the peasants would have to keep on propping up industry. It will be interesting to pause and consider this question, which, in the Congress, was only answered by general assurances that the maintenance of industry was a point of the highest interest, and that not least for the peasants themselves. Is it, on the whole, to be expected that the Bolshevists, under the conditions they have already created, and in view of a state of things that may be expected to arise in the near future, should be able to build up a prosperous industrial economy? The question is connected with another: What is the reason that industry, in spite of all that up till now has favoured its development, is, after all, in such a weakly condition? Are these factors of a more deep-seated nature, or is there any prospect of their removal?

The first of the factors that have prevented an industrial revival strikes the observer at once, viz. the faulty management. It was a step forward, of course, when, as has been already shown, the State gave up the attempt to control industry in detail and left this task to Trusts appointed for the purpose. But even this new system proved to be encumbered with serious defects.

In the first place, the Trusts and the industrial undertakings belonging to them acted, in directions where they were left to themselves, very often with distinct want of economic understanding. It was, of course, self-evident that all positions of control should be filled from the proletariate, and thus arose a state of affairs that has already been mentioned, when dealing with the Bolshevist State-mechanism as a whole: with all due respect to the proletariate, it was, after all, quite unable to provide really competent managers for about 500 Trusts and some thousand factories. There are undoubtedly, of course, quite a number of "Red directors," who, when they got used to their work, acquitted themselves most creditably, but that does not prevent the average standard from being extraordinarily low. The workman who had spoken like a man at the people's meetings and had fought like two in the Red Army was not up to his work as one of the heads of industry. To a certain degree, an attempt was made to balance this by placing at his side people with technical training, drawn from the former bourgeoisie, who, under the name of experts, were intended to exercise the real control of the undertaking; but the continual attitude of suspicion shown to this middle-class element prevented anything more than a very partial use of their possible power of management.

Consequently, the history of the Trusts is full of the most terrible mistakes. In spite of capable work now and again in details, the inexperienced industrial chiefs lacked the power to oversee the industries confided to their care. The Trusts worked away, trusting in the providence of God, or rather of the State; they could always fall back on that when things went wrong. What, for example, shall we say of an industrial management which—as Djersjinsky relates in one of his speeches—one day sends in a report to the State Supreme Economic Council that the industry was going on splendidly, and, the day after, sends a telegram begging for State help to enable them to pay the wages? Or of the management of the great coal industry in the Donom district; without thinking of such a trifle as possibilities of sale, they worked away for dear life until, one fine day in the summer of 1924, it was found impossible to get any customers; home industry was overstocked and in the foreign markets the price of coal had fallen below Russian cost of production; so there they were, in the twinkling of an eye, in the very midst of a crisis, whose possibility had never even occurred to them. This crisis at first produced a terrible upset and confusion, which, according to Djersjinsky, led to the compulsory paying-off of a thousand workers and from which the only possible escape was a resolution to export coal—at a loss!

Often, however, it is not only competence that is missing, but active interest and energy as well. However great their revolutionary loyalty and devotion, these Bolshevist officials have still not been able to fill the place of the industrial chief with a personal interest in his undertaking. "The administrative councils in our Trusts and the directors of our industries," so Trotsky complained in the twelfth Party Congress, "are not real managers who keep an eye on everything, who are heart and soul in the business, who make use of every minute, save every possible farthing, and pass their nights busied with the needs of our factories, our mines and our iron works." The value of personal interest could not be more strongly emphasized than is done here by Trotsky with wisdom, learnt in his experiences of Russian industry.

Real management is wanting. Its place is taken here, as in every case where it is a question of Bolshevist organization, by a heavy, impersonal, bureaucratic mechanism. Every Trust-management comprises a whole corporation in itself; every factory belonging to the Trust provides itself with another. Such an over-organization is beyond comparison. Officials, of all grades, rival the workers in number. Note this little example from the public Press: A workman in a comb factory describes how these works, employing a total of thirty-one men, have fifteen persons, from the director downwards, on the official staff; in times gone-by the factory was managed by the owner alone, with the help of one foreman. This man afterwards offered to take over the whole management for a certain percentage of the profits, but his offer was not accepted. The communication goes on: "The workmen are firmly convinced that the industry will be a losing affair." Of course, they are right; the industrial over-organization is an unreasonable burden that threatens to eat up the small profits.

But another result of over-organization is—as described above—an intolerable bureaucratic stiffness in management. Every industrial unit, large or small, Trust or factory, becomes a machine driven by paper, heavy and slow in working. The paralysing effect of this bureaucratic industrial management extends even to trivial details. The work-people themselves have often a very clear idea that everything is going wrong; time and again correspondents are to be found in the newspapers, writing from their work-places, sharply criticizing the absurd organization in their factory and suggesting simplifications; the factories' so-called "wall newspapers," hand-written papers, in which they give full vent to their desire to criticize, are filled with keen criticism of the over-organization which, quite unnecessarily, complicates work. Last autumn Zinoviev read in one of his speeches an amusing little communication that he had received from a workman in the Treugolnik factory in Leningrad, which has the reputation of being one of Russia's best-managed industries. "A bolt has fallen out of a machine," the workman writes, in a sketch which he calls "The Story of a Bolt." "It is a small bolt, 1½ to 2 inches long, worth about half a kopeck. To get a new one, the foreman has to draw up a written request that a fresh bolt may be put in machine so-and-so. Then the written application must be taken to the engineer for his signature, and then to the mechanical engineer, who sends it to the repairing-shop. The order-form is received, then a requisition has to be written. The requisition is written in triplicate, and afterwards taken to the foreman for his signature. He is not always just to hand, since the factory has a circumference of a couple of versts; he has to be looked for, and the looker goes round the factory to find him. At last he is found. He signs, and then it has to go to the engineer, and then finally to the store. But in the store no such bolts are to be found, only bolts 3 inches long. So out comes a knife and it is cut and put in its place."

These defects of system, now mentioned, are the inevitable consequences of the fact that the Trusts, although nominally acting on their own initiative, are only parts of the great Bolshevist apparatus, and, as such, labour under all the weaknesses inherent in it. If a remedy is desired, it can only be found by continuing along the road already trodden on one occasion, i.e. by lessening the dependence of the Trusts on the State by permitting them to fill up positions in the management, not on the grounds of Party merit, but on grounds of efficiency, even if such efficiency should happen to be amongst the non-proletarian class, by allowing them to build up an organization which is guided by reasonable principles, instead of being in accordance with Bolshevist schedules, and by permitting them to get rid of all that bureaucratic spirit which seems an inextricable part of Bolshevist organization. Meantime, however, an exactly opposite road is being followed; when the Trusts are impossibly unsuccessful, they are made more dependent on the central State organization. As we have said, the principle should be for the State to keep only the ultimate control over industry, but development in the past, and increasingly so in the present, has shown a tendency for Government again to get the management of industry more and more into its own hands—that is, there is a sliding-back into the system which, when it was first tried, made such pitiful shipwreck.

The chief control of industry is vested in a Supreme Economic Council, in reality a people's commissariat, although it does not happen to go under that title; it is assisted by a number of institutions with various names, the chief of which are the so-called Central Executive Committee and the Labour and Defence Council. The official duty of these Government organizations is to use their united efforts to plan out industrial activity and to fix the production programme for the different Trusts in order to prevent, as Djersjinsky puts the matter, an "anarchical extension of production on the part of individual Trusts"; but, in reality, they direct all industrial action in matters great and small, thus reducing the independence of the Trusts to a mere empty form.

Thus the Trusts are deprived of every possibility of growing into capable industrial organizations. As long as they still had a certain independence, there was a chance that they might gradually develop efficiency, power of initiative and business insight. In rare cases—as we have said—that has already happened. Now, when the Trust managers are more and more reduced to nothing but tools for carrying out the intentions of the Government organizations, these qualities have no longer any possibility of developing in them. Even the incentive of the work disappears before a State interference which is often gross in character. The Bolshevists are not yet so expert in their transformation of human psychology that they can prevent a Trust-management from losing heart when, after really getting their industry to go—as we have said, there are some such Trusts—they are suddenly ordered to slacken speedon ly because another Trust, working on the same lines, is doing badly and is in danger of having to pay off its hands. And it may be good Communism, but it is, very certainly, bad industrial policy when an electrical Trust—one where several useful inventions had been made, and which, thanks to them, was doing exceedingly well—is roundly abused because it had not, at once, shared the inventions with the rival Trust. I speak of rivalry because, although industrial competition is a capitalistic abomination, yet no power on earth can prevent the fact that whenever individual Trusts have really begun to succeed, their increased activity has always been closely associated with the beginning of competition on the part of others. "In many of our industrialists," Trotsky declared in the summer, "we notice an uncritical, sympathetic attitude towards competition as a factor of technical and economic development." In so far as the keen Government control now renders this competition impossible, it tends, indeed, to maintain the purity of communistic teaching but not the welfare of Russian industry.

Since the Trusts have been forced in this way to take a subordinate place, the industrial control is, in reality, wielded by central State organizations, created for this object. As regards this control, it must be acknowledged that these various central institutions, more particularly the Central Executive Committee, are not, by any means, badly equipped with industrial ability and skill, great part of it supplied by certain members of the former middle-class who have been taken into favour again, nor can we deny that the work in them is both alert and energetic. But that does not help much. Again we come upon the usual old Bolshevist story, viz. boundless over-organization with all its inevitable consequences. A number of different official departments with endless sub-divisions examine into and turn over the industrial questions in a way so detailed as to be perfectly absurd, at the same time lying in wait on each other to spy out their mutual incompetence. Even the dry report setting out how the yearly production programme for the various branches of industry is fixed, and given in *Pravda* by a Trust member during the summer of 1925, is splendid. It runs literally as follows:

"The programme is carefully considered for six to eight

months, and the scrutiny is carried on in the following way: The Trust sends in its proposal to the respective board of directors in the Supreme Economic Council. The Trust chief and a director in the Council go through the programme; then it goes to various sections and organs of the Supreme Economic Council, and the farther it goes, the greater the number of persons who scrutinize it. Then the programme goes to various sections in the Central Executive Committee. There all the work done by the Supreme Economic Council is put into the waste-paper basket, and the scrutiny begins again from the beginning. The number of critics increases. A great number of people join in, all dispute, and everything that has been done up till then is gone through again. Then the matter goes to the presidency of the Supreme Economic Council. From there it goes to the Labour and Defence Council, and if it is not unanimously approved, to the Council of People's Commissaries. The number of those taking part in the procedure in the Supreme Economic Council is 100 to 150; the number of departments through which the programme passes is more than ten—in the naphtha industry, for instance, it is thirteen. In every one of these departments the consideration of the programme requires several meetings and, in addition, specially appointed commissioners often work at it. And, further, to deal with special points in the programme, meetings are appointed in the Finance Commissariat, the Commissariat for Foreign Trade, the Industrial Section in the Supreme Economic Council, etc."

Of course, it is impossible to doubt but that decisions, arrived at in this way, represent the acme of industrial wisdom. The only pity is that industry profits so terribly little by it; as a rule, before all the procedure described can be accomplished, half the year has gone and the industry has, meantime, been compelled to work without any programme at all! For instance, the metal industry did not get its programme fixed for the year beginning October 1, 1923, until May 7, 1924—that is, when barely five months of the year were left With regard to the production programmes of the various Trusts for the year October 1, 1924, to September 30, 1925, Djersjinsky announced, in a speech in January, 1925, that "nearly all" had passed—"except a few cases"—the Supreme Economic Council. "With the exception of some," they had then been sent on to the Supreme Executive Commissariat, and some had "already" (four months on in the current year!) been scrutinized by the Labour and Defence Councils. The state of affairs during the present work-year has been perfectly preposterous, since, on account of the gross miscalculations—which shall be discussed later—the various production programmes had to be recast; now the first edition of these programmes has not managed to pass through all the departments before some of them are already at work in the scrutiny of the second edition; now we can read, in the newspapers, that in February the Labour and Defence Council has considered the metal industry's programme for the year (in the year's fifth month!) and is sending it on to a special commission.

"We get into hot water," the Trust member, quoted before, wrote to *Pravda* in the summer of 1925, "if we diverge from the programme fixed for us now, in the middle of the year concerned, although, with the best will in the world, we cannot work in accordance with it." What is true of the production programme is also true of all industry's dealings with the State management; things are moving on rapidly towards what is called "*glavkism,*" that insufferable condition during the early years of the revolution, when the above-named State institutions, *glavki*, smothered industry in their bureaucratic bosom.

* * *

Meantime, it is not only the management that is at fault; the most serious impediment to the creation of a prosperous Russian industry comes from the workers. The idea, given to them by Bolshevism, of their rights and duties makes normal industrial activity extraordinarily difficult. First of all, it is a fact that industrial discipline in the new Russia leaves terribly much to be desired. The total breaking-down of what industrial discipline still existed after the general confusion and upset of the revolution months was the Bolshevists' first proceeding in their dealings with industry. Before the experiment, described above, of industrial State management, they introduced into factories and work-centres a so-called "workers' control," which meant, in reality, complete anarchy in the industrial world. This resulted in a travesty of conditions which, during the first months of Bolshevism, was much talked of in Western Europe, but which there—although quite erroneously—was almost looked upon as a poor joke, as pure fiction, viz. the workmen lorded it in the factory to suit themselves, the management had to dance to their piping, and the head of the works had less to say about the matter and got worse paid than the lowest of his workers. The system, indeed, was certainly done away with very quickly and an attempt made—a decidedly firm one, too—to re-establish normal conditions, but the tradition left by these months has not been easy to uproot. The idea that the management has to control and organize the industry, and that the work-people's first duty is to work, is one that does not occur to the average Russian workman. He considers it his inalienable right not only to hold a very decided opinion as to how the work should be organized and carried out, but also, when his opinion differs from that of the managers, to persist obstinately in making his own prevail. The Russian workman, looking vainly in other quarters for any reality behind the talk about the supreme power of the proletariate, here unhesitatingly makes use of the logical conclusions of his reputed dictatorship, and defies anyone to come trying to order him about in his work!

Now, of course, it can never occur to anyone to deny the advantage to production if opportunities are given to the workers to express their points of view and put forward their ideas; this is especially true of Russian industry, where the management, as we have shown, is usually so utterly weak. Many an ordinary workman at his machine has, quite certainly, a much wiser judgment and keener eye for what will promote or hinder the progress of the industry than some of those who, on the strength of Communist Party merits, are put in positions of control. In so far as workers content themselves with making their voice heard in the regular way—at conferences called for this and similar objects—with reference to questions lying within their sphere, nothing but good can result.

But the fact is that the workers certainly do not content themselves with this. For one thing, they desire to have their say in questions of which they know nothing. "The workmen interfere in things that are not at all their business," even Djersjinsky owns; and with a sharpness in his tone which is an additional proof that conditions, in this respect, are beginning to get quite unbearable, he explains that it is the management's duty to keep them in their proper place. For another, they have no scruples in setting up opposition where the orders given are not to their fancy —even *Izvestia* recognizes this "abnormal phenomenon." But that is not all; the workman will not put up with any admonition or criticism of his work. An article in *Izvestia* reports: "A foreman writes to us that, when he criticizes work or points out to a workman that he must be more particular in what he is doing, he makes an enemy for himself. The result is that those whose business it is to supervise the workers become less scrupulous in their duty and turn a blind eye to defective work. If the ideas held by the workman as to his position make him so rebellious to any control, even when this is exercised by a proletarian comrade like his foreman, they, of course, do so even more when he sees above him his natural enemies —whom it is only his duty to defy—in the middle-class element whose technical knowledge industry is continually obliged to use in increasing measure. An engineer at one of the larger factories, a man whom the Bolshevists had shown themselves most anxious to secure on account of his well-known powers in organization, assured me as follows: "It is like driving one's head against a wall; the workmen look upon every idea of mine as a sly bourgeois invention and take every one of my orders as a purely personal insult." There has grown up amongst the workers a real "*eating of specialists*," the accepted term for the perfectly unreasonable obstruction, accompanied by annoyances of every kind, which they put up against technical knowledge and specially trained ability. Djersjinsky is obliged, again and again, to oppose these methods, which, according to him, are relics from the time when workers, in their relations with the specialists, "held a cudgel in our hands and had to make use of it to keep them from cheating us."

It is plain that a cudgel like this does not make any sort of lever for industrial work. Until the Soviet has managed to train for its use efficient proletarian skill, it is dependent on that of the middle-class, and if industry is to have the slightest prospect of getting on its feet again, this middle-class skill must have opportunity to make its influence felt—at present it is rendered almost completely useless.

The lack of industrial discipline is all the more serious, since it is evident that those in positions of control lack the courage to make a serious effort to remedy it. It is true that, in political matters, they treat the proletariate with but scant ceremony and any tendencies to political opposition are crushed without mercy. But that the workers should defy the middle-class element in industrial control is, after all, quite in accord with Bolshevist principles, and in the drawn battle between workers and management any general appearance of siding with the latter would, strictly speaking, really not quite do in a workers' republic. Djersjinsky and other leading politicians may, certainly, allow themselves to utter a sharp word now and again, but, as a rule, they dare not do more than offer, most cautiously, gentle suggestions. They recognize that the management often makes unlawful demands and advise the workers to keep a keen outlook for all arrogant tendencies in those in control. "Of course," *Izvestia* writes, "the technical staff must not go too far. By exercising too heavy or too sharp a pressure on the workers, they alienate them and open a gulf between workmen and management that can only be crossed with great difficulty. All work that the technical staff in any undertaking wishes done in the interest of production must have the consent of the workers' organizations. Orders from above without explanations of the importance and use of such orders are positively harmful." Tucked away in all these admissions, then, comes a little admonition to the workers. "If the demands upon the workers, made by the technical and administrative personnel, are imperative in the interests of production, and if such demands do not trespass on the workers' fundamental rights, they should be complied with."

Still more fatal than the worker's reluctance to submit to necessary industrial discipline is one other thing, viz. his aversion to real work. Now he has never possessed any unconquerable love of work; work-intensity in Russian industry was amongst the lowest in Europe, even before the war. But, at the present moment, conditions have become really incorrigible; never has the work been worse in Russia than under the workers' dictatorship.

Some of the figures given by the Bolshevists themselves in that respect are significant. "I am going," said Djersjinsky, in a speech in December, 1924, "to show by plain industrial figures how many workmen during the year 1923–4 were needed for work that in 1913 required a hundred men: in the coal industry 214, in naphtha production 213, in shoe manufacture 234, in chemical industries 292, in tobacco production 318, etc." One of the industries which offers somewhat more favourable figures—an increase only to 148—is, we may remark in parenthesis, the paper industry, but then that is also one of the most important for the Bolshevists. In the South Russian metal industry—the figures are still Djersjinsky's —the value of a workman's yearly production was in 1913 3,227 roubles; in 1923–4 its value, reckoned at pre-war prices, was 988 roubles; in the same industry in Ural in 1913, 1,370 roubles, now 700 roubles—in the south, therefore, now 31, in Ural 51 per cent. of the earlier value. In a number of machine factories a worker in 1913 produced, on an average, goods to the value of 1,740 roubles, in 1923–4 of 810 roubles; before the war there were working in those factories 99,000 men, and their production was worth 173 millions; in 1923–4 the workers numbered 80,000 men, but their production only reached a value of 62 millions. "You see," Djersjinsky adds, "how upsetting is the disproportion between these figures. The number of workers is nearly the same as before the war, but the production is only one-third what it was then." Still more striking is a picture of the metal industry published in 1924 in *Economecheskaya Jeezn*: "The same piece of work requiring, in Western Europe, 2–3 hours, in 1913, in Russia needed 5–6 and now 13–20!"

It is self-evident that it is not only the workers' poor work-intensity which is to blame for the very wretched production figures. Many factors, some already touched upon, contribute, of course, to this result. "The worker may strain every muscle," such is the charming little idyll from Russian factory life given by Zinoviev in one of his speeches, "but if the head of the factory is an ass who does not understand his job, if the foreman is incapable, if the raw materials are bad, if every roof lets in the rain, there will be no increase in manufacture, for all his efforts. But none the less the fact remains that the chief responsibility rests on the workman. "We must," Zinoviev says, with a softness in his voice suggested by the fear that imperious orders will not do much here, "be bold enough to tell the workers that they alone are responsible for 50 per cent. of the fall in production." The revolution introduced the eight hours' day, but at the moment there is very little question of eight hours' work per day. "In our principal cities, in Leningrad and Moscow, there really exists," so says Zinoviev, "an eight hours' day, even if not in all undertakings. But in quite a number of districts in our S.S.S.R. the daily work consists of four to six hours. That we cannot afford," he adds. "Of course, when Communism has conquered, we shall shorten the working-day to six hours or less, but we cannot think of that now."

Still worse than this severe shortening of work-hours is the generally recognized fact that, when the men really are working at their best, they only go at half-speed. The idleness, indifference and slackness which now characterize the average Russian workman form indeed a record. Everyone who has come in contact with Russian industry recounts fabulous instances of this, and even Soviet writers acknowledge it. According to one of these, a little time ago in the Leningrad factory Krasny Putilov, which has, on paper, an eight hours' day, only 58·5 per cent. of that time was spent in work: 1 hour 5 minutes was spent in smoking, 55 minutes in promenades about the works, the rest in prolonging the meal-time breaks. In other factories things are still worse. According to the same writer, the real work-time in the Krasny Uzborget factory did not exceed 1 hour 37 minutes; from the same source we learn that, in the Kolomna iron-works, 800 hours a month were lost in reading the papers and forming queues for getting their wages. Undoubtedly, various means have been tried to improve matters. Especially since the autumn of 1924, an uncommonly active campaign has been started to induce the workers to make reasonable efforts. Leading politicians, dealing with the subject in every speech, expressed the Soviet's anxiety and appealed to the workers to take pity on them. "There was a time," so runs an extract from one of Zinoviev's speeches, "when we and you demanded an eight hours' day from the Bourgeoisie, Tsar and Co.; but now the workers' State—i.e. all of us—beg of you an eight hours' day—an honest, real, genuine, sober eight hours' day—a thing we still have not got." The newspapers filled column after column with sermons on the subject. For instance, *Izvestia* writes: "The Soviet Republic has a perfect right to demand from the workers increased intensity of work, a maximum use of the eight hours' day, a decrease of wasted time and a greater feeling of responsibility in their work. A fresh spirit of work must inspire the Republic, as it has done, many tim es before, in moments of the greatest danger." And a mighty apparatus has been created to attain, in different ways, the desired end. "Fifteen committees work and two are busy organizing," *Izvestia* announced about Christmas, 1924. It is evident that such a concentrated tattoo must have a certain effect. The question is, however, whether it is, in fact, possible in this matter to obtain any considerable and really effective result.

To begin with, it is fairly uncertain whether the workers, under present conditions, *can* increase the intensity of their work to any appreciable extent. As long as they are paid an insufficient starvation wage, forced to live in dwellings unfit for human habitation, and, in general, to lead an existence which is nothing but a series of hardships and deprivations—I will return to these conditions later on—it is fundamentally unreasonable to demand any higher degree of intensity from them. They are simply physically incapable of putting any real strength into their work. "The worker's muscular system cannot do much more than it already does," was the declaration in the Federal Soviet Congress, held in the spring of 1925, of a workman from the Putilov factory. "The majority of the delegates dwelt especially on the workers' impossible housing conditions, which exercise a prejudical influence on industrial production," says the *Pravda* report of the same Congress. "One of the primary hindrances to industrial revival," Djersjinsky also acknowledges, "is the general housing misery, the unheard-of crowding together of our population, which deprives the worker of any possibility of sufficient rest after his heavy toil." In an Economic Congress in the autumn of 1924 a worker from distant Ural scoffed at the rulers' simple faith that production could be increased by agitation, bombastic speeches or utterance of the password: "Save your native country and strain your strength to the uttermost." "The means," he pointed out drily, "are a sound wage-system." He referred principally, in this connection, to the delay in payment of wages which, at one time, was general in industry, and sometimes led to the workers not getting their money for months, or even for half a year; but his remark is equally true as regards the terrible insufficiency of the current wages. There can be no thought of any real and substantial increase in intensity of work until the workman is properly paid and therefore able to raise his standard of living. And since, on the other hand, there can be no question of any really effective wage-increase so long as industry, mainly owing to poor intensity, is in such a miserable condition, the Soviet State is here caught in a vicious circle of a very unpleasant nature.

But one other thing remains, and that not the least important: it is still more uncertain whether the Russian workman *will* increase his speed. It is, first and foremost, true that, as long as the present system of underpayment continues, he feels it is simple injustice to ask increased production from him, an injustice he meets with a determined and methodical resistance. But he has also adopted and holds fast to the general idea that his right to slacken the rate of work until it suits his Slav indolence is one of the real gains of the revolution—a gain that he does not mean to let slip through his fingers, as he has been obliged to do with a number of others. Should he, the dictator, not have a right to take, not only a rest to drink his coffee, but one to read his paper and another for discussion ? Surely he has not made a revolution for his powers of work to be exploited even more than in the times of tsardom ?

" If one of the foremen represents to a workman that it is not right of him to sit in the dressing-room during work-hours, he gets, time and again, such a torrent of abuse in answer that his face flushes with shame at the worker." These are the words of a writer of an article in *Pravda,* in which he shows how important the dressing-rooms have become in the factories, now that they have been converted into centres for the most eager political and economic debates. The workers, too, expressed their opinion as plainly as could possibly be desired during the campaign to raise the work-intensity. It was not long between the occasions when they gave expression to their dissatisfaction with an agitation in which they often saw an unlawful infringement of their rights—a dissatisfaction which had a marked effect in reducing the agitation. Zinoviev, whose gentleness to the working-class was quoted above, pronounces in the same speech from which the quotation was taken, a warning against " wearing out " the workers by too much talk about the necessity of increasing their work-intensity and by piling on them reproaches which buzz like flies in the workers' ears with their " raise the production, raise the production." It has also proved very difficult to effect any real improvement in the wretched rate of work. Certainly, during that agitation campaign, they succeeded, at first, in raising industrial production by a not too inconsiderable amount. The ncrease from October, 1924, to May, 1925, was about

31 per cent. It ought to be added that, as a matter of fact, the improvement was no doubt due, not so much to the agitation itself as to the fact that, at the same time, in spite of the workers' determined opposition, piece-work wages were introduced to a great degree in industry. But then came "stop," and not only "stop," but "back." In the latter part of 1925, industrial production showed a steady decline; a worker's average daily production, which in the April to June quarter was worth 6 roubles 5 kopecks, diminished in the next quarter to 5.89 roubles and in the last quarter of 1925 to 5.78 roubles. Certainly this decline was not entirely due to the worker's low intensity of work, but was, to some extent, due to the fact that the industrial equipment then began to be so worn out as to exercise an adverse effect on the output. But, in great measure, the explanation is that the worker had already had enough of the somewhat forced speed. It was stated on all hands that shirking work—especially after pay-days—soon increased; a somewhat searching inquiry from the Ukraine reported that the cases of shirking during the last quarter of 1925 had increased in number and importance to double and three times their previous record. From a factory in the Donom district—to quote only one of many newspaper instances, taken from *Pravda*, March, 1926—comes a report of "a great increase" in malingering and shirking. There are, it states, workmen who "work only ten to fifteen days in the month; there are cases where a worker explains he can only come to work for fifteen, afterwards he is ill. Consequently the factory can only carry out its production-programme with difficulty and has to keep 15 per cent. workpeople in reserve for every emergency." It adds: "Afterwards we can see the invalids sitting in the beershops." There were also bitter complaints in political speeches, the Press, and economic conferences of different kinds that industrial discipline was slackening and far from what it should be. *Pravda*, in an anxious leading article in February, 1926, speaks of the "sickly processes in our industry," which have assumed the character of evidently dangerous and chronic sufferings that are a menace to all our economic

plans and calculations." The situation is so much the more disquieting, as the increase in work-intensity which, at any rate, has been attained in comparison with 1924, has turned out to be of the very slightest economic benefit to industry.

To begin with, the increase in production is, to a certain extent, apparent only; the worker, it is true, has increased the quantity of his production but has indemnified himself by reducing its quality. Moreover—and yet more important—the gain is neutralized by a special circumstance.

The fact is that although—as we have already said—there is, under present conditions, not the slightest possibility of raising the insufficient wages to a reasonable standard, yet the Soviet State is compelled, again and again, to give a small increase. The wages shall—that is the rule—from year to year move up by just the merest fraction—an increase not large enough, however, to turn them into a living wage—but this regular increase has a psychological effect on the workers which the Soviet State cannot dispense with, and therefore it cannot inquire as to whether industry is able to bear the higher wages or not. And in the midst of the great campaign started for the purpose of increasing work-intensity and thus decreasing the price of production, it has been necessary to give the workers an increase of wages which swallows up the profit that the increase in working power would have brought with it. What industry, on one hand, by dint of great effort, has managed to get out of the workers in the form of increase in productivity, it has, at the very same moment, to give back to them in the shape of an increased wage. In the beginning of the great campaign, the increase in productivity was really greater than the increase in wages, but after the summer of 1925, when a number of increases were given and, at the same time—as mentioned above—the workers slackened in intensity, the curves of productivity and increased wages present a perfectly terrifying picture for industry; for each rouble paid in wages, the workman daily produces less. It is easy to understand why Djersjinsky himself sums this up as "a very alarming state of affairs."

* * *

If, taking the factors already mentioned into account, the future of Russian industry appears somewhat dark, there is yet another circumstance, by no means least in importance, to be considered. In the course of the year 1926 industry enters, namely, into quite a new phase of its development when problems of an entirely fresh nature, and more critical than before, present themselves for solution.

It has already been shown that the Russian industry has been living on the inheritance left behind by tsardom. It has been spared all worry as regards new buildings and equipment. Wherever it has been possible to widen the industrial activity, they have only to an increasing extent made use of industrial equipment which was already available. But now the inheritance is beginning to come to an end. To begin with, when any industry wishes to extend beyond its present limits, there are no longer ready-made factories and machines standing there, waiting to be used. The very last of those, hitherto unused, were set going this year; as a matter of fact, they are gathering up the last fragments that remain and putting up with what has, until now, been considered quite impossible to use, such as factories with old-fashioned technical equipment or situated far away in remote corners where it is difficult to get raw material. "What is now being put in use is the old worn-out factories and machines," *Pravda* states in the beginning of 1926. Industry will continue to have to put up with less exceptional conditions; it will have to put up factories itself before it can begin to turn out goods. Moreover, during the past years, it has given its equipment such rough usage that it is worn out; it is all very frail, for only the most essential repairs have been done and practically no attempt has been made to bring any of it up to date. Some time ago the *Economecheskaya Jeezn* described the Zormovo factory, one of Russia's most important iron-works, as no longer a giant in the metal industry, but a cripple; the buildings are old, tumbledown, and covered with soot; the roof rusty and a good many of the windows nailed up; only 4·5 per cent. of the furnaces are in a good condition; 62·5 per cent. of the other technical equipment is in need of great repairs A similar or worse state of affairs exists in most places, with the exception of a few exhibition works that are shown to foreign Labour delegations. It is a situation that becomes every day more hopeless. First of all, it affects industrial productivity; that this is now so unsatisfactory is, as we have shown, mainly due to the workers' low power of intensive work, but, in addition to this, the defective industrial equipment is a powerful contributory factor. "Without replacement of the old, worn-out and antiquated equipment there can, of course, be no question of any definite solution of the problem of productivity," *Pravda* definitely states in February, 1926. The same factor also explains, to some extent, the low quality of the manufactured goods, for, even with the best will in the world, it is impossible with the present available means in machinery, etc., to reach a faultless standard. And the work with the existing industrial apparatus also exposes the worker to continually increased danger for life and limb. To sum up, then, a complete new industrial equipment is necessary, not only for the further development of industry, but even if the present *status quo* is to be maintained. Now, if industry has had a struggle during the last few years, when it only had to carry on with the machinery inherited for nothing, then it is plain that it has no very rosy prospects of success when it is a question of also providing the necessary new premises, repairs and modern improvements at a cost of many milliards of roubles.

Nor is the way in which this new stage in the Bolshevist industrial history has been started very promising. It was intended, as a little beginning of the great reconstruction work, to devote the first milliard (1,020 millions) to industry; about 200 millions of this to go to new factories, 700 millions to putting old ones in thorough working order, and 100 millions to the erection of workmen's dwellings. But it has not been possible to accomplish even this programme, although it was exceedingly modest when compared with the greatness of the need. The idea was that about half should be defrayed by funds which—inasmuch as their provision by the State treasury was more or less disguised

—were designated as industry's own. But it has been hard to produce these funds. "Industry is experiencing," so *Pravda* says, "such acute want of capital and such financial straits as only occur in the most critical moments." To take half a milliard out of the empty purse is, under such circumstances, no easy matter. The other half-milliard the State was to pay under different forms of direct Government subvention. *Pravda* writes in the beginning of 1926: "To carry out the new building programme from their own resources without the active support and co-operation of the State treasury and the credit system that is at the Government's disposal is a task beyond the power of industry; it demands the utmost efforts of every department of national economy." But even the funds that the Government was to give fell very far short. When in autumn, 1925, it was thought it would be possible to give industry half a milliard of money for new equipment, this was counted as part of an economic programme, calculated on a Russian export of 1,059 million roubles; in this they had, on the grounds of the relatively good harvest of the autumn of 1925, especially reckoned on a considerable export of grain. But the Russian peasants, as we shall show later on, put a stroke through these calculations. In a very short time the rulers had to give up all hope of the 780 million poods of grain which they had thought that the State apparatus for the purchase of grain would be able to get together; the amount had to be reduced to 600 millions, and even that amount proved difficult to obtain. The grain export had, therefore, to be brought down and the total amount reduced from the above-mentioned 1,059 millions to about 800. Under such conditions, the State has been unable to give industry more than a part of the subsidies allotted to it. As a result of all this, the industrial programme for building and repairing has been several times severely curtailed. The amount, originally fixed, of 1,020 millions was first cut down to 932 and then to 746. Under these circumstances, the 200 millions for new factories has been diminished to 110, the three-fourths of a milliard for repairs and fresh equipment to one-half a milliard, and so on. These figures are those put forward in the beginning of 1926; how far they will materialize remains to be seen.

In spite of the drastic reductions in the industrial work-programme for the year 1925–6, necessitated by the curtailed plans for renovations, a certain increase of production in comparison with last year is to be expected. The old machinery is, at any rate, still holding together, even if the cogs do creak and some of the wheels, standing still hitherto, have this year, as previously stated, been set going again. It is credible that the manufactures may reach a total of about 95 per cent. of the pre-war production. But then comes the real struggle. Next year, when the need for new industrial equipment makes itself felt in good earnest, then indeed the racer will have his first opportunity to show what he can really do. The preliminary heats, run whilst enjoying a number of illegitimate privileges, do not inspire the spectator with any great confidence in his powers.

CHAPTER IV

STATE TRADING AND NEPMEN

ALTHOUGH the Bolshevists look at the industrial position with an optimism which strikes an outsider as inexplicable and which doubtless is not so very deep-rooted, they do not, on the other hand, hide their anxiety at the difficulty of putting commercial negotiations on a satisfactory basis. "We do not understand commerce," Djersjinsky plainly declared in his report at the Federal Soviet Congress in the spring of 1925. "Have we made any advance in this direction?" he asked, about the same time, at a commercial congress, and answered: "As a community and as individuals, we must say this is the department in which we have learnt least; we must own that our advance in the field of commerce has been the very minimum." Of course, there are a number of Western travellers to Russia who, even in this point, report complete success of the Soviet policy; possibly Djersjinsky's repeated assurances may be considered to bear a testimony opposed to theirs.

It is scarcely worth while to discuss the first Bolshevist attempt to arrange a system of distribution of goods on a basis satisfactory from a Communist standpoint, and to clip the wings of private capitalism. Private trading was forbidden; the State, by means of its organization, created for this special purpose, would—without the medium of money—negotiate an interchange between the town manufactured goods and the country agricultural produce. This turned out the most amazing failure. That the country districts practically got no manufactured goods at all was certainly not the fault of the distribution machinery, for, by reason of the industrial upheaval, there were no goods to distribute. But to provide the towns with agricultural produce was a task completely beyond the power of the State distribution system. According to figures—quoted by Bucharin in the summer of 1925—of the exceedingly limited supplies received by the towns in the year 1918–19, only 42 per cent. came through State mediums; the remaining 58 per cent. were brought in by "sack-carriers," private jobbers who bought up the peasants' produce in villages and then sold it in the towns at most exorbitant prices. It was simply the private smuggling—the term is not an apt one, for this private trading, although forbidden, was carried on openly enough—that during these years of "war-communism" acted as Russia's real trade mechanism. This was what the Bolshevist commercial policy achieved in its first stage.

In 1921 the whole economic system, of which this commercial policy formed a part, collapsed. The peasants refused—as will be shown later—to give up their grain without receiving something in exchange, and, to satisfy them, the State had to recognize their right to dispose, as they chose, of that portion of the land's produce which was not taken by the State in taxes. They were given permission to sell their grain, and then, of course, if this permission was to have any practical result, they must also be allowed to buy something in return; freedom of trade had to be reintroduced. This was the "new economic policy," "*Nep.*"

As a matter of fact, all this was by no means a new economic policy, but a return to an old one, tried for centuries in capitalistic States. In the ranks of the Party opposition, sternly silenced as they were, it was the fashion for a time to interpret the three letters *n e p* as "new exploitation of the proletariate." Meantime, the authorities did not wish to remove entirely limits already fixed. They were compelled to take away trading restrictions, and, in order to get a new and effective commercial system established, forced to open, not only the back door as before, but the great gates as well for private enterprise and private capital. But even though they set high hopes upon its help, they did not, therefore, intend private trading to get too important a place. Before anyone else, the State itself was to assume the chief position in the Russian commercial spheres, its representatives being, on one hand, the sale-mechanism of Government industrial Trusts and, on the other, the Co-operative movement, which, after a series of disputes and controversies with those in power, had been turned into a purely Government institution with nothing but an empty show of independence. Private trade was only to be granted to that small section of commerce with which the Government organs at first were not able to cope, chief amongst this being a portion of the retail trade. And private enterprise, with its superior training and experience, was, at the same time, to act as a kind of "pace-setter" for the somewhat inexperienced State undertakings which were to acquire from it commercial principles and methods.

But, on the other hand, care was to be taken that, even if private capital was allowed to enter the Russian market, all capitalistic exploitation was to be kept outside. The State's own appearance there would be a guarantee against the development of all unsound tendencies.

The Bolshevist policy failed in both respects. The Government trading organs have had enormous difficulty in holding their own against the superior rivalry of private trade; for a time, they certainly succeeded, by the help of the police, in keeping down private trade, but the method did not prove a happy one and had to be given up. Nor have they been, in any way, able to shut out exploitation and speculation; on the contrary, these flourish freely and under quite as objectionable forms as in capitalistic countries.

* * *

From the very moment when the Government, in 1921, with a grand flourish invited private enterprise to enter the market, they tried all available means to ensure its keeping in the modest place reserved for it. By heavy taxes, difficult credit conditions, administrative annoyances, etc., the authorities endeavoured in every way to reduce its power of competition.

The result, however, was not what they expected. The difference between the qualifications of the private and State trading was too great to be neutralized in this way.

As regards private traders, on their legal appearance

in the market after their concealed activity—which was, however, as we have said, often carried on quite openly—they were in possession of a capital of considerable value which the Bolshevist State was powerless to take from them. They were indeed badly off for a circulating medium, in the form of cash, but they owned what was of greater worth, viz. alertness, energy, adaptability and smartness. Only people with a good share of these qualities, whether they came from the old trading-class or had served their apprenticeship as jobbers during the time of crisis, could have found their way through all the stumbling-blocks of the past; the conditions under which they had been compelled to work had brought their qualities to perfection. And those who came in later were elements of the same kind; only those who were really adaptable and smart dared to throw themselves into the market to wrestle with the almost insuperable difficulties that met them there. And, at the same time, private traders had, from the beginning, a living interest in their work; their business, from the first moment, was a kind of exciting game of chance, and they went to work, urged on by its keen spur.

What the Government business men had to show in comparison with all this was insignificant in the extreme. The faithful Communists, who were commandeered for the trading movement as, in earlier times, they had been commandeered for service in the Red Army or for propaganda work, were, to begin with, as a rule, without any business qualifications, without training and with the most hazy ideas about commercial matters. "When Lenin pronounced the dictum, 'Teach yourselves to trade,' none of our economic officials," so Bucharin states, "could do it. 'To trade' seemed a completely mad occupation to a Communist." It was, as we have said, the rulers' knowledge of their weakness in this point which, in great measure, made them let in private traders as a whole, since part of their task was to teach the Communists how commerce should be carried on. And the Government traders, for another thing, lacked the motive that spurred on the private business men; they were, after all, only officials without personal interest in the undertaking.

In any case, however, this was not the worst of it, for, by degrees, business qualifications might be developed and Party discipline might help to keep things going briskly when interest was at a low ebb. Something else was worse; the private trader's adaptability and smartness was replaced by the clumsiness and lack of agility that, from the beginning, marked the Government commercial mechanism, which, in this respect, is a typical product of the characteristic Bolshevist deficiency in power of organization, of which we have already seen so many proofs.

To begin with, the cleavage, already mentioned, in the State trading organization is absurd. For the distribution of manufactured goods there is, on the one hand, the sale-mechanism of the Trusts, on the other the Co-operative stores. The latter, like the former, are, in reality, Government sale agencies. That these stores, in spite of their name, managed and directed by the State, as they are, down to the smallest detail, should be anything but a purely State organ, not even the Bolshevists themselves seriously maintain. "We consider the Co-operative organizations," says a writer in *Pravda*, "or rather their relation to us, as an integral part of the State institutional system. The situation now reached is that Co-operation in the country districts enters the market, not as a representative of the peasant class endeavouring to obtain the best possible conditions for their employers, but as the agent of an institution trading with the peasants." So the whole arrangement is a true Bolshevist organization, viz. two parallel institutions instead of one, with all the inconveniences that arise from the duplication. Most important of all these is the increased cost. How is trade to maintain two great sale agencies, neither of which can have all the business it could manage, but which, to a great extent, bring but little grist to the mill? Of course, the cost falls back very heavily on the goods. Next comes all the confusion which arises when the two get in each other's way and trample on one another's toes, as must inevitably be the case. It is indeed a most original spectacle to witness the drawn battle between State Industry, which naturally desires, in the first place, to provide its own sale agency with satisfactory supplies, and State Co-operation, which is dependent on State Industry for its supply of goods. "It might be thought," says *Pravda*, "that the executive board of the leading State and Party organizations, when it recognizes the Co-operative agency as the most important channel for the distribution of manufactured goods, would guarantee it a sufficient supply of goods. Experience, however, has proved the reverse. The stock of goods held by the Co-operative agency is reduced; the system for supplying it with them has failed." "The attempts of the *Centrosojus* (the Co-operative central management) and of the chief Co-operative Societies to bring about some ordered arrangement in the mutual relations of Co-operation and State Industry by means of a general agreement," *Pravda* goes on, "has always met with insuperable difficulties." And the paper tells how the *Centrosojus* negotiated for four months with the metal industry—with a negative result; for three months with the salt industry—with a like result, although the Commissariat for Internal Trade acted as mediator. It is not without reason that the newspaper thinks such a state of affairs "most abnormal." "It is," so it says, "plain, from the standpoint of national economy, that the existence of two parallel agencies, neither used to utmost capacity, is a meaningless extravagance." And not an extravagance only; it is clear that these peculiar relations within the chief controlling powers of State trade will not exactly increase its working efficiency or power of competition.

Then, too, the usual weak points of Bolshevist organization mark the apparatus right to its uttermost ramifications. Everywhere there are extensive establishments with masses of officials—the least little Co-operative store is a complete bureaucratic business activity. Identically the same picture met my eyes, time after time, in the villages: in the temporary little hut where the country shopkeeper—once a rich man and owner of some of the biggest houses in the village, now ruined and deprived of all his property—has taken up his work again on a small scale, I saw him himself, possibly assisted by a boy or two, standing behind his counter, selling for dear life, sweat pouring down his face and his mouth working—he had now to fall to work again under different conditions. But farther on, in one of the village's best buildings—appropriated for public use—the Co-operative Store had taken up its quarters in great style. The smart chief walked about with his hands in his pockets, smoking a cigarette and superintending his staff; three or four assistants behind the counter, cashier, accountant, errand-boys, etc. Jakovlev describes how, in one village, he came upon a

THE VILLAGE SHOPKEEPER OF FORMER DAYS.

Government business managed by a Red officer. It was quite prosperous, but the private village shopkeepers, who were making continual headway at its expense, laughed. If they had the Government shop's resources, they assured him, they would crush all competitors in the twinkling of an eye. One of them, before the war, had had a turnover of two millions and employed seventeen assistants; the State shop had not one-fifth of that turnover but a far larger staff; there were ten officials in the office alone. Even the Government manager himself saw this was not as it should be. "I asked him," Jakovlev narrates, "how many men he would keep on if he was the owner of the business that he now managed for the Government. He undertook, in such case, to reduce the staff to one-fifth its present number." This distension of trade-mechanism is all the more serious since it has grown beyond the control of the management, particularly in one respect; it has proved impossible to free these great establishments from the unhealthy tendencies which have increased at an extraordinary pace in them. It is in the very nature of things that such tendencies should easily take root there. Thousands of young men, who have never before had anything to do with finance, suddenly get large sums of money passing through their hands. A great many of them have got their commercial posts as a reward for praiseworthy Party-service, and consider it quite within their rights, when the financial benefits of such posts do not come up to their expectations, to improve them by suitable extractions from the tills. "The thefts," a correspondent in February, 1926, quite frankly declares, "are not thefts, but a natural supplement to provide a living minimum (!)." The reasoning is typical of these rulers of society who consider that they do not need to keep so strictly within the limits recognized by ordinary people. The consequence is that, if Communists in general—as has been already shown—have a strong inclination to misuse their public posts, these inclinations find a culminating point in the commercial agencies; and when these have developed, the authorities in control have a very difficult task in effectually combating them. Above all, in the Co-operative agencies away in the country, where the control is particularly weak, a state of affairs exists which, even in Bolshevist quarters, is stigmatized as frightful.

A *Pravda* correspondent writes: "In equal proportion with the undeniable growth in size of the Co-operative agency, we find, within its ranks, conditions that fill us with fear. There is misappropriation, robbery, pilfering, disappearance of money and goods. That has assumed a multifarious character, has, so to speak, become part of the Co-operative character. From the distant villages news comes of 'epidemics' of thefts, of 'the chronic disease of the Co-operative agencies,' etc. The whole truth about the real Co-operative position must be told, the evil exposed in all its extent and horror."

Fresh complaints from different quarters in the Press continually confirm this wrong condition of things. Here is a complaint from the Tver gubernia of an exposure that has been made in the Co-operative net of "epidemic robbery and all kinds of abuse of power on the part of the officials and management of the movement." "But," it is said, "the local Co-operative management consider this as an unavoidable evil and joke about the simply fabulous knavish tricks." An inspection that was instituted revealed an enormous number of scandals, but when, for example's sake, in May, 1924, the matter was taken to court, it was hung up in the legal machinery—even in June, 1925, it had not got so far as trial. Here is an indignant contributor from a town in the Kursk gubernia, who says: "The director of the Co-operative business in the town of Korotya Ivanov consumed from February 8th to March 21st 138 bottles of ale alone, without payment. And that in winter, when it was cold. How much more did he not finish up during the summer! And did he stop with beer? I wonder. All that could be got at was taken and stolen until the Co-operative store went bankrupt." In another part of the same gubernia, a village, after the revolution, managed to get six different Co-operative stores, one after another. They all failed because their employees made a clean sweep of everything, cash and stock. "Not one of the thieves has been sentenced or, for that matter, even tried."

Numberless complaints in the Press bear witness that the thefts often assume the form of the Co-operative employees taking or giving out goods on credit on such terms as, from the very first, preclude the possibility of payment. "Who gets the goods on credit?" is asked in *Pravda* in February, 1926, in a description of conditions in the Ukraine. The answer runs: "The leading men's friends and their relatives, as well as the authorities; and after sure provision has been thus made against any chance of inquiries, then the heads of the Co-operative management and the very employees take goods on credit. The great majority of these debts are hopeless. They are not collected energetically enough and the collection is difficult, as the amount of debt is very many times the total wages of the person who has incurred it." In the Ukraine country Co-operative trade in June, 1925, the goods out on credit amounted to 2,300,000 roubles, whilst their whole share capital was 1,600,000 roubles. According to a calculation in *Pravda*, October, 1925, the different kinds of theft in the Co-operative Society amounted to 12 million roubles yearly, and figures published in the same paper in January, 1926, showed that, in some districts, robbery was discovered in 50 per cent. of the Co-operative agencies. In one district of the Ryazan gubernia robbery and pilfering have taken place in thirty-five agencies out of seventy-four, and the sum total stolen amounted to almost 20 per cent. of all the local Co-operative Society's capital. "The Co-operative Society, both in town and country," says another *Pravda* contributor, "suffers in the first, second, and third place from want of honourable, devoted and experienced people."

* * *

Such were the two rivals that, in 1921, began to compete for the Russian market. On one hand, the heavily handicapped but agile and smart private dealers; on the other the State traders, favoured by all kinds of illegal privileges, but clumsy and hampered by the bureaucratic shackles on their legs.

From the very first, the former class showed their superiority. Before the good Communists in the State agencies had even managed to master the ordinary commercial terms, whilst they were still, as Bucharin expresses it, "chafing against the collar," the private traders had got practically the whole market into their own hands. In a moment, 80 per cent. of the wholesale and over 90 per cent. of the retail—particularly nearly all the country retail trade—was in their hands. When the State traders began, at long last, to set about business, their task was considerably increased; now they had to try to push out a rival who, in certain quarters, had already worked his way in.

The same superiority continued to distinguish the activities of the private traders. In the struggle for customers they have been triumphant throughout. Besides, who would have anything to do with the clumsy State mechanism when there was the attentive and quick trader just at hand? Before the State adopted the violent measures to be described later, it must gain, to begin with, the wholesale trade. Things had gone so far, in that respect, that the Government's own institutions, in their commercial dealings, for a long time preferred, in great measure, to use private traders as intermediaries. But they had, and still have, to gain—and that in a special degree—the retail trade as well. Here the superior methods of the private business men all along secured them the advantage. Everyone who has, at any time, visited as a customer the Government and private shops is struck by the colossal difference in the attention given to customers' requirements. In the private shops the customer finds often—even if far from always—what is wanted, and even gets a little choice as well; in the Government shops he has most wonderful experiences of what those concerned look upon as included in the term of a well-stocked shop. He continually comes across the absence of the commonest things, whilst, at the same time, he finds the most unnecessary articles. I saw myself a typical little instance in Moscow in August, 1924: for several days no sugar was to be found in any Government shop in the capital, not even in the smartest warehouse of all. There were tropical fruits, caviare, preserves—as much as you like—but sugar—no, not a bit, whilst all the sugar you wanted could be bought—at an extortionate price certainly—in the little private shops. Time after time complaints are to be seen in the papers from workmen of the way in which shops cater for their needs. For instance, a *Pravda* contributor complains that his Co-operative store has in stock, it is true, powder and eau-de-Cologne, but not the simplest everyday things. That the Government agencies in this question of stock have been so outdistanced by private traders who, in spite of the impediments put in their way, have managed to solve this difficulty remarkably well, is, of course, the result of the bad organization of the Government trade, its absence of adaptability and its want of a business man's psychology. That people should be content to be able to buy what the Soviet State offers them seems to be the maxim they favour, no less in higher quarters than in the shops themselves. Out in the villages, the officials often complain that they depend for stock on their superiors' "compulsory assortment," in which those in control palm off on them the most impossible things. Here comes a complaint from a little village of how the Co-operative up there gets from the central supply thousands of fashionable ladies' shoes, marked "shimmy," materials at seven or eight roubles a yard, scents, etc.; here comes an account from another quarter that 50 per cent. of all the goods the Co-operative shop is compelled to accept are "completely useless"; here they tell how the local official's protest against having to accept in the little village Co-operative Store cigar-cases, mirrors, and playing-cards is met by a declaration that it is necessary to spread enlightenment in the villages and, therefore, to sell all kinds of things. And still more important is something else, viz. that the private shops understand that they must treat customers in a fairly business-like manner, whilst the Government agencies do all they can to frighten them away. It is perhaps possible to meet in one or another public institution in Western Europe with the same uninterested, indifferent and bungling service as is meted out to customers in Russia, but most certainly not in any business undertaking that wishes to pay its way. Customers—my own personal experience specially includes a series of Government sale agencies in different Russian towns, but also quite a number of other shops both in principal cities and country places—have a very strong feeling that they are not dealing with business men who wish to sell, but with worn-out officials who are certainly paid to give the undertaking a certain portion of their time, but who will take good care not to give it one ounce of their interest. The customer is an intruder, and he is made to know it. With what a bored look one of the gossiping or tea-drinking employees leaves his place behind the counter in the great empty shop to place himself at the disposition of the customer whom he has long completely ignored! With what indifference he receives the order! How unwilling he is to help, if asked for advice! What satisfaction it gives him to declare that the article wanted is not in stock, even though it may be set out in the window! The customer may be thankful that he does not get a regular reproof for some simple question.

In the spring of 1925 a discussion about Co-operation took place as a sequel to the fact that the Russian proletarian poet, Demyan Byednyj, in one of his very apposite poems, overwhelmed the Co-operative Society with the choicest abuse. One of those taking part in this discussion writes: "Our Co-operative workers are often indifferent to everything that goes beyond the horizon of the eight hours' day or that touches their 'dignity.' How should it be possible for him to give himself any trouble for a customer or to move a little more quickly behind the counter? He is a complete contrast to the sellers in the private shops, who are always obliging, courteous and busy; he is always crusty, indolent and bad-tempered." Zinoviev, too, in a speech last winter, declared that: "It would be a great help if the Co-operative employees learnt to treat customers politely, like rational beings." "I saw lately," he adds, "in a paper a picture that put our Co-operative Society in a comical light. The clerk in a Co-operative shop spoke politely to a customer. The astonished chief or his vice said: 'Our clerk is evidently not quite normal; see how he speaks to customers; he surely has a screw loose.' Such," adds Zinoviev, "is sometimes the character of the Co-operative agencies, and for that reason workmen's wives won't go to them." And the general public follow the women, and betake themselves, when opportunity offers, to the private shops, where the customer does not have to beg pardon for the trouble he gives. Of course, there might be an effective way of attracting the public, in spite of everything, to the Soviet agencies and of competing with private traders. The customer would not mind running the risk of a reproof if only he got his goods more cheaply. What is the state of things with regard to the prices in Government and private markets?

* * *

As a general rule it may be accepted that the prices that Russian goods fetch over the retail counter—whether in a Government or private shop—most undeniably fleece the public. Even the wholesale prices are unreasonably disproportionate to the cost of production; and although a certain improvement has been obtained in the matter, yet the retail trade-additions to the wholesale prices are always perfectly abnormal. The official figures alone are suggestive enough. According to a table put forward by the Economic Commission in April, 1925, the retail addition to the industrial wholesale prices averaged 40–45 per cent., i.e. two to two and one-half times greater than that before the war; in country districts, according to the same source, this figure rose to 50–60 per cent. As regards the metal industry, Djersjinsky stated at the same time that the retailers sometimes put on more than 100 per cent. During last winter this addition—in union with the prevailing scarcity of goods—increased still more. "The retail traders' addition to the price of goods," so Rykov states as lately as March, 1926, "reaches simply fabulous dimensions." In Moscow itself, in November, 1925, it was on an average 62 per cent., in December 69 per cent. As regards some kinds of goods much more even, viz. in the shoe trade 88–90 per cent., and china goods 207 per cent.; and in this connection it must be noted that the retailers' enormous additions appear in the Soviet statistics only in a very greatly modified form. Especially away in country places, where the control is weaker than in the towns, the retailer seizes the opportunity to take prices that would certainly cost him a considerable stay up in the northern gubernias if they came to the ears of the highest authorities, but, as a rule, they remain a matter only between himself and the circle of customers whom he fleeces.

Yet even the official figures are of a nature to turn the rulers' hair grey. During the last two years particularly, constant complaints have been heard over the traders' unreasonably high prices for goods. As related in the last chapter, the Russian authorities, ever since 1923, have brought about a number of considerable reductions in the factory prices for their goods; this they have done, on the one hand, to set industrial production on its feet again, for it was threatened with stagnation—the former industrial prices being beyond the public's purchasing power—and, on the other, to calm the dissatisfaction with the high prices—a dissatisfaction that found, especially amongst the peasant population, very pronounced expression. This reduction of factory prices, which, to a very great extent, resulted in the factories selling the goods under the cost of production, threatened, at first, to prove quite ineffectual, since business men, especially in retail shops, appropriated the percentage of the reductions and sold the goods at much the same price as before. "The campaign, still going on, to reduce the price of the most important necessaries, has certainly had a great effect as regards wholesale trade but an exceedingly poor one as regards retail," *Izvestia* acknowledged even at the end of 1924, a year after the price-reduction campaign had been started. "A considerable amount of the advantage accruing from the lowered prices does not get beyond the trade mechanism; the importance of the reduction must not be too much emphasized, for the peasants do not feel much of it," was said in *Pravda* as lately as April, 1925. In order to make the reductions in price really perceptible to the general public, it was necessary, thanks to the retailers' obstructive action, to go much farther in screwing down factory prices—to the distinct detriment of industry—than had been contemplated at first. Djersjinsky also complained bitterly: "If we are to carry through a price-reduction policy in industry, only for the peasants to have to pay later three times as much, we are not exactly encouraged to lower prices. This depresses us. When a man works in the factory, straining every nerve to cheapen and improve his goods but, at the same time, knows that the peasant has to pay a treble price, he loses all inclination to work." And when, after all, the State had succeeded at last in the attempt to bring prices down so far that people can manage to buy, in no time it was as bad again. The increased demand brought about a scarcity of goods, and this gave retailers an opportunity to force up prices again—this has just happened in the last few months.

If an explanation of the unreasonably high prices is asked, it is of a twofold nature, as far as the private trader is concerned. First, the high prices are the natural consequence of the fact that if his business is to pay, he must cover his expenses by high prices. So far, then—and this goes a good deal of the way—it would be unfair to speak of any unlawful exploitation of the public on the part of the private shopkeepers. But secondly—and that in the majority of cases—there is another cause for the forcing-up of prices, viz. a genuine, unblushing, profiteering spirit which is quite as marked in proletarian Russia as in capitalistic countries. As long as the private undertakings still ruled the wholesale trade, this profiteering spirit indulged in great orgies and led to the most shameless speculations. "We know," says Djersjinsky, "that in the crisis of 1923, when prices were forced up to such a height, one of the causes was speculation; the goods went from hand to hand, and again and again fresh increases of price were piled on to them." And even if this was stopped by the exclusion of the private trader from the wholesale markets—as will soon be shown—yet all the time there went on in the retail trade what the Bolshevists call a capitalistic plundering of the half-starved Russian proletariate.

After all, this is really only what might have been expected. Under the given conditions it would have been a miracle, if Russia had had a body of traders working on sound commercial principles.

To a certain degree, the present salesman's morality undeniably dates back to far-gone times. A pronounced tendency to exploit the public has always distinguished the Russian commercial world; a reasonable profit and honest treatment of customers would be of fairly tardy growth in such environment During the ten years immediately before the war, however, a change for the better became apparent, a certain improvement had taken place, and in the towns particularly, tradesmen began to work along more modern lines. This development was brought to a stop by the war. Next to the officers, no class of society had such destructive treatment by the Bolshevists as the business men. And those who, in spite of it, saved themselves were not the best and most worthy, but, on the contrary, the sharper element; as a rule it was the poorest fish that were slippery enough to escape through the meshes of the Bolshevist net. It was, therefore, these who, when trade was freed, again appeared in the market, reinforced by a number of "sack-carrier," types who had learnt the art of trading during the years of crisis. They were all, as we have already pointed out, slim, smart folk, but at the same time an exceedingly unscrupulous, crooked species from whom any moderation in the profiteer's appetite would be the last thing to be expected.

And this so much the less since the conditions under which they had been, and still were, obliged to work did not encourage them to adopt another idea of the alpha and omega of business life. Nor had they, to begin with, any reputation to lose, as their business had always been nothing but robbery. Even if, at the beginning of the new economic policy, private trading had been proclaimed a lawful means of livelihood, yet, after all, traditions from the time when individual freedom of trade was looked upon as a repulsive feature of capitalism were still in the air. To tolerate the return to the capitalist economic system implied in *nep* was, alas! compulsory, yet it was not necessary to go so far as to look upon the *nepmen* as anything else but capitalistic blood-suckers and exploiters. It was no matter how they conducted themselves, for they were branded beforehand, and the *nepmen* have to be pardoned if they considered it not worth while to try to be better than their reputation. And, moreover, there was the fact that sound and sterling business methods were incompatible with the practical conditions that Bolshevism gave to private traders. To try to work up a business by honourable means, to be content with a reasonable profit, and, instead of making huge gains, to try to gain public confidence and so get a secure and steadily increasing turnover—all such action would have been completely senseless, since there was no guarantee, when the solid foundation was at last laid, that the Bolshevists would not come and shut up the shop, destroying, in the twinkling of an eye, the result of years of toil. There was an increasing tendency for the situation to become such—I will return to this shortly—that traders could, with certainty, reckon on the fact that those in power, sooner or later, would have their knife in their business. Their motto, then, must be :—as quick and large profits as possible, and no work with an eye to a distant future. Sooner or later the catastrophe will come, and they must see that they have safely harvested something before it does.

If, thus, all factors have combined to turn private trade into a shameless exploitation of the public, it seems that the Government trade will now have a brilliant opportunity. Since it is exempt from the burdens that press upon the private traders, and since no one, of course, would credit it with a wish to fleece the proletariate, it ought to be able to supply goods at prices that will completely capture the Russian public.

But what do we find ? The level of prices in the Government shops was far and away higher than that of the private traders. Complaints are still heard about this. " In the last meeting of the Leningrad Soviet," Zinoviev said, in a speech in June, 1925, " the workmen and women declared in their speeches that our Co-operative Society always sells things at a higher price than the private shops." " In the private shops we can get everything and at considerably lower prices," a contributor from the Pultava gubernia declared at the same time in *Pravda*. In other quarters the comparison was more favourable to the State agencies. An inquiry, held last summer in Moscow, showed that although Government traders might be dearer than the private dealers in many things, yet, in most cases, they could show a reduction, even if only an extremely insignificant one. An inquiry by the Co-operative headquarters, reported in *Pravda* in January, 1926, with regard to conditions in the Ukraine, Ural and a number of other districts, showed that in the Co-operative agencies there the prices were 8–10 per cent. below those of the private traders.

The State therefore takes, at any rate very nearly, the same shameless prices as the private traders with their voracious desire for profit. How can this be explained ? Very simply: The State trading organization and its manner of working are such that they force up prices to the same high level. The same prices that give the private traders gains literally equal to those of war-profiteers, in the Government concerns barely suffice to cover working expenses. There is the greatly increased personnel to be paid; the losses from the substitution rendered necessary by the so-called "compulsory assortment" described above (*Pravda* states that the goods, not required, lie littering up the Co-operative shops for two or three years and then are sold, with the greatest difficulty, at half-price); there are other losses of the most various kinds that have to be made good. Here, for example, *Pravda* gives instances of increases in price due to unpractical methods of distribution: "It often happens that goods on their way from the Co-operative head stores to the local Co-operative agencies are loaded and unloaded unnecessarily several times and also go by an unnecessarily long, roundabout road." *Pravda* also complains that the purchasing is done without method, without reckoning either requirements or sales; describes how the Co-operative shops, in buying some trifle that could just as well be sent by post, dispatches a special messenger whose journey has to be paid; and states that the Co-operative officials like to make their purchases in comfort, and, therefore, in negotiating something worth a hundred roubles or so, "travel to town, go to an hotel, and make a claim for the day's expenses." "When the State enters the market with a great quantity of goods," Kalinin states, "neither artisans nor peasants get much gain from it. For the State has new young organizations that are still almost without experience. The profits that capitalistic sale-agents put in their pockets are, to a considerable extent, eaten up by the State working expenses." What a crushing condemnation of Soviet trade frankly uttered by the very head of the Bolshevist Government himself!

* * *

Thus the Bolshevist State-trading has, in all points, proved its hopeless inefficiency. It is plain that if conditions had been allowed somewhat free development, it would have completely broken down in face of competition. Even the Bolshevists saw, at quite an early stage, that the restrictions, with which they had tried to modify the freedom of action that private concerns obtained in 1921, were not severe enough, and the continual question, since then, has been to what degree they could be further increased.

The years immediately following 1921 mark a steady increase of severity in their policy with regard to the private traders. The position these had gained at one blow, as we mentioned above, of 80 per cent. of the wholesale and 90 per cent. of the retail trade, struck the Bolshevists with horror. They had not dreamt of anything like that, and it was indeed grist to the mill of those forces that had, from the first, opposed the *nep* policy. A determined campaign was started against the *nepmen*, as they were called. Repeated blows followed. Their taxation increased to a perfectly abnormal degree. Some figures, published last summer from the Leningrad gubernia, show that 75 per cent. of the business men's turnover was taken in taxes, the Government tax being 45 per cent., the Commune tax 22 per cent. and other taxes 8 per cent. of their income. Nor was this all by any means; taxation was supplemented by credit withdrawals, great annoyances with regard to the purchase and transport of goods, and finally—especially from the year 1923 inclusive—direct police interference. Great numbers of business men, big and little, were arrested and banished to the northern gubernias, sometimes as speculators, sometimes quite simply as a "non-working" element—a designation which would, most certainly, have been more applicable to the mass of slackers amongst the Bolshevist employees who held their comfortable sinecures behind Soviet counters. In the summer of 1924 the campaign, aided by the fiery zeal of the Press, political speeches, and the stage, reached its highest point. The feeling in those business circles with which I came into contact was one of unmitigated panic. No one felt safe; business people kept, like terrified rats, in their holes and tried to make themselves as inconspicuous as possible, whilst, at the same time, they utilized their reprieve to get as enormous profits as they could and sought to lengthen this reprieve by scattering bribes amongst people who might be thought to have some influence as regarded their fate. Even at a very early stage of this campaign, the Bolshevists succeeded in crushing the private wholesale trade, for here only a relatively insignificant number of persons were concerned, and they could be the more firmly handled, since the State soon enough thought itself able to find substitutes for them in their own organization. The campaign against the widely-spread net of retail trade was less easy to carry to a successful issue, and, at the same time, more hazardous as well. The Government had, after all, to own that it was not equipped to take their place. But, even in this direction, they took quite energetic measures and reduced the share of the markets that the private traders had succeeded in gaining to about one-half.

But then came the reverse. The Government had thought that their own retail traders would surely have learnt a considerable amount during the past years, but events proved that the greater the tasks laid upon them, the higher was the degree of their astounding incompetence. More especially evident was the rotten state of affairs that marked the Co-operative agencies throughout the land. One after another came to utter grief, sometimes as a result of poor economic management in general, but most often as the result of simple dishonesty. Public complaints of the Government method of distributing goods became louder and louder, and even those in power became aware that the time was not ripe for dispensing with private enterprise.

So it was resolved to stop the campaign against private traders and even to make a show of friendly invitation to those whom they had just been persecuting. If they were compelled for a time—how long no one knew—to harbour the snake in their bosom, they determined to handle it so that it spat out as little poison as possible. Private traders were to be allowed to work under something like endurable conditions—perhaps then they would drop their worst tricks. The hot fire against the *nepmen* is dropped ; again and again the newspapers emphasize the fact that they form a class with a full right to existence. The administrative persecutions have already ceased at headquarters; the local administration, which has—as is so often the case after the complete reversals of Soviet policy—not kept pace with the new turn of events, but still continues its constant castigation of *nepmen,* is emphatically reminded, again and again, that such a line of action is unfitting. "It would be exceedingly harmful," said Rykov in April, 1925, "to prevent the development of private trade by any form of administrative pressure, a thing that has been practised, here and there, during the last few years." Representatives of private trade are summoned to confer with those in power who protest their good intentions towards them; their burden of taxes is lightened, more facilities given them to get their goods, etc. Factories, banks, and also tax authorities are to modify their activity as regards private traders, and make conditions more favourable for them than they have been hitherto, is Rykov's dictum. In other words, the *nepmen* have become a greatly favoured section of the community; and *Pravda* writes a long article exhorting everyone, authorities and private individuals alike, to cultivate a little pleasanter attitude towards them. It does not do to thump the table with your fists, take them by the collar and drive them out, so that they fly like bombs through the door. Now, whether it will be possible, in this way, to give private business men such a feeling of security as will develop into a private trade movement of a firm and solid character, that does not only calculate on each day's enormous profits, is indeed more than uncertain. They know, of course, quite well that the abolition of private trading is the ultimate aim of Bolshevism—an aim it will endeavour to realize as soon as it perceives that the State agencies have cast off their present incompetence and are in a position to take up the private traders' task. In the Proletarian Republic *nepmen* are, in any case, only strangers and visitors who at any time may expect to be turned out. "The private business men must not forget," was the candid declaration of the chairman at a public meeting to discuss private trading, "the difference that exists between them and the working population, and must give up the thought of any political rights, once and for all." The *nepmen* are, and remain, a pariah class, and their activity is somewhat what one might expect from such a class. A profiteering private trade and an incompetent State trade—such are the achievements of the Bolshevists in the sphere of commercial activity; and, for the present, it is not likely that they will be in a position to give anything better to the Russian proletariate.

CHAPTER V

THE BOLSHEVISTS AND THE MOUJIKS

In the spring of 1925 the fourteenth Bolshevist Party Congress passed two significant resolutions as regarded their peasant policy. On the one hand, they officially protected the Russian country districts from any more attempts aiming at the regulation of life there on something like right Bolshevist lines; now, instead, in the hope of pulling them up financially, all available means were to be taken to favour the development of something so anti-Bolshevist as a well-to-do peasant bourgeoisie. On the other hand, a reduction was made in their financial demands on the Russian peasant class; the taxation-total, to be taken from them, was diminished by a third, i.e. from 470 to 300 millions a year.

The resolutions betokened the final crash of the peasant policy followed by Bolshevism up till then. No matter what difficulties they had encountered and what abatements they had been obliged to accept, so far they had not quite given up any items of the Bolshevist programme. Now one and all were utterly renounced. And stubbornly as they had pursued their aim of squeezing out of the peasants the means required for financing the Bolshevist experiment, in spite of the peasants' obstinate attitude of opposition to Bolshevist ideas, yet now they were forced to make an appreciable modification of their demands in this direction. This was the end of a chapter which in its entirety may perhaps be considered the most ignominious in the history of Bolshevism.

* * *

The first item in the Bolshevists' agrarian policy, the eviction of the landowners, undeniably turned out indeed a complete success. In that they still had the entire peasant class on their side, or, to speak more accurately in that the peasants had themselves begun to realize the Bolshevist programme, before they had even heard of Bolshevism and whilst Lenin was still hiding in a hayloft in the marshy tracts round Petersburg. When the peasants, after the February revolution, were put off by the parties then in power with promises that their interests would certainly be considered, if only they would have patience, they began soon enough, from fear that they would have to wait in vain, to take the matter into their own hands, to drive away the landowners, and divide their lands and belongings amongst themselves. The debutant Bolshevists gave full sanction to this, the peasants' initiative. Lenin declared it was not only the peasants' right but their duty to take the land from the landowners, thus assuring to his little band of 35,000 men the support of the 100 million members of the peasant class.

After the Bolshevists had really come into power, the campaign for the extirpation of the landowners went on at full speed—the peasants worked to the Bolshevists' complete satisfaction and showed they had a real Bolshevist streak in them. We have had any number of descriptions of this, the first stage in the Bolshevist agrarian policy ; it is only when we get out into the Russian villages that we fully realize with what systematic thoroughness and precision the policy was carried out in its time. In village after village we pass over ruins of what must once have been one of the Turgenev noble strongholds, and fancy we are walking in one of the battlefields of the Great War. Not even the stone foundations of these landowners' buildings have, as a rule, been spared from destruction ; heaps of stones mark the places where they once stood. And all around there are gigantic clearings, sometimes over whole acres of land ; hundreds of bare tree-stumps, endless numbers of young broken stems. These are the estate gardens and parks, the Tchekov cherry orchards that have been brought to destruction, not to get fuel—the forest is only a few stonethrows away—but simply to satisfy their noble lust of destruction. From a purely practical point of view, one would indeed think that they really ought to be able to make some sensible use of these abandoned estates.

For example, in villages where the school is housed in some wretched hovel a few square metres in area, one would think the big house might be adapted to a school. But no! Here and there, perhaps, an estate still exists, converted into a rest-home for town artisans, but this is the exception. No compromises with revolutionary convictions—away with the bourgeoisie abominations!

And we go round into the cottages in the little village; here and there we find trophies taken from the big house; the greater part of its contents have indeed been devoured by the flames—old libraries with valuable hoards of books, art collections, antique pieces of furniture, etc.; the Bolshevists have saved but an extremely insignificant part of these memorials of a fine old culture to which they are more than indifferent. But one or two things the peasants had appropriated as war booty. In cottages where men, domestic animals and all kinds of creatures still lower in the scale lived together in true Russian fashion and in communistic harmony, I saw, here and there, an antique armchair, a wonderful icon of some saint, or an old Swiss clock—it went so badly, said its possessor, that he had thought of throwing it on the rubbish-heap. The walls in a little room that a peasant gave me for my night-quarters were decorated, not only with a number of cuttings out of the papers, pictures from the Japanese War, Nicolai Nicolaievitch, Lenin on his bed of state, etc., but also with some extraordinarily beautiful little landscapes in oils, whose gilt frames had evidently tempted the desire of acquisition. And we talk to the peasants about their last settlement with the landowners. There they sit, good-humoured and friendly, with us round the samovar and tell, as if it were the most natural thing in the world, how they burnt the master and his family with their house. The remembrance of how one member of the family tried to save himself by jumping out of a window on the second story of the burning house but killed himself by the jump induced a general smile, and one of them describes—evidently for the hundredth time, but none the less to his hearers' great edification—how with a hayfork he put an end to another of the unfortunate people who had managed in some way to escape from the flames. Had they borne the master at the big house any special grudge? "No, certainly not. He was like a father to us—a real father," comes the answer in chorus. But he was a *barin*, a gentleman, and gentlemen had to be put an end to!

But there was also another upper-class element in the villages that the ordinary peasants, encouraged by the Bolshevists, did away with at the same time. This element was the so-called *kulacks*—close-fisted, as the word really means—undoubtedly a most uncongenial peasant bourgeoisie—peasants who, by all kinds of unscrupulous means, had worked their way up and who, profiting by the general misery in the villages, had got the other peasants into their clutches financially. With these, too, the peasants settled old accounts—many had to share the *barins'* fate, and, in every case, they were deprived without ceremony of both land and substance.

In this way the village upper-classes disappeared, but when the question arose as to the disposal of the inheritance they left, the Bolshevists, for the first time, met with opposition from the peasants. Lenin had certainly promised them the land, but he had not at all meant by that what the peasants thought. Instead of the millions of small individual holdings in the country districts, on which the peasants, even if they managed to make them a little larger by partition of the landowners' estates, would lead a miserable existence, whilst, at the same time, becoming more fixed in their own personal habits of thought—instead of this, the intention was to institute giant farms, conducted on factory lines, collective holdings where the land and its cultivation should belong to all members of the community and where the products of their common work should be divided amongst them. In this way it would be possible to make the best use of capital, effects and live stock, as well as to combat the peasants' individualistic tendencies and to train them in proletarian solidarity and discipline.

Such was Lenin's agrarian programme, and, as a first capitulation to the peasants, he had unreservedly to give it up. The peasants would not hear of Lenin's great holdings; they suspected an attempt to deprive them of the land at the very moment when they had realized the dreams, inherited through many past generations. It was such solid opposition that the Bolshevists did not dare to defy it. When they issued their first land decree, it contained a complete acceptance of the peasants' demands in regard to the land, as they had been formulated by the peasants themselves and presented by the Social-Revolutionaries, who later became such bitter enemies of the Bolshevists. Even though the land was declared State property, it was, nevertheless, left in the peasants' hands on such conditions that they might well look upon it as their own. The individual peasant, it is true, was not allowed to sell or mortgage the land allotted to him, but as long as he worked it with the help of his own family, it could not be taken from him. This was complete capitulation, and Lenin recognized it openly. "We cannot," he declared, "oppose the masses' decision, even though we disapprove of it." One small consolation they did allow themselves. In order to facilitate a future transition to the great farms of which they had thought, the peasants should have a practical demonstration of them. At the distribution of the land, the State reserved for itself a number of the best estates, amounting altogether to about 4 per cent. of all the Russian arable land, and set up on it model farms, built on large-scale principles. These "Soviet households" were equipped with the best machines, stock and seed that could be procured and loaded with privileges of different kinds; the brilliant results expected from them would be a general summons to the peasants to imitate them. This was a little piece of the wreckage of Lenin's agrarian ideas that he tried to tow to land; later on we shall see how this too went down miserably.

Thus the peasants succeeded in carrying out the programme of which they had dreamt ever since the abolition of serfdom. The landowners' estates were divided amongst the peasants in the adjacent villages, and, in connection with that, there took place a general redistribution of land in which even the *kulacks'* and other better-to-do peasants' larger portions were portioned out—a levelling, it is true, not of all the country district, but of the land possessions in each separate village.

* * *

The Bolshevists' first defeat in their agrarian policy with respect to the peasants was soon followed by another. Lenin had been obliged to let the peasants keep the land in the shape which they themselves desired, but the peasants soon found that he had not, with the land, given them the right to keep and dispose of, according to their own ideas, all that grew upon it. "The peasants demand," Lenin said in a speech in January, 1919, "freedom to sell their grain. They do not understand that freedom to sell bread means freedom to speculate. We shall never allow that. We will all rather die than yield on this point."

According to the economic system which was then established, the peasants could only keep for their own use a certain amount of the corn; the rest they were to give up and get industrial products from the towns in exchange. The system, however, would not work smoothly, even from the very beginning. During the general industrial anarchy that soon occurred, the towns had no manufactured goods to give to the peasants, so the latter had to give up their corn without getting anything in exchange. They cannot be blamed if they were not very delighted and that the gain in land, which the revolution had given them, struck them as quite worthless, since its produce, in any case, was taken from them. "The land is ours, but the corn yours; the meadows are ours, but the hay is yours; the forest is ours, but the wood is yours." This was how a peasant in a congress summed up, in the very faces of the Communist leaders, the result of the Bolshevist land policy, as viewed by peasant eyes.

The feeling grew more and more bitter. The peasants turned a deaf ear to the eloquent appeals made by those in authority to the peasant revolutionary solidarity. The town workmen! what were they to them? Peasants would be much better off if there were no towns at all! And so they began to offer resistance. In part, this was active. When artisans came out into the villages to take the corn they were to have, the peasants beat them and sent them home empty-handed ; when armed troops were sent out into the villages to take by force what was not given willingly, they were met by the peasants with shining weapons. The memory of the regular battles fought then, in which the Red soldiers successfully used methods learnt during the war against the White Army, still lives in the minds of the peasants and does not increase their affection for the Bolshevists. In part, however—and this was more dangerous—the peasants offered to the Bolshevist exaction of corn a passive resistance of the most fatal nature, i.e. a cultivation-strike. They did not sow any larger areas than would give them just the amount which they had a right to keep. Not only the newly-acquired estate grounds had to lie untilled, but great parts, too, of peasant land lay fallow. According to the Bolshevists' own reports—which, however, are greatly wanting in uniformity—only about one-half (according to responsible people's calculations, only about one-quarter) of all Russian land was cultivated. The result is universally known, viz. the terrible famine years in Russia of 1920 and 1921—years of famine which cost Russia millions of lives and which would have cost many times more, if Europe and America had not stepped in and averted the worst consequences of the Bolshevists' agricultual policy. The Bolshevists, it is true, give two other explanations of the famine. On the one hand—as thanks for the help sent them from foreign countries—they have impressed upon the minds of the Russian proletariate that it was the capitalistic world that caused the Russian famine by its blockade ; and, on the other, they throw the blame on the certainly most unfavourable weather, that caused a bad harvest on such land as really was under cultivation. Since, however, all the Russian land under present cultivation-methods produces a harvest that, in normal years, just about feeds the Russian nation—the Russian grain export has always been based on the semi-starvation of the peasants—it was self-evident that the substantial reduction in the area sown must, quite apart from the weather, result in famine.

Faced with such a situation, the Bolshevists, in spite

of all Lenin's solemn vows, had to beat a retreat. Two years after the declaration of his programme, just mentioned, Lenin, in the tenth Communist Congress, 1921, was compelled to put forward another. "The peasants are dissatisfied with their present relation to the State, so it cannot continue. We are great enough realists to say: Let us revise our policy touching the peasants. Before this evening is over we must send out a wireless message through the world to make it known that the Congress has decided to abolish the requisition system and replace it by a system of taxation. By taking this step the Congress sets right the relations between the artisans and peasants and expresses its belief that the good relationship will remain firmly established."

Instead of giving up their excess of corn, the peasants were to hand over a part of it as a tax; the rest, whether much or little, they might keep and deal with it as they wished, i.e. sell it. This was the resolution that Lenin, in spite of energetic opposition even from his staunchest followers, succeeded in getting passed. Thus, once more, the Bolshevist land policy had been obliged to surrender to the peasants; but the capitulation was this time the more serious, inasmuch as it resulted in consequences affecting the whole of the Bolshevist economic policy. The very fact that the peasants were allowed to sell their grain and also to buy something instead—a right that must naturally be conceded if the sale was to be of any benefit to them—meant the end of the economic system, established in the earliest days of Bolshevism, which had banned everything in the nature of trade. In its stead came the *Nep*, or New Economic Policy, which we have already discussed.

* * *

The Bolshevist peasant policy which led in the first four years to such mortifying defeats had now to introduce important modifications into its programme. The authorities had to be content, on the one hand, with trying to prepare the ground for a future advance of the agrarian front, and, on the other, with compelling the peasants meantime, if they could not be a source of satisfaction to Communism in any other way, at least to pay what Communism was costing Russia.

As far as the first of these tasks goes, it is not worth while wasting many words on the verbal and printed agitation that was to convince the peasants of the superiority of the Communist agrarian principles; the Bolshevists have not made many proselytes by this. If anything was to be gained, it must be by a more convincing propaganda. It was the consciousness of this that prompted Lenin to establish the collectivist model farms mentioned above. After their agrarian policy had come to grief in other directions, the Bolshevists fixed great hopes on these. The question is, then, how this experiment succeeded.

It is no exaggeration to say that, amongst all the unsuccessful Bolshevist experiments, this attempt of Soviet housekeeping is amongst those that turned out worst of all. The workers from the towns who, in these great farms, conducted on collective principles, were to teach the peasants rational land cultivation, were, to begin with, utterly ignorant of the most elementary things in farming; secondly, they, like the industrial artisans, introduced into agricultural work a much curtailed and badly utilized eight hours' day; and thirdly, in the usual Bolshevist manner, they provided themselves with organizing agencies that greatly multiplied the working expenses. The result has been that Soviet housekeeping, instead of proving an instructive example for the peasants, alternately aroused both their indignation and laughter.

I went to some villages that had Bolshevist model farms for their nearest neighbours, and was able to verify the fact that the peasants there had less respect than any others for communistic farming methods or any wish to follow their example. Although the Soviet households enjoyed advantages of which the peasants themselves would never have dared to dream, they got no farther than "spoiling the ground," so ran the judgment pronounced by the peasants. The latter were annoyed at this, but, at the same time, could not help laughing at the tales of the Soviet farming which were in general circulation. Now, of course, the peasants' judgment in this case must be accepted with a certain amount of caution. Their scathing criticism may be partly the result of their well-known mistrust of all that is new and partly of their dissatisfaction that the Soviet households had got land to which they laid claim themselves. I will return to this dissatisfaction later on. But this criticism receives confirmation, even from Bolshevist quarters. Some examples, given by Jakovlev in his books, leave nothing to be desired in their graphic descriptions. Here is a Soviet household in the Kursk gubernia. Of the 81 dessiatines which it had at its disposal, 28 in former times had belonged to one landowner and brought him in a yearly income of 3,500 roubles; now the whole property, three times as large, does not give a single kopeck of profit. Or here is a model farm in the Tambov gubernia, a property of 786 dessiatines—about 100 ordinary peasant portions—generously equipped with implements, 40 ploughs, 7 drills, etc., and provided with a mill which all the peasants living in the neighbourhood must employ, since it is the only one in the district. But still both ends do not meet. All the farming is done anyhow—the land ploughed at the wrong time, the seed put in too late; in 1923 the autumn grain is so poor that the peasants round about have eight times as good a crop. The ground is not manured, agriculturists are not employed; on the great pastures only ten cows are fed. The barns are tumble-down and the hay is rotting in them. The peasants give in chorus their account of the methods of work: the worker yokes two oxen to his wagon and drives and drives, till at last he drives into a glen; there he lies down to sleep till the inspector comes; then up he jumps and begins to work as if he had been at it all the time.

But there is another reason why the Soviet households, even if they could, by way of exception, have anything to teach the peasants, completely fail in their pedagogic mission. Partly as retaliation for the aversion which the peasants, from the very first, have shown to the model farms and their inmates, whom they look upon as intruders from the town, taking possession of their land, partly as a manifestation of the Communist disposition—already mentioned—to bully the despised peasants, the workers in the Soviet households, instead of trying to guide and teach the peasants, take every opportunity of annoying them.

The peasants talk about this whenever they can find a listener. Every little assistance that the Soviet farms, with their greater resources, could, without any difficulty, give to the peasants, and which the latter, after all, used to get from their *barin*, is refused or given only at a heavy price. And, at the same time, their arrogance towards the peasants finds triumphant expression. At a meeting arranged by Jakovlev's Inquiry Commission between representatives of a Soviet household and the peasants of the district, the latter formulated no fewer than thirty separate complaints of the model farm, some of them remarkable enough. " There never was," so they say, " a worse neighbour than a Soviet household. If a herdsman is driving his beasts and a single horse gets on to the Soviet land, they make us pay for the damage as badly as any landowner in the old times. A poor peasant woman, leading a hungry child, goes to the Soviet farm and begs to get milk for a week on credit, as her own cow is ill. But the inspector drives her off, with 'We don't keep a dairy for you.' Why, a *kulack* wouldn't do a thing like that! What sort of example is that for folk? Greve Stroganov—the former *barin*—didn't let the peasants into his park so that they shouldn't disgrace his property with their moujik faces, but the Soviet farm doesn't let the peasants into their park either. And to keep the children from sitting on the stones the inspector has had them tarred. And yet there's nothing valuable in the park—the peasants won't begin gnawing the Soviet farm trees, do you suppose?" In the famine of 1922, when the peasant could scarcely keep body and soul together, but went about like a tortured fly, the Soviet household made use of his hunger to speculate; they gave him 1½ poods of rotten grain for a sheep. "The model farms have never taught the peasants anything. What sort of example is it for the peasants when they are never invited there without being threatened with the knout and driven off with foul abuse if they come on to their land? We and they live like cat and dog. The Soviet farm ought to be a help both to the State and to us peasants. The Communists explained to us that that was why the State keeps the Soviet households. But they only do us an injury; that's all we've seen in them."

The question of the winding-up of these doomed institutions has also in recent times constantly recurred. It was greatly discussed in the spring of 1925. Even *Pravda* states that the situation was such that the model farms threatened to become models in the wrong directions, examples of how farming should *not* be done. Here and there the workers on the model farms, without more ado, let out farm-land to peasants in the district or established their own private little farms on this land. Everything required for starting the year's work was wanting. To prevent the necessity of the Soviet households resigning their "agricultural and revolutionary" work, the State made them a little gift of 5½ million roubles, in part as a loan. In the beginning of 1926 this sum had again been duly spent, and the question of the Soviet farms' continuance or non-continuance was once more in the order of the day. Probably the State will again have to lose some millions to escape the reproach of being compelled to abandon this Lenin idea as well.

The attempt, then, to give the peasants a taste for communistic housekeeping by a practical demonstration has failed. The experiment, however, has, after all, been made on a very small scale, and this fiasco, however disagreeable it may be, cannot be written down amongst the greater Bolshevist defeats. Something else is more serious, viz. the Bolshevist failure in all their policy aiming at the gradual creation in Russian villages of a basis for a future communistic development.

From the very first the Bolshevists had felt it a pressing matter to fan the flames of class-warfare in the villages; only in the atmosphere of class-warfare could the Bolshevist teachings be expected to take any root there. After the landowners and *kulacks* had disappeared, however, there was a danger that the peasants, if they were left to themselves, might lose in their lives the stimulus of class-warfare; it was therefore essential to see that they were benefited by this and to find a stratum of the village inhabitants whose proletarian instincts could be developed in strife with the other village elements and who might be trained to become the allies of the urban proletariate.

The first step taken by the Bolshevists with this object in view was to mobilize the very poorest element to fight against the village community as a whole. Why, it was,

THE VILLAGE KULACK.

of course, the lowest class in the villages, those most deeply sunk in misery, that formed the real proletariate; they must be upheld in opposition to the others and in this way made into a basis for Bolshevism in rural districts. All the power in the villages was put into the hands of the so-called "poor-committees," composed of such elements. During the corn requisition days, when the main thing was to extort as much grain as possible from the peasants, it certainly was an advantage to have at the head of the village authorities people who had no grain themselves to give and who, therefore, were not prevented by any egoistic motives from exercising the greatest zeal in dealing with such supplies. The project of stirring up class-hatred in this way was, to a certain degree, a failure because, in many quarters, the village community had a strong enough hold over those who had hitherto lived on the alms of others, to prevent this section of the population from ever venturing, in spite of their official position of power, to act in an aggressive manner. In another, the method succeeded only too well—the "poor-committees" misused their power in an incredible manner and contributed more than many another cause to develop that solid dissatisfaction amongst the peasant class which, at last, nearly led to a regular peasant revolt. Neither development was satisfactory from a Bolshevist point of view, and the "poor-committees" were, shortly after, discontinued. The Bolshevists had, as they recognized later on, backed the losing side.

Instead of taking in hand the somewhat hopeless lowest class of the village proletariate and playing them off against the other inhabitants, they now turned their attention to the village so-called middle-class, which, at bottom, also consisted of quite good proletarian elements, and egged them on against the *kulacks.* It is true the real *kulacks* had long since been rendered harmless; as we have shown, the peasants had dispatched them about the same time as the landowners. Those who were now included in that term were the small percentage of the peasant class who, even under the desperate conditions then reigning, had been able by efficiency and industry to raise themselves a little above the average misery. Against this section, then, the Bolshevists proclaimed their holy class-war, and they themselves set the peasants a good example in the matter—the local communistic administration neglected no opportunity of oppressing the better-to-do peasants; burdens of all kinds were loaded upon them; the right of voting at the Soviet elections was taken from them, this last, considering the nature of this right, being, however, but a somewhat modest loss; and, at the same time, an energetic agitation, both verbal and written, was set on foot against them.

Inoffensive Russian peasants who, in the majority of cases, had done no other evil than working and keeping themselves up to the mark, figured in this agitation as vermin, parasites, blood-suckers, etc.

As a rule, certainly, the Bolshevist village agitation fell on promising ground; in such cases, as soon as an appeal was made to the envy of those who were a shade better off, it met with a ready response. In the villages there began—no one can deny this advance of Bolshevist policy—a general persecution of the most self-respecting section. The peasants, in general, set about watching with strained attention individual villagers' attempts to improve their position. It was only necessary for a peasant to work his way up—be it ever so little—by industry and thrift, to get the means to have two horses when the others had one or none, to manage to buy a proper plough when his neighbours had a Russian *socha* or no ploughing implement at all—and, in less than no time, he was stamped as a *kulack*—a wolf in the fold. Taunts and abuse pursued him; he was harassed in a thousand ways and his life made a burden to him in every manner conceivable. The common life is so intimate in the Russian villages, the peasants are so dependent on one another, that his position became completely untenable. I met several peasants who had undergone this martyrdom, and I well understood them when they declared that, henceforward, they would take good care not to work too hard. During this Bolshevist persecution campaign against the *kulacks*, the atmosphere in the Russian villages became such that honest successful work was a misfortune and a curse.

The Bolshevists rubbed their hands for a long time at the sight of this promising development; it was indeed evident that the proletarian class-consciousness was beginning to awaken in the village. But, by slow degrees, they grew at last a little thoughtful. As long as ever the Russian peasant rôle in the Soviet State was to finance practically the whole of the Bolshevist movement, it was, first and foremost at all events, a serious matter that their economic standard—in any case a low one—should, in this way, be reduced to a still lower level. Where would it lead to, if energy and efficiency were not allowed to assert themselves? These doubts of the wisdom of the course they had pursued increased in force in proportion as it began to be apparent that the peasant class neither could nor would any longer consent to the economic bleeding to which they had hitherto been subjected. Before we pass on to consider what fruit was borne by these doubts, we must dwell, for a little, on these economic relations between the Bolshevists and the peasants.

* * *

To extort from the peasants a maximum amount of the sinews of war has been, as we have said, during the last few years, the chief aim of the Bolshevist agrarian policy. A little time since, a leading Bolshevist authority confessed, with all the candour that could be desired, that Soviet finance looked upon rural Russia as a colony whose resources the motherland exploits.

As we study this "colonial" policy, the very first question that arises is: What has been done to put the colony of the rural districts in a position to fulfil the claim that is made upon it? We have seen how the State, with neverfailing generosity, poured out millions for industry, which was a direct source of loss; we might surely expect that it would bestow greater tenderness and interest on agriculture, which, in quite another way, possessed qualifications enabling it to repay the care expended on it.

On this point it is evident that the side of agrarian policy has never been able to rouse any great interest on the part of Bolshevism. Great plans and ideas have certainly been propounded, but there it has stopped, as far as practical action was concerned.

The Russian rural districts must be electrified. This was a plan which, at a very early stage of Bolshevist rule, already greatly occupied the minds of those in power; during Lenin's last years it was the one of his pet ideas to which he returned again and again. The electrification of the rural districts was the means by which the antiquated Russian farming was to be improved in a moment to a degree hitherto undreamt of. Cartloads of printer's ink have been squandered on the project, and fine placards, representing Russian country districts transfigured by the help of electricity, have suddenly appeared in great numbers in the villages. In the same way we see, in our mind's eye, farming carried on with the help of the most modern present-day implements, and tables are drawn up of the constant increase in the thousands of tractors to be distributed every year through the rural districts, when the art of making them has been mastered. A small number, that up till now have been produced, have swallowed fabulous sums for their manufacture.

But whilst they thus dream of raising farming to an American standard, it is allowed, for the moment, to sink far below the old Russian level. Whilst waiting for the millions of horse-power that the future is to place at the disposal of agriculture, this agriculture has now, to a very great extent, to manage without any horse-power at all. The want of draught horses in the villages is enormous. The war and famine years heavily reduced the stock of horses, and not the least of the peasants' complaints is of the Bolshevist ruthless requisition of their horses during the civil war. But even since then the decrease has continued. According to the statistics published in *Pravda* at the very beginning of 1926, in the Ukraine, in 1921, 19 per cent. of the peasant households had no horses; in 1922 the percentage increased to 34; in 1923 to 45; in 1924 to 46, and the percentage in 1925 will presumably be higher. For the whole country, as Rykov in the beginning of 1926 estimated, the number of farms without horses is 30 per cent. According to one calculation, Russian farms now have a supply of horses numbering about the same as in 1850.

It is only necessary to point out very shortly the effect this must have on the farms' productive power. "A peasant without a horse is like a fish without water" is what the peasants say. The peasant who has no horse has to yoke himself to the plough. "I am my own tractor," a peasant said to me. Everywhere in the country, at harvest-time, the harvest may be seen carried home on hand-drawn carts, generally dragged by the women—

methods which are not exactly compatible with rational farming; or else the peasant, who has no horse himself, has to hire his more favoured neighbour's. But, as a rule, this is a very losing transaction, for either the hire is paid in grain, which most perceptibly reduces the peasant's own portion of his harvest—already a small one—or else it is paid by days of work, the result often being that the peasant has, in the busiest time, to work for someone else and neglect, meantime, his own husbandry; moreover, the owner of the horse must use his animal first for his own requirements, so his neighbour is often kept waiting till the right time has passed. Another consequence of the scarcity of horses in the villages is that those to be found there are used to the very utmost and become so worn-out that their work is of little value. It is only necessary to see the particularly wretched, broken-down animals that form the horse supply of Russia's rural districts to understand that no really effective farming can be done with them. The Bolshevists have shown great indifference with regard to this crying need of agriculture. Whilst doomed industry, year after year, has drawn its great subsidies, the peasants have not even been able to get the credits that would have put them in a position to increase, even to the most modest extent, their supply of horses.

It is just the same with farming implements. All the vague plans for a new agricultural equipment—the last word in technical perfection—in the future profit the peasant but little, since, for the moment, he cannot get his need of the most elementary implements supplied. First of all, it has, of course, not been possible to think of meeting the deficiency which, for tens of years, has been the weakest point in Russian farming—viz. the want of proper ploughs. This is the need that is responsible, in great measure, for all the terribly bad harvests, those visitations which, from very far-away times, have with chronic regularity occurred in rural Russia. A proper working of the soil that enables the roots of the corn to make their way down into a deeper, moister layer is, in the Russian climate, of vital importance for the harvest.

But such working, owing to the want of ploughs, has never been given to any great extent. The peasants have not received any help in this respect from the Bolshevists. Besides, with the present miserable supply of horses, modern ploughs would now be a very small advantage, for their worn-out animals would not have the strength to draw them. But now the peasant is not sufficiently supplied with even the old-fashioned agricultural implements that he used to own, above all, the *socha,* that antiquated old thing which, strictly speaking, cannot plough at all and is only responsible for turning over a little earth in the very topmost layer. Even with this the peasant, to a very great extent, is not supplied. In the Ryasan gubernia, to take an example from Russia's chief agricultural district, last year 458,900 peasant households only possessed 250,400 *sochas* and 43,000 modern ploughs ; thus over a third of the farms had no plough at all. In the Ukraine, the number of peasant holdings without a plough increased from 24 per cent. in 1921 to 42 per cent. in 1924. The peasant has to make up for his lack of farming implements in the same way as for his want of horses, i.e. he has to hire his implements under oppressive conditions and at unsuitable times for successful farm-work. And in this connection the peasants are fully justified in accusing the Bolshevists, not only for the lack of interest which they have shown in their requirements, but also for being the direct cause of the miserable state of affairs. The importation of cheap implements, which in earlier days, to a great extent, provided for agricultural wants, has been almost completely stopped by the Bolshevists, partly to preserve the trade balance and partly in the interests of Russian industry, and the State goods have at first been so highly priced that the peasants simply could not think of getting even the most necessary farming implements. Besides, they were manufactured in such insufficient numbers that it was often impossible to buy them for money, even when it was forthcoming.

Just as the Bolshevist policy has done but little to remedy the difficulties that have arisen in the last few years and that now paralyse Russian agriculture, so they have—if we except continual high-sounding speeches—accomplished extremely little when it was a question of combating the more chronic ills which, for tens of years, have been so closely associated with Russian husbandry and have contributed to its decay.

The first of these is that veritable canker of agriculture caused by the method of land division that has gradually developed in the Russian villages. From olden times, indeed, in Russian rural districts, the village community has apportioned to the peasants the amount of land which it was considered ought to fall to each one, and the ruling principle was that the most scrupulous justice should be observed. This laudable principle has, however, in practice, led to extremely disastrous consequences. The first of these is the constant redistribution of the land that recurs after a certain number of years, the idea being that whoever chanced to get poor land at one time should be indemnified by getting a better portion the next. The result of this has been the complete destruction of all interest in the land and death to all individual initiative. What did it profit the peasant-farmer to get his land into good cultivation when, at the next land distribution, his present fields would be taken from him in any case and he would run the risk of getting his neighbour's neglected land in their stead? Secondly, this strict application of the principle of justice led to a grotesque splitting up of the land. So that no injustice should be done, each peasant must have a bit of every kind of land belonging to the village—a bit of sandhill, a bit of marshland, a bit of clay field, etc., so that, in the end, his portion of land was scattered round about the village demesne, seldom in less than twenty to twenty-five, often in thirty or forty, different places, some of which might lie ten to fifteen kilometres from each other. This system made all scientific farming impossible, especially as these land portions very often had the most unsuitable shape; for instance, strips of land which might measure several hundred metres in length but only a few steps in breadth, barely giving sufficient room for the plough to turn, and which could only be tilled from end to end, and not across.

Stolypin's land reform, which made it possible for every peasant to go beyond the village community and get his portion of land in one collected whole, opened a way out of this madness. Whilst interest on the part of the peasants quickly increased, great numbers of land surveyors during the last ten years of tsardom were kept busy with a sensible plotting-out of the peasant land; more than 1½ million peasant holdings, comprising 16 million dessiatines of land, were, during the years 1907–16, handed over for distribution. The revolution annulled practically the whole of this work. The addition to the area of the available lands necessitated a fresh distribution, and, moreover, the peasants who, during the years before the revolution, had gone outside the village community, and in consequence had, as a rule, begun to prosper, were now amongst those who were stamped as *kulacks*, and upon their land the other villagers threw themselves greedily.

However, the idea itself had managed to win such general approval that the peasants, especially in certain parts of the country, now returned to it again, and after a good deal of vacillation, first on one side and then on the other, the Bolshevists too resolved to favour its accomplishment. But in what way? In a village that I visited, the distribution proceedings had just taken place, and the peasants described how the matter was managed: two and a half years' writing, preposterous costs, a year's almost complete loss of harvest (since, whilst waiting for the result of the distribution, every peasant only did the minimum of work on his old portions of land), and, at last, a visit from a Bolshevist surveyor, who was not only entirely incompetent, but took bribes in the most shameless way from some of the peasants, and arranged the new boundaries in a way that plainly defied the most elementary justice. Now that all was clear, the peasants saw that they were obliged, in spite of fresh delay and more expense, to try and get the allotment set aside. Great numbers of villages had the same experience. "It is necessary," Jakovlev writes, "to draw the Party organizations' attention everywhere to the fact that, in this direction more than in any other, we still find relics of the past in the shape of unnecessary delays, corruption and the like."

Even in other directions the peasants have seen very little of the Bolshevist endeavour to pull up Russian agriculture from the decay of centuries. Now we must certainly say that perhaps the great majority of the peasants have not the slightest wish to learn any new ideas as regards their method of tilling the ground, those old-fashioned principles of farming that have been handed down from generation to generation from times immemorial. To all the hampering superstition and prejudice that form the principal ingredient in their stock of agricultural knowledge, to all the obstinate unchanging routine that distinguishes peasant-husbandry, most of them cling fast with a hopeless, mule-like pertinacity, and are thankful to have no interference with their inheritance from the past. But yet in some directions an inkling that it no longer does to go on in the old way begins to peep out here and there amongst the peasant masses; also a great number of peasants, when prisoners of war in Germany, had the opportunity of seeing something of scientific farming and brought home accounts of it. But the desire—which is thus becoming apparent—to get instruction and guidance in a more sensible husbandry remains, in the great majority of cases, unsatisfied. We have already described the upshot of the so-called Soviet holdings, which, according to communistic ideas, were to demonstrate to the peasants modern farming methods. And, in spite of all that has been said and written about the epoch-making activity that the Bolshevists have started by sending round to the villages agricultural experts to instruct the peasants—amongst other proofs of this activity, pictures are to be seen at short intervals in the newspapers of the special trains, filled with such experts, laden with material for agricultural instruction and even painted outside with edifying pictures, as they speed along the railway tracks to teach peasants the new husbandry technique—yet, in spite of all this, most villages have not caught a glimpse of the Soviet agriculturists, and often do not even know what sort of apparition an agriculturist may be. Nor is this difficult to understand, since, according to Jakovlev's report, there is at present one expert for 40,000 peasants, and the majority of them never set foot in a Russian village, but are swallowed up by the many Moscow offices.

Moreover, the Bolshevists, not content with having left the peasants unassisted in a number of economic points, have, in addition, put impediments in the way of the peasants' own attempt to cope with economic problems by the help of Co-operation—one of the most effective means imaginable. The Soviet Government, fearing the independence of the Co-operative organs, during the earlier years completely crushed the Co-operative movement and destroyed the possibility of improving the state of agriculture offered by this movement, which, in the years immediately before the war, had begun to get a firm footing in the villages. And when, after the introduction of the *Nep* policy, the broken mechanism began to be put together again, it became something which did not deserve its name of Co-operation, namely, a State institution under the control and mismanagement of Soviet officials, regulated to the last detail by the State—a dry bureaucratic, lifeless apparatus, and consequently looked upon with mistrust by the peasants and without any influence on Russian farming. "The peasants," so Rykov affirms in February, 1926, "to a great extent look upon Co-operation as a Government affair, not as their own."

The Bolshevists showed quite other powers of initiative and energy than those they displayed in increasing the power of agricultural production, as soon as the question arose of utilizing this production. "The peasant is a sheep; whoever wants his wool, shears him. The tsar used to shear us before, and now the Bolshevists do," say the peasants. And the Bolshevists are incontestably masters in the agricultural art which consists of clipping the peasants' wool. The new kind of instrument that they principally use for this purpose is, of course, taxation. When the Bolshevists in 1921 were compelled to relinquish their claim on the peasants' grain production, and decided instead that the peasants should give up a certain amount of their corn as a tax and have the free disposal of the remainder, they, in great measure, indemnified themselves for their concession by considerably increasing the amount when fixing the tax. Several modifications of the tax were made during successive years. At first the rulers made a number of taxes—about twenty of them—and their collection scarcely gave the peasants any breathing-space; then they were all united in one. At first the tax was taken in kind; after the stabilization of the coinage it was required, at first partly, and then entirely, in cash. In one respect alone these modifications never showed any change, that is in the terribly heavy burden of taxes that rested on peasant shoulders. Now, it is true the Bolshevists saw to it that the tax demanded was not appreciably greater than under tsardom. The direct tax was certainly half as great again, but, on the other hand, many indirect taxes were dropped. In this connection, however, it must be noticed that even if the Bolshevists might not exploit the peasants to a greater degree than tsardom had done, yet this was no proof that they dealt gently with them; on the contrary, in so far as they followed in tsardom's footsteps in their taxation of the peasants, it was a clear proof that they robbed them terribly. Moreover, it is evident that these taxes, now that agricultural conditions had become so much worse, were heavier to bear than before. Every pood now demanded from the peasant was taken, not from his surplus, but from the small quantity that he was allowed for food. In addition to this, the tax was collected with a severity never practised before. Every delay brought the peasant heavy fines, which often ran up to an amount that doubled his tax. Stalin told in one of his speeches in the summer of 1925 how the rural district administration sometimes went so far in their zealous collection of taxes as even to tear the roof off the house of any dilatory taxpayer.

A few concrete examples, drawn from the account that Jakovlev writes of his inquiries, give an illuminating picture of what the tax meant in these years to the peasant. A peasant, the owner of 4 dessiatines of land, had reaped 35 poods per dessiatine. As he himself had no horse and had to hire his neighbour's, 15 poods per dessiatine was deducted from his harvest for ploughing, 7 for carrying in. The amount he kept thus amounted to 13 poods per dessiatine. Of these the tax took more than half, 7 poods per dessiatine. "Now I have to choose either not to pay the tax or to die of starvation." A peasant woman who, in the same way, had to use hired help, came, in April, to the end of her last measure of corn, and had to sell her calf to get the means of living herself; it is not strange that she felt bitter at the thought of the 21 poods of corn that the State had taken from her. Things had got so far with a third, even in February, that he had to begin by selling his belongings; the State had, in autumn, demanded 64 poods of corn from him. Or take a fourth case: a widow, with six children, had to employ hired labour for her land. Taken all in all, she got a harvest of 119 poods; of this she had to pay 21 for ploughing, 18 for getting in the hay, and 17 poods went for autumn sowing, so 63 poods remained for food. The State demanded 40; she did not pay in time and was sent to prison for the sum. It is, as we have said, an investigation instituted by the Soviet authorities themselves that gives these figures; in village after village that I visited the peasants gave me similar or worse pictures of their economic state.

The Bolshevists had, however, at the same time another, almost more effective, implement for the sheep-shearing in the villages, viz. that which, for long, went under the name of "the scissors," a term originally used so effectively by Trotsky. Immediately after 1921 the prices, upon which the peasant's economic condition depends, began to move in opposite directions; these prices were, on the one hand, those at which he could sell his corn, and, on the other, those which he had to pay for the manufactured goods that he required. In order to improve the artisans' conditions of living, the State tried, in every imaginable way, to keep down the price of corn. On the one hand, under pretext of the necessity of making speculation an impossibility, a very low maximum price was fixed for corn, and, on the other, after the peasants had begun to pay part of their taxes in money, the State bought up their corn at a low price immediately before the tax was due, when the peasants had to get ready money, and afterwards, in the market, competed with them in the sale of any corn they might have left—a policy that ended in the price of corn falling to half what it was before the war, or even lower. At the same time, the prices of manufactured goods rose. Imports from abroad were stopped, and Russian industry, then starting again, produced goods which, as long as they were to be sold for profit, necessitated terrible prices, which were still further considerably increased—as has been shown—in the process of trade distribution. This decrease in the price of corn and the increase in that of manufactured goods—a double movement in prices which, as Trotsky pointed out, made the two curves look like a pair of scissors with wide-open blades—naturally contributed, in a very special degree, to the utter exhaustion of peasant resources. The necessary articles that a peasant could obtain in earlier days by selling a sack of corn, he could only get now by selling ten or twenty; to get a little clothing he had to drive to the town with a whole cartload, and to buy some farming implement he was compelled to empty his barn. All this was quite rightly considered by the peasants as an indirect tax which pressed more hardly than that levied directly.

* * *

For about two years after the capitulation of 1921, Bolshevism went on calmly in its policy, as regarded the peasants, along the lines described above. Then they were obliged to beat a retreat again.

To begin with, they were compelled to press together the scissors' greedily gaping jaws. They had opened overmuch, and, in consequence, at last they cut nothing but empty air. The method of squeezing out the peasant's last resources by forcing him to use the miserable pittance he got for his corn to buy Soviet manufactured goods at fabulously high prices proved, in the long run, impracticable; the peasants ceased to prop up Russian manufactures in this way. They left off buying, chiefly because they simply could not, and partly because, even if they could have possibly scraped together a few coins for the most indispensable articles, they would not do it; there arose a general buyers' strike, in part involuntary, but in part, too, of set purpose. The result was that described in a former chapter: the industrial turnover came to an end, and one branch after another was faced with the necessity of a complete stoppage of output. How this crisis was surmounted has been already told. To satisfy the peasant class and to set industry going again, the prices of manufactured goods had to be reduced, even if this meant that industry would, in the future, have to work at a loss. In this way, one of the scissor blades was pressed down; it is true that it was stopped to a certain degree—as we have shown before—by the impediment that the retailers, to a great extent, preferred to take advantage themselves of the lower industrial prices, instead of allowing the public to profit by them.

To be compelled in this way to yield in face of the peasant buyers' strike was, naturally, a most serious blow to the Bolshevists' policy, even though they did put forward the reduction of the selling price to a level below the cost of production as a brilliant economic artifice. But even this sacrifice did not suffice. The peasants' dissatisfaction continued and increased; the autumn of 1924 was indeed a very critical time for the Bolshevists in Russian rural districts. The peasants began again to show plainly—as they had done three years earlier—what they thought about the Bolshevist policy. To a very great extent they boycotted—as we have already related—the Soviet elections that took place towards the end of the year, and throughout the rural districts there broke out a veritable epidemic of murders and attacks on Communists, especially on the so-called village correspondents, i.e. the Communist newspaper reporters in the villages, whom the peasants considered as nothing but Soviet spies. Reports came from every quarter that the feeling in the rural districts grew more and more alarming. The Communists grew very nervous, and this nervousness was clearly reflected in the speeches of the leading politicians and in the anxious reflections of the Press. "Eyes front to the village!"

became the daily cry that resounded without cessation, and a number of attempts to calm the peasants were planned and carried into effect.

An effort was made—this has already been shown—to allay the peasants' dissatisfaction, in so far as it arose from a feeling of political inferiority, by proclaiming a free vote—although it was but illusive—at the elections for the Soviets which were announced. But it was seen that, before all else, the efforts at conciliation must be of an economic nature. It would not do to continue the policy of extortion that had found expression in the heavy taxes. In spite of all their efforts, they had not succeeded, during 1924, in getting more than something over 300 millions of the total taxation of 470 millions. Thus, in the spring of 1925, the Bolshevists decided to capitulate on this point by contenting themselves with levying a tax on the peasant class of 300 millions, and also by abstaining in its collection from the extremely compulsory methods hitherto employed. This really meant that they gave up all hopes of getting more than a fraction of this sum.

The retreat before the peasants even on this point was, in itself, a most serious matter for the Soviet economy; it was, however, to have still more serious consequences. Up till then, the peasants, as soon as the harvest was carried in autumn, had been obliged to sell the greater part as quickly as possible to get money for paying their taxes, and the State could then purchase what corn it required on practically any conditions whatever. Now that the tax-pressure was somewhat diminished, the peasants began to show a disinclination—disastrous in the highest degree for the Bolshevists—to throw their corn straightway into the markets. As the harvest of 1925 had been a relatively good one, the Government had expected to have at their disposal more than enough corn for their needs; they reckoned that the State agencies for buying corn would be able to collect 780 million poods, and they built on a substantial corn-export to bring in a sum that would enable them to give a very effective contribution to the new industrial equipment that was so very urgently needed. It proved, however, that they had reckoned without the peasants. The mighty State agency for purchasing corn—which, in parenthesis, we may say was a typical Bolshevist organizing monstrosity—from the very first met with a decidedly obstinate peasant obstruction. The quantity it managed to procure in no way satisfied their calculations, and to get any corn at all it was necessary to pay prices of which they had never dreamt. When the peasants were no longer in fear of the lash to the same degree as before, they refused to half-starve for the benefit of the Bolshevist finances and began to eat up the corn themselves; and when they might have sold without going short themselves, they often did not trouble to do so. The Bolshevist money had no attraction for them. It has just been shown how the price-reductions, made after 1923, for a time put the peasants in a position to buy manufactured goods; this increased demand soon exceeded the industrial power of production, and a scarcity of commodities ensued, with the result that, since the autumn of 1925, manufactured goods have been, on the one hand, difficult to procure, and, on the other, have commanded prices which the peasants will not pay. Hence they do not convert their corn into money to buy industrial products. And they take good care not to sell their corn to get a store of money—they have no confidence in the Bolshevist *tchervonetz*, and prefer to keep the corn in their barns. So the hopes of getting 780 million poods of corn had to be abandoned; they reduced their claims to 600 millions, a quantity of which, in January, 1926, they had scarcely got a half. The result was that the glorious export programme had, at various times, to be severely cut down and the grant to industry, upon which they had reckoned, to be reduced over and over again—a fresh defeat for the Bolshevists in the drawn battle with the stubborn *moujiks*—and surely not their last!

Still worse, however, is an absolutely fundamental capitulation to the peasants which the Bolshevists have had to make during the past year. All the difficulties that they have had in the course of years in their economic dealings with the peasants compelled them—as we have indicated above—to go seriously into the question of what was the real reason why the rural districts could not fill their rôle as the object of Government exploitation. They turned their eyes to the policy—already described—which directed class-warfare in the villages against the best and most self-respecting section of the community and paralysed them. It was now recognized that this, more than anything else, had hindered economic development in the rural districts and thereby prevented them from becoming the Bolshevist financial base. And so this policy, on which such great hopes had been founded, was then in a moment utterly condemned. The authorities vied with one another in showing its impossibility in all respects imaginable. All sections in the village, they now stated, were dissatisfied with it—more than any others the *kulacks* themselves, who were hindered in what the Bolshevists now recognized as entirely loyal efforts to improve their position. "Hitherto," said Bucharin, "if a peasant has put an iron roof on his house, he has been for ever declared a *kulack*, and that was the end of him. If a peasant has wanted to buy a machine, he has done it so that the Communists might not see it; to improve farming has seemed a sort of conspiracy." But it was maintained that even the poorer peasants were discontented. In the past they had got their living by working as day-labourers for richer peasants; now, when richer peasants were not allowed to exist and the use of hired labour was forbidden, they were beginning to starve. "The poor man says: 'It is a very good thing that you grind down the rich, but then take me on at the factory; if you can't give me a place there, give me one somewhere else. I cannot live by eating proletarian decrees.' The whole thing," Bucharin affirms, "is a wrong economic strategy."

And in the Party Congress of April, 1925, they set about putting a complete end to the strategy. The class-warfare against the *kulacks* was entirely stopped. If the village community had but just before been egged on against these "dirty bloodsuckers," it was now represented to them with considerable sharpness how unfitting it was that peasants, who were pure idlers themselves, should harass industrious and thrifty husbandmen, who were, most undeservedly, branded as *kulacks.* And the Congress solemnly confirmed the resolution of those in authority that all hindrances that had been put in the way of these peasants' honest work should be put an end to. Now they introduced what was called a *nep* policy for the rural districts as well. All that the better-to-do peasants could desire, they should have. More land? Just help yourselves! The right to rent land, abolished after the revolution, was brought in again for their benefit, and, so that they might feel quite secure in their tenancy, the lease was fixed for a period of twelve clear years. Hired labour? Take what you want! The employment of hired labour, hitherto strictly forbidden and branded as exploitation, was allowed to an unlimited degree, "with suspension, if necessary, of the eight-hours day." That a rich peasant should use in the summer, if need be, ten temporary workers for the season in no way prevented his being a good member of the proletariate; such was the assurance of a writer in *Pravda.* Many of the revolution gains, once so vaunted, thus went the way of the world. But what more? It was essential to create a well-to-do peasant bourgeoisie, for that is, after all, the economic backbone of the peasant class. This now became the Bolshevist principle. Stolypin was, twenty years before, of precisely the same opinion.

"What is the use of saying that we must bring in socialism when we are going at full speed towards pure and simple capitalism?" was the question put by one speaker at the Party Congress. It is natural that such a catastrophic defeat for Bolshevism as was implied in the acceptance of this new policy should give rise to several bitter reflections of the same kind and arouse opposition, that found strong expression as early as the April Congress, and afterwards made itself even more strongly felt in the Party Congress of December, 1925. But on both occasions this opposition was ruthlessly beaten down. Larin, one of the leading radical Bolshevists, met with special silencing when he openly declared that if they now allowed the building-up of capital in the villages, they would have to be ready, in a few years' time, to confiscate the total amassed. This cost him a sharp reprimand from Rykov himself. Such things ought not to be said; every speech about confiscation of capital did more than anything else to scare off the foreign capital of which Russia was now in such pressing need.

Officially they assumed, instead, an appearance of cheerful satisfaction. Just as at the introduction of the new economic policy in its day, so now the decision to introduce *nep* into the rural districts as well was not a step back but a gigantic stride forward. The creation of a class of small capitalists in the villages will contribute to economic improvement in the rural districts; the rural districts' economic improvement will give the State increased financial resources; increased financial resources for the Soviet State implies that it can work with much greater energy for Communism and look after the proletariate's interests; therefore, the creation of a capitalist bourgeoisie in the villages means a great advance for Communism and for the proletariate.

Such is the line of reasoning. The radical Bolshevists observe that, when the Party now coolly sanction village capitalism, it reminds them very much of the mediæval priests who on fast days ate meat, to their hearts' desire, after they had first said some prayers over it and called it fish. And, sure enough, it is quite certain that, from a Bolshevist point of view, it is indeed a very indigestible piece of meat that they have just swallowed. The *nepmen* created by the new policy of 1921 have already been, as we have shown, very difficult to keep in check—this, too, although they have never made any effort to take any part in politics, and, moreover, in great part, had their sphere of action in the towns, where the Communist Party is, comparatively speaking, strong and they can be kept under somewhat effective control. The *nepmen* in the rural districts, who have now got a free hand, are, without doubt, far more dangerous. The very fact of their being allowed to take in peace and quiet an assured economic position helps them to become those with most influence in the villages. The poorer peasants, who, of necessity, are economically dependent on them, in other respects, too, easily come under their control. The village *nepmen* have, therefore, all the qualifications for becoming what the *nepmen* in the towns have never dreamt of, viz. the organizers of public opinion. And if the Bolshevists have already had so far a precarious position in the Russian rural districts, it will certainly not be improved by this additional counterweight to Bolshevist influence. The optimism of the Bolshevists seems to rest on somewhat insecure foundations when they proudly dismiss the idea that these peasant bourgeoisie, one fine day, when they have managed to grow strong enough, may take into their heads to deny their political faith in and obedience to communistic principles.

Bolshevist peace with the peasant bourgeoisie was thus an accomplished fact. It had a sequel of a very original nature. Although the leaders had swallowed the great capitalist lump of meat, they wanted, at least, to follow it up with a tasty little dish of fish. They felt the need of showing all ill-disposed critics, who, instead of looking upon the whole business as a great victory for Bolshevist policy, saw in it a somewhat ignominious retreat before capitalism, that Bolshevism did not betray its principles, but was still the great capitalist destroyer. By diligent search they hunted up a few isolated remnants of the Russian landowner class who, by a miracle, had saved themselves during all these years. Some few former landowners whom the peasants had spared, and who, in their respective villages, lived a peasant's life amongst the peasants, received a share of land, like the other members of the village community, and even "wormed their way into the peasants' confidence." What a frightful danger for the proletariate was thus disclosed! Here indeed quick and radical measures were needed! To build up a new capitalist class of some hundred thousand men was good Communism, but to allow a few hundred former capitalists, who had now turned into peasants, to live in peace on their modest holdings would indeed have been a betrayal of Communist principles. With a great flourish of trumpets they marched to the attack and made a clean sweep of every one. The land was taken from them and they themselves sent into exile. Who could now come and say that the Bolshevists had retreated before capitalism? The manœuvre was effective enough. What does defeat matter when the vanquished understand how to cover their retreat in such brilliant fashion?

CHAPTER VI

THE LIFE OF THE PROLETARIATE UNDER PROLETARIAN DICTATORSHIP

HAVING now examined the Bolshevist achievements in some individual points of the social fabric, we will pass on to another question: To what extent does this building, the result of eight years' restoration work, as a whole, offer more tolerable conditions of life to its occupiers? What improvement in their material position have the proletariate made under the supreme power of the proletariate?

As far as the present class is concerned, the answer has, to some extent, been given in the account of the Bolshevists' peasant policy. We have seen how that policy—in part by failing to support the productive power of agriculture, in part by levying heavy contributions on this production—has placed the farmer in a very difficult position; in both cases it has—as we have shown—aroused such pronounced dissatisfaction amongst the peasants that the Bolshevists have been compelled to retreat before it. The question, however, remains as to whether the peasants—in true peasant fashion—have not cried out a little unnecessarily, and whether, in reality, a summing-up of the peasants' revolutionary gains and losses would not give quite a good credit balance.

"The Bolshevists, after all, have given you the land; that's a gain you cannot deny," we say to the peasants, after we have heard them pouring out, far and wide, how their position has been made worse by the revolution.

The peasants have their objections quite ready, and assure us that it is not quite such clear gain as all that. In this connection, as a rule, they do not, first of all, call attention to the truth that, as a matter of fact, the land does not belong to them, but to the State. The restrictions that ensue from this do not press upon them in general, and they really feel themselves to be the masters of the land, at any rate one seldom hears any complaints in that respect. With one exception, however—and this they emphasize so much the more—they have been deprived of a part of the land which they needed just as much as the fields, viz. of the forest; for the State keeps a very firm hold of the forests, and is exceedingly niggardly in any share that it allows to the peasants. In times gone by the peasant simply took what he required out of his own, or, much more often, out of the landowner's forest. The peasants have always considered it one of their most inalienable rights to steal timber without penalty; now they talk till they are hoarse of all the endless trouble they have to fetch a load or even a few sticks from the Government forest. They do not understand how to fulfil all the intricate ceremonies required, under the Bolshevist rule of papers, to get permission to cut some timber, and to take it without leave means frightful fines for them. The only possible way, they say, is to bribe the Bolshevist forester, who is grasping and insolent, like Communists in general.

This first complaint is followed by another: the peasants, so they assure us, have never got the best land; that the Bolshevists have kept for their own use. They mean by this the Soviet holdings, previously discussed. This fact, that the Bolshevists have taken peasant land to support idlers from the towns, arouses the peasants' deepest feelings, especially since the husbandry of these model farms has proved to be a sight for gods and men. Naturally this indignation is greatest in villages that have the model farm close at hand and have been directly deprived of the land upon which they had reckoned. But even in other villages, that only know the Soviet farms by report, the peasants, when we talk to them, show a predilection for the subject of how the Bolshevists have filched the peasants' land, and they absolutely refuse to believe that they could have done so with any other object than to maintain their own people at the peasants' expense. The loss which the peasants have suffered in this way seems, in itself, somewhat insignificant. In Russia proper the peasants had, before the war, about 76 per cent. of the land and the landowners and Government 24 per cent.; now the peasants own 96 per cent. and 4 per cent. the State has kept for itself. Only the sixth part of the land, which, before the revolution, was not in peasant hands and which they laid claim to, has been withheld from them. The percentage of the land which has been withheld at the distribution to the peasants is still less in the Ukraine; here the peasants, before the revolution, owned only 55 per cent. of the land, whilst landowners and Government had 45 per cent.; now they possess 96 per cent., so that the Soviet has only claimed a tenth part of the land available for distribution. And even if the loss now falls heavily on a not inconsiderable number of the peasant class, who, owing to the Soviet holdings, have not got a hand's-breadth more land, the whole matter scarcely seems worth making such a to-do about.

When, then, the peasants, after all, do so, it is because of its connection with another matter—a matter that is the chief explanation why the distribution of the *barins'* land, of which the peasants have dreamt for generations, has by no means aroused very effusive satisfaction amongst them nor inspired them with any warmer feelings for the Bolshevists. That the slight reservation made in the general land-distribution has assumed such importance in their eyes is due to the fact that the whole land-partition has been a great disillusionment for them.

It was self-evident that this must be so. For tens of years they have fixed jealous eyes on the landowners' fields and persuaded themselves that there would be an end of all their trouble on the day when these rich bits should be portioned out between them. The parties who sought their favour never had courage to set them free from this illusion. And yet—quite apart from the fact that the Russian peasants with their present methods of husbandry must remain poor, poverty-stricken creatures, even though all the land in Europe were distributed amongst them, and that the only way of escape from their misery is a sensible cultivation of the land—it was evident that the landowners' estates formed such an insignificant portion of Russia's acreage that the peasants' gain at its distribution must be a quite modest one. Taken all in all, 50 million dessiatines have been distributed amongst the peasants, certainly in itself an enormous quantity of land, but, in any case, not particularly much for a population of 100 million peasants. On an average the peasant's portion of land has been increased by one-third, whereas he himself expected it to be three times as large as before. And this increase has not come to those who stood in most need of it, viz. to the peasants in Russia proper. The lion's share has been taken by the Ukraine, where the peasants, who were already fairly well off, on an average got their land doubled. The peasants of Russia proper, on the other hand, had an insignificant enough increase of land. In some parts of the country, where the landowners had been but few and far between, the peasants got no share whatever in the distribution of land.

If the gift of land, in itself, proved a disappointment, the gain in economic respects which the land-distribution, in any case, incontestably implied was further diminished, during all these years, by the fact that the produce of the land was taken from the peasants. "The land is ours, but the corn is not ours." This expression, which, as we have said, was coined in the days of the requisition system, has, even since the system has come to an end, embodied the peasants' summary of what they consider their revolution gains. We hear it repeated wherever we go, in village after village. "We are the landowner's, but the land is ours," was the phrase in the days of serfdom. "The land is ours, but the corn is not ours," is the present version—in both cases a little hitch in the possession of the land which, most perceptibly, reduces its value.

The methods by which the corn was taken from the peasant class have been described in the foregoing pages; we have also touched upon the ways in which the peasants have, again and again, forcibly brought about modifications in such methods. That their complaints, however, have been well-grounded up to the very last is shown by the Bolshevists' own figures. If we confine ourselves only to what has been taken from them by way of taxes, it is apparent from the calculations of the Supreme Economic Commission, quoted by Djersjinsky in a speech in the beginning of 1926, that the peasant class, in the year 1924–5, had to pay in taxes, not only every kopeck that they got for the corn they sold, but 38 millions in addition which they had to raise from some other source than their chief article of diet. It was not until the year 1925–6, after the taxation reductions obtained by the peasants' forcible methods, that the corn sales were reckoned not only to cover the tax payments, but also to leave a surplus to the peasants of 297 millions—that is to say, 3 roubles per head. It is hard to prove that the peasants have complained without good cause !

And if we now consider what the Bolshevist peasant policy, as a whole, has effected with regard to better social conditions for the peasant class, the result is, at least so far, anything but brilliant ; what may be the effects of the modifications in this policy that have been obtained by the peasants' defiant attitude it is still too soon to judge. It is, of course, a well-known fact that the Russian villages have at all times presented a picture of poverty and need. However hardened we may have become through former acquaintance with them, we are always completely paralysed as soon as we get out into the real rural districts. We come to villages that, from the church to the last hut, present throughout one single, unbroken picture of hopeless decay, where the houses seem to have difficulty in standing up, with windows in which repulsive rags take the place of glass, with roofs on which the thinning thatch hangs in loose tufts, and stuck up in the middle of all this wretchedness, the name-plates with grandiose revolutionary names, absolutely grotesque pieces of work with which the Bolshevists have adorned the indescribable village streets. We are surrounded by peasants who only partially cover their nakedness by fantastic rags, their trousers of torn sacks fluttering round their legs ; and in village after village we get evidence of how the peasants have to feed in a way which, even if it is a little better than during the catastrophic period of starvation a few years ago, in no case deserves any other name than famine.

I have, on various occasions, lived in Russian rural districts, but such general and continuous underfeeding I have only seen in years of actual famine. In a number of villages that I visited in the summer of 1924, villages that did not belong to that year's bad harvest districts, but where the harvest had been so good that in the opinion of those in supreme authority it would suffice to feed, not only its own population, but also those who were suffering from a failure of crops—in such villages the peasants' only food consisted of a heavy black bread, quite indigestible for ordinary stomachs, tea of roasted carrots, and a soup made of nothing but potatoes; they had had no meat since the Christmas before, and there was an utter want of any kind of fat. Every sort of implement was in an indescribable state; broken things of all sorts were, as a rule, lashed together with old rope; nails were a luxury that had to be used sparingly. They had to try and manage without the simplest manufactured goods. One of the first drivers that I employed could not drive at more than a walking pace; when, at last, I grew impatient, he showed me that his horse had only two shoes; he had no means of getting the other two that were missing. In this special case, it is true, the want was supplied, for he fleeced me for the drive of a sum that would have been enough for the shoes of a whole stable of remounts. "There are," said Zinoviev at the end of 1924, "districts where the simplest things, such as workers in the towns would not think twice about, are an unheard-of luxury." And he gives an example. "I asked," he says, "a representative of Baku, 'How much does paraffin cost in your parts?' and he answered, 'Four kopecks a pound.' It may be thought," Zinoviev continues, "that the price is not high, but anyhow tarred sticks are still burnt in the district round Baku. All about there they have a sea of paraffin, but the peasant is still so poor in the Baku gubernia that he burns tarred sticks because he has not the means to pay four kopecks." And although, of course, there are also districts where conditions are better, yet a few cold official figures showing the consumption of various necessities, both in 1925 and before the war, give a certain idea of the all-round reduction that has been forced upon the consumers. (The figures apply to town and country together; since under Bolshevist rule the towns have always been looked after best, statistics for the rural districts only, if such could be procured, would be still more striking.) The amount of cotton material used per head, before the war, was 20·6 ells; in 1925, 12·7; cast-iron goods, 66 pounds, now 22·4; sugar, 19·3 pounds, now 11·6; glass, 8 pounds, now 2·7; paraffin, 14·9 pounds, now 10, and so on.

Conditions are not least miserable for the peasants in cases where they have to rely entirely upon the provision made for them by the authorities. A splendid illustration of this in the one department only of the care of the sick is given by no less a person than Semasjko himself, the Commissary in the People's Commissariat for Public Health.

Taking as his starting-point the watchword so constantly repeated during the last year of "Eyes front to the village!" he states in an article in *Izvestia* a year ago that in this department the authorities have, up till now, kept not their eyes but their backs turned to the village. Hospitals have been closed throughout the land. In the Tver gubernia, for instance, they have been reduced to 69 per cent.; in a couple of districts in the Samara gubernia ten of the twenty-nine hospitals have been closed; twenty-eight of thirty-six so-called "barber-surgeon," centres have been shut down, and even in the Leningrad gubernia 3,000 hospitals have ceased to exist.

"And these," continues Semasjko, "are only bare statistics. In reality the situation is still worse. In an overwhelming number of cases, places registered under the name of hospitals are some old half-ruined buildings wretchedly provided with linen, equipment and medicines. And the staff, who have not been paid for several months, are busy farming to get a living." In the Ryasan gubernia the hospital generally consists of two rooms with an unheated waiting-room; the patients lie there in their own clothes—i.e. in their sheepskins—and 15 kopecks a day are allowed for their maintenance; in the Pskov gubernia this allowance is 10 kopecks a day; and in the Samara gubernia no food at all is given to the patients, but they must have it sent to them from their homes. In some places the hospital tries to improve its financial position by taking payment from the patients. The latter are, so Semasjko affirms, exceedingly dissatisfied with this and say: "In the time of the *semstvon* (the tsaristic rural council) we were nursed for nothing, but under Soviet rule we have to pay for everything; the artisans have sanatoriums and health resorts, but I cannot get even my finger tied up anywhere." "As things are," Semasjko states, "the whole hospital situation in rural Russia is catastrophic in the fullest meaning of the word." And, even although Semasjko later on, in February, 1926, feels able to bear witness to "something like a certain improvement," he, at the same time, gives the information that 20 per cent. of all the Russian volosts are without any medical help whatever, and 40 per cent. have only that provided by ambulances. "We have," he adds, "only made infinitesimal progress in comparison with what ought to be done."

The position is catastrophic; the curtain, however, is firmly drawn up on a pleasant little side-scene. The imperial castle in Livadia and a few other palaces down in the south have been opened as peasant sanatoriums; people interested in art have made every effort to get the imperial castle transformed into a museum, but no, a great blow must be struck here in the cause of Russian national health. Some hundreds of peasants can now loll about in the imperial halls; there, one can see for oneself how tenderly the Soviet cares for the peasant class. "The establishment of peasant sanatoriums," writes Semasjko in *Pravda,* "is something new and unknown in the world's history, the importance of which, in every respect, it is difficult to imagine. Neither medical nor social history has, hitherto, known such a thing. For this reason the peasant sanatoriums have attracted the attention, not only of politicians, but of medical professors (!) as well. In establishing them we have had an eye to their undoubted political significance; the peasants who come and are cared for in the tsar's castle get a practical lesson in the real meaning of the Soviet Government, the supreme power of the proletariate. . . . I believe that the establishment of peasant sanatoriums is also of great international significance. May the peasants of Europe and America learn what is implied in the dictatorship of the proletariate! It is an additional argument why the European class should take the side of the proletariate in their contest, It is essential to spread the news of the peasant sanatoriums as far and wide as possible amongst the international peasant class." Would it not be well at the same time to spread the news of the Soviet's hospitals where the patients have a maintenance allowance of 10 kopecks a day?

A cleverly organized propaganda can now make the very most of the fact that a few hundred peasants contentedly stretch their limbs in the imperial beds. In the health resorts season of 1925, the number of peasants looked after there was 800 all told. For all that, it cannot be denied that the 100 millions of the Russian peasant class live in terrible conditions in their back-yards. "Worse than before" is the peasants' unanimous opinion of the material position they have got under the Bolshevists; and anyone who sees their life is obliged to grant that, at least, it is no better.

One thing more must be added: this distressful life is all the more bitter for the peasant, since at the same time he has a rebellious feeling that he has been treated like a stepchild. "In the villages," Zinoviev announced last autumn, "there exists a certain jealousy as regards the town workers. In tens of letters that I have had from peasants they say: 'Two classes are in power in our country, the artisans and the peasants. The Government ought to try to give the same position to peasants and artisans alike, but it only looks after the advantage of the artisans." In intercourse with the peasants, fresh proofs of this jealousy of the artisan class are constantly to be found. Great numbers of tales go the round, in the villages, of the thousands of advantages that fall to the share of the town worker; to a great degree, after all, nothing more than an echo of the Bolshevists' own enraptured descriptions of the wonderful gains accruing to the artisan class from the revolution. "The artisans," so say the peasants, " suck the Government like calves whilst the peasants starve; the artisans live like fighting-cocks," or, as the more rustic phrase runs in Russian: " They lie like cheese in butter." It is their firm conviction that it is the peasants who have to carry the whole load, whilst their comrades in the towns take very good care not to lift a finger to help. And even with reference now to the rulers themselves: not even those at the very top, whose portraits are distributed in the villages, to replace the icons that they want to induce the peasants to throw on the dust-heap, escape the accusation of spending the peasants' money in their own riotous living.

* * *

We will pass on to the artisan class. It is not only the Russian peasants, but people much nearer home, who never tire of describing their fortunate lot in the Bolshevist " butter-jar." Are these descriptions well-founded in fact?

It is well known that the economic position of the Russian working-class before the war was a terrible one. A more sweated proletariate has scarcely existed in modern times, I imagine. It was the ruthless exploitation of the working-class rather than the political oppression that brought the Russian revolution to a head. So much the greater should we expect to find the gains that this working-class—whose hands accomplished the revolution and who at the moment wield supreme power—now have to record.

Let us begin by dealing with the main point: What change have they achieved in their wages? How far have they outdistanced tsardom's wretched starvation pittance that has scarcely known any increase since the beginning of the century? The answer is one that, having regard to the industrial situation, is indeed only natural, but, having regard to all the fine pictures that have been given, is wellnigh incredible, viz. not by the very least step. After eight years they have at last reached the beggarly standard of tsaristic times by means of the regular small increases of which I have spoken before, and which the authorities have been compelled to give the workmen to keep up their spirits, irrespective of whether industry could stand the increases or not, but they have got no higher; according to Bolshevist statistics, the figures now, in the beginning of 1926, are more or less 100 per cent. In a few industries where before the revolution the wages were quite incredibly miserable—as, for instance, in the provision trade—they are somewhat above this, but in others somewhat below instead. The average workman thus earns a wage of about 27s. 9d. a week in English money—and that, too, with a lower purchasing power than in England; and, moreover, the prospects of a continued wage-increase are but poor, when we consider the industrial position which has been already described. The increases given during the latter part of 1925, which brought up the wages to their present level, occurred during a period of temporary economic optimism, when, in consequence of the relatively good harvest prospects, the economic experts reckoned on a brilliant corn-export, which would make it possible for Government to give such substantial help to industry as would result in a great trade revival; a larger advance in wages—about 25 per cent.—was given than ever before and prospects held out of more in the near future. But this economic programme suffered shipwreck, as we have already shown, and now the working-men will most certainly have to be content for a long time to come with the somewhat precipitate increase which they then received. As lately as March, 1926, Rykov, in one of his speeches, declared that when in the preceding autumn they had promised the workers improved wage-conditions, "we have miscalculated the contents of our purse. I think," he said, "that for the immediate present, any increase of wages is impossible."

If the wages are insufficient, this fact is neutralized—so we are assured by travellers to Russia—by all the advantages enjoyed gratis by the worker—advantages for which his West-European colleague has to pay dearly. A workers' legislation which, it is insisted, is the best in the world, looks after him in sickness, misfortune, old age, etc.; the payments for this system of assurances fall entirely on the undertaking where he is employed without his having to contribute a kopeck himself. He has holidays fixed by law, and is then sent, should his health require it, to a rest-home in the country or to the watering-places—frequented in former days by the upper-classes—in the Caucasus or the Crimea. He gets his enjoyments for nothing—after working hours he can visit any one of the fine bourgeois palaces that are at his disposal, these " work-homes " or whatever they may be called, where, without limit and without charge, he can refresh himself with communistic literature, listen to communistic lectures, or take part in other communistic diversions. Reckon all that and much more of a similar nature in money, and the Russian workman's wage-advantages take on a very different complexion. Of course, these privileges are valuable enough, but a very considerable part of their value is seen to be exceedingly small on closer examination. The good intentions are beyond all argument, but the realization falls not a little short.

As regards the much-vaunted workmen's assurance scheme, there are already signs of retreat. It is true that it has never been effectual to any considerable degree. " The scheme of relief and pensions," says a contributor to *Pravda*, " has never yet reached a scale sufficient to cover completely the needs of those insured "—a cautious statement of the fact that it has proved insufficient to the very highest degree ; e.g. the sick-pay for complete inability to work was in the spring of 1925 on an average 12 roubles (27s.) a month. The contributions to the insurance funds have been, as we have said, the payments made by the respective industrial undertakings—the sum paid per workman has averaged 15·7 per cent. of his wage. The scheme, however, has failed ; many industries have not been in a position to meet their liability to the insurance funds. " In spite of energetic action in collecting payments to the insurance funds, the metal and mining industries, as well as the transport trade, have always had to be written down as being in arrears. It has become evident that they cannot pay such a high percentage." Consequently the amount has been considerably reduced, viz. to 10 per cent. of the wage for the heavy industries and to 12 per cent. for the transport trade. And the Council of the People's Commissaries, who passed this resolution, do not show great confidence in the result when they express their hope that these reduced amounts will be paid properly, so that no further reduction in the contributions will be found necessary.

Even less proportionate to the colossal boasts made of the rest-homes and sanatoriums is the workers' participation in them. According to the statistics given in *Pravda* in 1924—I have not seen the figures for 1925—the grand total of 221,654 invalids were received in country rest-homes, and of these only 70 per cent. workmen, as large a proportion as 26·5 per cent. consisting of Soviet officials, in whose favour, of course, the workers had to give way. And in 1925, 112,000 men were sent to health resorts, but how great a part of these consisted of Soviet officials does not transpire; as regards the preceding year, *Pravda* stated in this case as well that a large number of the guests had been "responsible" officials of various ranks who "travelled to the southern watering-places not to get cured, but to rest and enjoy themselves." Hence the invalids received by the State do not form a very imposing part of the 15 million members of the working class, and, moreover, it must be added that the care given to them left various things to be desired. The watering-places are somewhat falling into decay. An inquiry undertaken by a special commission reports, in the beginning of 1926, that "the utmost lack of all modern methods as regards arrangement and the primitive character of all scientific sanitary equipment is a characteristic feature of the majority of our health resorts"; it also reports on the monotony of the fare, the weakness in management shown in some, the want of a qualified medical staff, etc.

And even if all this care in rest-homes and health resorts is an evident step forward, in comparison with former times, yet the progress, with regard to the care of the workers' health in other respects, is, to say the least, a debatable matter. The artisans are certainly not so miserably off in this respect as are the peasants, and undeniably a certain advance has been made, but the results obtained do not, in any case, call for any great self-glorification on the part of the Bolshevists in their attitude to the backward West. A report from the Ukraine in *Pravda* of February, 1926, may deserve quotation as being of a very illuminating nature. "The position with regard to the medical care of the industrial districts in the Don basin is," so it says, "exceedingly difficult. In Gorlovka there is no dispensary or surgery for 18,000 workmen. To some pits, 8 or 10 versts from the town, a visiting doctor comes twice a week." Even in Gorlovka a doctor sees as many as a hundred patients a day. This doctor is a specialist in all branches of medicine, from gynæcology and surgery to venereal diseases and eye affections! In the consulting-room there is not even a washhand basin; the doctor who examines a venereal patient puts his unwashed hands into another patient's mouth or eyes. In another place they have arranged as consulting-room for 3,000 workers a former stable, which still, to this day, only has a mud floor. It is easy to imagine the hygienic conditions under which consultations and examinations take place. The hospital in Makejeva is intended for 3,000 patients and now receives 14,000. Medical assistance has a difficult time, not only in the basin of the Don, but also in other industrial centres. Even in Kiev and Kharkov, where they have at their disposal a large enough medical staff and sufficient equipment, the arrangements are anything but good. There are queues for the doctors, an heroic contest to be put down for an interview, and the doctors can only manage to visit sick people some days after they have been summoned. Under such conditions, it is the less surprising that in Krivoy Rog, for instance, there are neither ambulance bearers nor ambulance, and that those who have met with an accident in their mining work have to be carried on planks for 3 versts to get treatment, and conveyed in a pit cart for 20 versts to reach the hospital.

Still worse, however, than the fact that the advantages stated to have been gained by the working-class are not without evident defects, is that these advantages are counterbalanced by considerable deterioration in other departments of the proletariate's conditions of life. In one point particularly, the Bolshevist rule has completely failed to satisfy the workers' most modest requirement, i.e. in the housing question. As we have said, it is, of course, a good thing that some 10,000 workmen can sun themselves for one month in the year by the Black Sea—and it gives material for the most attractive pictures in the Russian illustrated papers; but this, very unfortunately, cannot appreciably help the Russian artisan class to bear the fact that, in everyday life, he has to put up with housing conditions that are without parallel in the civilized world.

The housing accommodation, which, from a sanitary point of view, ought not to be reduced, has been fixed at 16 square yards floor space per individual—to be sure, such an area does not give much space to move about in—and the 16 square yards are designated as "shortage standard." But even this "shortage standard"—which not many a Western worker would allow himself to put up with—proves, according to the pronouncement of the People's Commissary for Home Affairs, as lately as January, 1926, "in a number of districts an unattainable ideal." "We have," he said, "instances where, in some cases, the actual floor space allotted to a workman is 4·5 square yards—five men or more in every room." In such conditions, packed like sardines, according to the figures given for 1925, 13·2 of the population live in Nijni Novgorod and 31 per cent. in Jekaterinenberg; perhaps it may be a certain comfort, in such circumstances, that the rent is cheap. The Russian average rent, in the beginning of 1925, was 44½ kopecks a month per square yard, a figure which, however, was raised in the middle of the year to 60 kopecks, and which, in accordance with a resolution of the Council of the People's Commissaries in January, 1926, is to be advanced to an amount considered adequate to cover upkeep and repairs, reckoned at about 2 roubles per square yard. The conditions are not least terrible in Moscow, where, owing to the conversion of the city into the Russian capital, the population has been increased and is still growing by a quick influx of fresh inhabitants, and where, at the same time and for the same reason, the best houses have had to be given up for the Government offices. At the end of 1925 the housing accommodation was 13 per cent. less than before the war, whilst the population had increased 20 per cent. To visit the Moscow big city houses is like coming into an ant-heap. Stumbling over numberless dirty youngsters, we make our way up the narrow kitchen stairs and read on the doors: " Ring once for Petrov, twice for Ivanov, three times for Pavlov . . . ten times for Andrejev " ; in one and the same set of rooms ten families may be stowed away. And when we have aroused the inmates' attention by hammering in this way—the bell has long since given up work on the plea of over-exertion—we are led in through an indescribable kitchen, where preparations are going on simultaneously for several families' dinner, through overcrowded rooms and passages lumbered up with all kinds of rubbish, on to the square yards in the dwellings which are at the disposal of our acquaintance. If he is of the bourgeoisie, it has given the house-committee special delight to give him housing conditions still worse than his fellow-lodgers of the artisan class.

It is scarcely possible, at any rate in Moscow, to speak any longer of Russian homes, since people live all together in a genuine communistic collection. The authorities certainly try to regulate this by benevolent instructions. It is forbidden, so it literally runs in their issue of " Rules for Living Together," " to keep in the dwellings pigs, goats, sheep, rabbits, pigeons, or birds of any kind except in a cage; it is forbidden to saw or chop wood in the room; tenants are obliged to take measures to get rid of parasites and vermin; screams and disputes are prohibited from 11.30 p.m. to 9 a.m.; any tenant coming home between midnight and 7 a.m. has not the right to require other tenants to open the door for him ; a tenant coming home between these hours must go quietly to his room and especially respect the night's rest of those tenants by whose room he passes," etc. But it is self-evident that in these barrack-like conditions any kind of home-life is unthinkable, and all hygiene suffers, whilst immorality flourishes.

I got a little temporary glimpse of how life goes on in these communistic dwellings during a few July evenings, as I sat working in the house of a well-known Moscow scholar over some manuscripts that had found a refuge on his bookshelves, which had otherwise been entirely cleared. His little hole of a study looked out on a dark back-yard, and exactly opposite lay the tenement house, a great five-storied barrack-like building. Evening after evening it was the same tale. As soon as ever the inmates returned from their day's work, a quickly increasing cacophony began to issue from the hundreds of windows opposite, thrown wide open in the oppressive summer heat. A few loud-tongued disputes from a number of windows, first here, then there, set the measure; more and more of the black gaping windows joined in, and soon there resounded, from above and below, just one wild hundred-voiced quarrel. The strongest expletives in the language chased one another through the air, mighty explosions from rough bass voices, pattering volleys of women's shrill trebles, to an unbroken accompaniment of children's crying. The house was only silent, now and again, to listen to the noise from some one point, where the quarrel had gone on to blows; a noise of overturned furniture, crashing glass, hysterical women's screams pierced the air. And so it went on hour after hour, evening after evening.

To a certain extent this barrack system undeniably agrees with the rulers' ideal in the housing question. Zinoviev in one of his speeches points out the advantages of people being obliged to live together in big houses; otherwise they so easily develop their narrow individualistic possessive sense, their taste for "home comfort," etc.; "they say," he adds, "that in small houses men often beat their wives and say, 'Here I can beat her, for this isn't a communistic house.'" And Bucharin, in one passage, dwells on the fact that every great barrack-dwelling is important as a strategic unit in the social revolutionary battle. But, as the system has now developed, they cannot, however, deny that it has gone too far; they grant that these strategic points are each very apt to develop internal strife, and the papers complain of the endless disputes and scandals that keep the House Committees and People's Courts constantly employed. The worst of the tenants' aggressions certainly never come to the knowledge of any authority, as they are directed against the bourgeois element, who, in this common life, are the hopeless victims of their fellow-tenants' persecutions, but never dare to breathe a word about them.

Quite especially horrible are the workers' housing conditions in those parts where they have their quarters at their working centres, as in the coal district of the Don basin, the Ural mining industry, etc. They enjoy free lodging—more's the pity—but of what a kind! A certain idea of the matter is given by the following description—taken from *Pravda*—of a couple of Government workmen's barracks in Novorossiesk:

"A long low room, with dirty walls and ceiling. Along the side, against the wall, there stand sixteen wooden truckle-beds, covered with torn newspapers or rags. The barracks consist of two such rooms, chiefly occupied by Komsomol members, commandeered for the work here from the Don district. On a bed in the corner a young man is sitting cross-legged, using all ten fingers to scratch his head with undisguised enjoyment.

"'How do we live? We have no washstand, nor towels or soap either. We come in from work—nowhere to wash ourselves. No cupboards for our belongings; everyone throws his traps under his bed. There is no one to tidy up for us; we have to do our own sweeping or sit in the dirt, and generally we sit in the dirt. There is no time for sweeping. But the worst of it is we have to live in the same room with married folk—not so few either, eight families. We bother them and they us.'

"The living conditions in the other barracks are still worse. The room is small and low; twenty workmen live in it. We had scarcely closed the door before we were met by a heavy, strong smell of damp and sweat. A rope was stretched from opposite corners of the room and someone had hung on it dirty rags and underclothing to dry. There were marks of damp on walls and ceiling.

"'Yes, it is a most miserable state of things,' says the

chairman of the factory committee. 'As soon as it rains, the men complain that they are lying in a lake. That's the fault of the roof.' At any rate, in this barrack there is a washhand basin, soap and two towels—one, it is true, has been already stolen. There is a woman to sweep up, but there are no cupboards, and all the workmen's belongings lie tossed under the beds. The light is poor—one electric burner for the whole room."

"The work-people live," so runs a description of a factory in the Vladimir gubernia, published in *Pravda* in the autumn of 1925, "in dark, damp, tumbledown dwellings. Some workmen live in barracks in company with others who are suffering from venereal disease. The conditions in the barracks are incredible; in the winter cold, in the summer water pours through the roof. The buildings are tumbledown and might, any moment, fall down. There are great pits in the passages, the wind blows in through cracks in the walls, the stairs rock, here and there a tread is missing, and now and again someone smashes himself to pieces on them. Inside the bedroom it is stifling and full of smoke, and there they have to eat, as there is no dining-room; there the underclothes and babies' napkins are dried, and there are the buckets of rubbish with the children's night slops. They are not human dwellings, but dog-kennels."

What makes this housing misery still more gloomy is that no ray of light whatever can be found in the situation. A great many plans for the alleviation of the house shortage have been discussed; some quite important proposals for house-building have been put forward lately and a certain number of houses started by co-operative building. But it has all been utterly ineffective; the proposals have been unattainable, and they have come to grief over the proper organization of the work.

"We have," Djersjinsky said in the spring of 1925, "done something in this direction, but I wish to call attention to the fact that we do it very badly. I am afraid the millions that the State spends on building operations will not give the result they ought to. Of all departments in our State housekeeping, that of building is the most badly ordered. There we still find, in greater degree than elsewhere, relics of the old régime of robbery, thefts, and want of economical straight-dealing. Taken as a whole, the upbuilding operations that are carried on are not large enough even to prevent a continual increase in the shortage of houses." In Moscow, according to *Pravda*, the building results cannot keep pace with the birth-increase. And throughout the country it is true that the housing accommodation gained by fresh building is less than what is lost by the decay that takes place at a constantly increasing pace. The Russian Government houses after ten years' misuse are, in the majority of cases, beginning to fall to pieces. The People's Commissary for Home Affairs gives some examples in his speech just quoted: "In Tula we have, all told, about 18 per cent. of houses that do not want repairs; in the Ural district 7 per cent. of the dwellings lie in ruins and 80 per cent. are in need of radical repairs." "In different parts of the principal cities and in nearly all the provincial towns," *Pravda* states in February, 1926, "decay continues in the majority of cases." Simply to maintain the *status quo* in housing accommodation it would be requisite to build for 120 million more persons than is done at present.

Although, then, material conditions for the average of the Russian proletariate—in spite of various privileges—are such that they, without the least doubt, can only be designated as unfit for human beings, there is, amongst the proletariate, a considerable percentage whose misery is still greater. Chief amongst these are the unemployed. For a couple of years now their number has been round about a million; in the summer of 1924 it was 1,400,000; it sank in October, 1924, to 775,000; rose again in April, 1925, to 900,000; in September, 1925, to 1,300,000; and in February, 1926, the Press reported that the unemployment figures had remained much the same during the winter. Now, in these figures there are included, it is true, on the one hand a certain number of the bourgeois class, on the other a certain number of peasants who have poured into the towns in the hope of sharing in the superior position of the artisans, upon which the village folk look with envious eyes, but the main part of the unemployed army is composed of former artisans, trade-union men. In spite of the fact that industry, in the autumn of 1925, had shown an appreciable increase in the numbers employed, partly in consequence of the industrial improvement that had taken place during the year, and partly owing to the hope of still more, as a result of the favourable trade prospects in the following year, yet, according to *Pravda's* statement in February, 1926, the number of trade-union men out of employment had increased, during that winter, from 600,000 to 800,000. For where fresh workers were taken on, industry opened its doors, first of all to the demobilized soldiers of the Red Army, and then to those who were less well qualified but also less exacting in their demands than former workmen, i.e. to peasants from the villages and young men not yet belonging to any workers' organization, etc. Eight hundred thousand unemployed members of the trade unions! Since the trade unionists in the beginning of 1926 numbered 7 to 8 millions, this means that more than every tenth member were without work.

And the position of the unemployed is desperate. Only 34 per cent. of the whole number get any assistance at all, and the assistance given amounts to 7 or 8 roubles per month, i.e. a pittance upon which it is quite impossible to live. There are only very few organized work-centres for the unemployed. The State contribution for these, in 1925, was 7½ million roubles—not even 10 roubles per man. And the help that the unemployed get in this way is dearly bought; these centres enjoy, throughout Russia, a constant reputation of the very worst kind. A contributor to *Pravda*, describing the unemployment centre in the town of Kiev, writes: "It is just as if no industrial laws whatever were in existence. Brutal treatment, cheating of the workpeople, delay in payment, contempt for the most elementary rules for the protection of the worker—these are what the workman gets as supplement to his scanty wage. It is dangerous to complain, for it means either dismissal or removal to harder work somewhere else. Land workers—amongst them many women—sometimes work standing in water up to their knees without rubber boots. Even in winter, in four degrees of frost, work was done under such conditions; as the result of such exploitation, in one and a half years there were more than forty invalids who had become entirely incapacitated, not to mention the larger number of those whose power of working has been reduced." As we have said, the majority of the unemployed get neither money relief nor chance of work at the unemployment centres; their position is practically hopeless. The time when industry shall have improved sufficiently to be able to employ these crowds of unemployed is quite certainly far distant. The fact—as we have already shown—that all industrial equipment left by tsaristic times will shortly be entirely worn out, will form a serious impediment, for a long period, to any industrial extension or employment of an increased number of workers. If industry is really to be set on its feet again, it will be better to think of turning off a good many of the hands now employed and compelling those left to work properly. In the past the workman, shut out from the factory, had a place of refuge in the village, where he was always a member of the village community and land stood at his disposal; now, however, the land is distributed, and besides, the peasants—with the ever-increasing feeling existing between peasants and artisans—are anything but disposed to receive him. Thus his position is hopeless; in most cases he sinks to the lowest stratum of society, takes refuge in the gutter, and joins the quickly increasing ranks of the cities' beggar-proletariate.

Thus in the streets of the large towns great numbers of the proletarian "supreme rulers" are to be found; and the unemployed find there—beside great hosts of the former bourgeoisie—other proletarian reserves, and this the category most to be pitied and with least hope of any redemption—the father- and motherless children. The World War and the civil war deprived endless numbers of little ones of their parents; in numbers, calculated by the Commissariat for Public Health at the fabulous total of 2 millions, they wander about the streets and slums, friendless and homeless, begging a livelihood, sinking into vice and crime, and ending in physical, psychic and moral ruin. Teachers and doctors are unanimous in assuring us that, in the overwhelming majority of these children, who sleep in the sewer-pipes, in asphalt cauldrons, in doorways of deserted houses, there are already the seeds of various kinds of spiritual and bodily diseases. Many of them succumb to these diseases, and those who survive become walking infection-carriers. Begging and pilfering are their usual lawful employments. They sit on the pavements with the sober looks of adults, smoke cigarettes, and share the booty of their " work " in the streets, at the tramway stopping-places, in the markets and queues. Often they go even farther on the downward path, get into dens of vice, and become acquainted with the darkest sides of life. A workman, describing some travel impressions, in *Pravda*, at the beginning of 1926, says : " I came to the town of Omsk ; there, at the very station, neglected children were lying quite naked ; I certainly counted more than thirteen of them, but on the market by the station I saw about ten more like them, running about naked, collecting all kinds of refuse and eating it. Afterwards I came to Samara, and as soon as I entered the station—and it was at least midnight by then—I saw stark naked children lying on the bare ground cowering together in the cold."

Even in the question of taking in hand these crowds of young proletariate the Soviet Government falls short. It is true that the endless newspaper columns written about them bear witness to undeniable sincerity in their tender sympathy with these unhappy children ; it is also true that amongst the first things shown to strangers visiting Moscow are a couple of model children's homes where clever doctors give the visitors a little lecture on the new methods that have been devised for the treatment of these complicated cases. But they are fine plans without any particular practical significance. " Where have we got," inquires Semasjko, the People's Commissary for Health, " the institutions that can give these children what they need ? " " There are scarcely any at all," he replies to his own question. The great overwhelming majority wander about continually, running quite wild and doomed to ruin.

The help, then, that the Bolshevists have been able to give these proletarian millions, who are suffering such shipwreck, is insignificant to the last degree. One positive gain they may perhaps report when all is said—at least, if the Russian Press is to be believed—and this is, that when, sooner or later, the prison doors open for them, they no longer find inside them the holes of tsaristic imprisonment, but really comfortable places of recreation. If the papers speak truly, it is here—but not much sooner—that the successful realization of the Bolshevist proletarian paradise is to be found.

CHAPTER VII

THE PROLETARIATE'S PROFIT-SHEET

"LAND and liberty!" For tens of years before the war this was the watchword in which the Russian peasant class summed up their longing of centuries past. On one side, then, a position of economic security, which, according to the peasants' opinion, could be obtained only by a distribution of the land amongst them, on the other, freedom from the oppression of tsardom and its hirelings, from landowners and bureaucracy. Improved economic conditions with political and social freedom, in the same way, formed the desire of the Russian artisan class. And both peasant and artisan class expected the fulfilment of these desires from Bolshevism.

We have already seen how they were disappointed in both these points. The liberty that Bolshevism has really given them has proved not enough to satisfy the most modest claim, whilst the economic conditions have become worse rather than better.

The question then arises, What has Bolshevism really given to the Russian proletariate? Something it must evidently be, or else it could not be still existing now, in its ninth year. And something quite significant, too, seeing that, in any case, practically quite large numbers of the Russian proletariate are attached to it, not only from compulsion, but from devotion, and even with an enthusiasm bordering on fanaticism. What are these gifts and what have the people received that can make up for the other disappointments that they have suffered at the hands of Bolshevism?

The first gain that certain sections of the proletariate, at least, have won in the course of these years, is this: a certain sense of power—a pious, unreasoning, invincible belief that the dictatorship of the proletariate really means a complete change in their position. All the bitter experiences they have gone through during this time have not been able completely to annul this gain.

The hypnotism exercised on their minds by the revolution catchword is still not entirely wanting in power; the high-sounding phrase, "the supreme power of the proletariate," has not yet quite lost its enchantment; the golden letters on the banner, under which the proletariate went to battle, still keep their brightness, diligently polished, as they are, by capable hands. Does not the talk of the proletariate's enormous gains from the revolution meet the people at every demonstration in which they have to take part, at every meeting they are forced to attend, in every paper they open? It is impressed upon them, on all sides, that Russia's freed and sovereign proletariate are the most fortunate people on earth, to whose happy lot all the enslaved and down-trodden proletarian classes of the Western world look up with longing sighs. They hear it to-day, they heard it yesterday, have heard it now for eight years; it is not surprising that some of it has taken root in their minds.

All the profit that can be shown to accrue from the fact that the revolution has given to the Russian proletariate a position of which no other people can even dream is magnified to such proportions as may well dazzle the eyes of simple folk. Where has a proletariate been called to exercise such direct influence on its country's political and social work as in Soviet Russia; they lavish praise on the faultless merits of the Soviet system and hold up to scorn the old, antiquated parliamentary system of the West, until the astounded proletariate almost forget that in all the agencies by which they can exercise their influence they do not get a word in edgeways. Where in the whole world does any proletariate enjoy such unique privileges? Where is an imperial castle transformed into a peasant sanatorium? Such a thing, according to the People's Commissary, Semasjko—whose words we have already quoted—is without parallel in the world's history; that alone shows, he declares, what the supreme power of the proletariate really is, that alone is of such a nature that the peasants of Europe and America will most certainly desire to follow the Russian proletariate's example, when they get to know about it. Every little privilege which the proletarian enjoys as an extra to his starvation ration grows, in this way, under the Bolshevist magnifying-glass, into a sumptuous feast. To be sure, this ethereal food cannot satisfy his hungry stomach, but it undoubtedly tickles his gustatory nerves and strengthens his feeling that, after all, he really is seated at a splendid banquet.

It is all an illusion, of that there is not the slightest doubt. But even illusions, too, have their value. As regards the artisan class, it is plain what this illusion during the past few years has meant for them. The whole type of Russian workman has undergone a metamorphosis; since the revolution he has perceptibly straightened his back and raised his head; the crouching trait in his character and his browbeaten manner—the inheritance from the time of serfdom—have disappeared; he has acquired a greater feeling of human dignity, a feeling which certainly may, at times, swell beyond due proportions, but which, taken as a whole, is all to the good. It is a development which sooner or later, of course, will prove a danger to the Bolshevists, for its effect must be that, when the working-man sees clearly the empty nature of the illusion, he will begin to feel the Soviet roof too cramped for him. But the illusion which, in this way, has managed to add an inch to the working-man's spiritual growth still holds him firmly under its spell and, in some degree, helps to reconcile him to his rôle of dumb supernumerary.

As regards the other section of the proletariate—the peasant class—the matter is somewhat different. The revolutionary phrases have never had the same fascination for the peasants as for the artisans. The peasants have not enjoyed the advantage of consistent guidance in looking upon the result of the revolution in the way that the rulers wish to find in the proletariate. And if even they did, for a moment, believe that they had reached the goal of the desires they had cherished so long, disillusionment proved quicker and more effective for them. Thus they view the situation coldly and soberly as it really is, without any illusive embellishment.

* * *

If, then, the leading portion of the proletariate, at any rate, constantly clings firmly to and derives consolation from the belief that its position has been changed for the better in a way that is, indeed, no less than epoch-making, this illusion is also greatly strengthened by the incontestable fact that the proletariate is, at all events, the most favoured section of society. Granted that the working-man has not much room in which to turn, yet, after all, he is cock of the roost; granted that his privileges in that position are but few, yet, at any rate, no one has any more—above all, not those upon whose favoured lot he used to cast a jealous eye, for the former middle-class suffer immeasurably more than do the proletariate. To see their suffering and to lend a hand himself to intensify it, even if it has no direct power of satisfying, is still a pleasant mental relish.

The ideal gain which it may be for the proletariate to get a new class below themselves, the blackness of whose evil fate forms a background against which their own grey existence stands out in dazzling brilliance, such a gain has undoubtedly been given, in rich measure, to this proletariate. There are, as Zinoviev is accustomed to say in his speeches, two and a half classes in Russia at the present moment; the half-class, he adds, is nothing to trouble about. Beside the artisan and peasant classes there exists another class, already half-exterminated—a class deserving no consideration and whose remaining half will gradually come to share the fate of the first, viz. the fragment of the former upper and middle classes, the despised bourgeoisie—a pariah class, more down-trodden and oppressed than the lower-class ever was in days gone by. The contest against this bourgeoisie still goes on with unabated energy. The idea, which seems to have found a certain acceptance in Western Europe, that the class-warfare in Russia has now come to an end and that the former middle-class who have loyally adapted themselves to present conditions have also got the right of citizenship in the new realm, is completely erroneous. The warfare still continues, and indeed has only now reached its most repulsive stage.

In one respect this campaign is entirely senseless, for this class of society is no danger whatever for the Bolshevists. The middle-class opposition to Bolshevism has been crushed, once for all ; it was overcome in the first stage of the class-warfare, when the fighting was certainly fierce, but at any rate honourable fighting, in which the conquered themselves took the chances of war. The middle-class element still to be found in Russia are, on the one hand, those who from the first took up a neutral attitude in the contest, people who belong to the silent of the land, to whose nature, in general, any thought of active political strife has always been foreign, and who now suffer Bolshevism with the same Christian patience as they displayed under tsardom. On the other hand, there are—and this is specially true of quite considerable sections of the former so-called *intelligentsia*—those who, even at an early stage, accepted Bolshevism, if not with their heart, at any rate with their intellect, since they saw in it the natural product of the Russian historical development and the only chance—even if a desperate one—of salvation from the prevailing chaos. And if, in addition to these two categories, there is also a section to whom Bolshevism continues to appear madness and ruin, the past years have so broken their power of resistance and destroyed their will that every thought of kicking against the pricks is now very far from them. At most, they still harbour a silent hope that Europe may come and save them—I often met with this illusion—but they are themselves too paralysed to lift a finger against the Soviet power. The whole matter gives a firm impression that the rulers can scarcely feel safer from any quarter than they may from this bourgeois element.

Under such conditions one would think that the strife and the persecution of the middle-class might well be brought to an end. The authorities ought to be able to do this without risk, to gain for some useful work in the social fabric a class whose qualifications they certainly try in every way to diminish, but which, after all, are perhaps not quite unserviceable; and, above all, they might, by so doing, take a step in the direction of that social justice which Bolshevism, in solemn moments, declares itself called to realize.

But there can be no question of the conclusion of such a peace. Of course, there are exceptions. Even if we except those members of the bourgeoisie who won their spurs in the Communist Party even in tsaristic times—almost all the leaders in the Party are drawn from them—and of whose bourgeois descent no one, of course, thinks any longer, we yet find a couple of categories of those taken into favour. To begin with, there are—in spite of all, and annoying as it is—amongst the despised bourgeoisie some whom the Bolshevists not only have to put up with, but whose help they positively have to beg. These are people whose special knowledge or technical training even the brilliant natural gifts of the proletariate cannot dispense with. Especially have they sought high and low for specialists in banking and finance, and some, too, in industrial capacities. A few they have found in self-imposed exile, others in prison, from which, however, they were taken—without in these cases hesitating either over bourgeois birth or even over bourgeois opinions—to occupy responsible positions in the Soviet State. To be sure, the reconciliation is not so absolutely sincere; this bourgeois element know quite well in their hearts—and also hear it quite openly—that when the requisite competence has been trained from the proletarian ranks they will be sent about their business again. But there is also another category of the middle-class who have slipped through the Bolshevist doors and taken a firm seat inside, namely, individuals of the climbing and place-hunting type, with strong elbows and elastic consciences. No inconsiderable percentage of such persons have crept into the Communist Party, and have found, in its troubled waters, fish to their liking. They go on there from strength to strength, and purchase absolution for their bourgeois birth by taking so much the more zealous share in the persecution of that social class from which they themselves have sprung.

But otherwise the bourgeoisie are kept strictly down in the pariah position ; the lower they are pushed down, so much stronger is the proletariate's feeling of their own exaltation. It is, to begin with, a self-evident fact that the bourgeoisie must be shut out from all the political rights and social advantages—such as they are—which fall to the share of the proletariate. Then in all departments of social life they are put into a badly treated class by themselves.

Equality in the eyes of the law is an unknown idea ; the same offence for which the member of the proletariate gets no punishment brings to a bourgeois years of strict "isolation." Even the protection of the law is denied to the bourgeois, especially if the one who injures him is a member of the proletariate. A bourgeois had been murdered and the offender was condemned—so the judgment ran—to five years' "isolation," but, it was added, in view of his proletarian birth, the punishment has been reduced to two years, and with regard further to his well-attested service in the Red Army, the court feels able to reduce this to one year's "isolation." The house of a friend of mine in a Russian country locality had been broken into ; my friend went himself, the next morning, to the police-station to notify the fact. Here he was subjected to a long examination : what were his parents, his political views, etc. He felt the whole time, he told us, that he was looked upon as the real culprit, and accounted himself happy when, the examination over, he was allowed to go home again—he had, at last, believed that the matter would end by his own arrest. The guilty parties were, of course, never caught, probably never looked for. The bourgeoisie are shut out—as I shall show more fully later on—from all public educational opportunities : these are the monopoly of the proletariate ; schools shut their doors to bourgeois children, and students of bourgeois parentage are cleared out of the universities. And this is only one example of the general tendency ; the bourgeoisie must, to as great an extent as possible, be prevented from earning a living and be starved to death. And, at the same time, there goes on for the edification of the proletariate a never-ceasing, determined running-down of everything bourgeois. The proletariate's former feelings of hatred towards those who were, in earlier days, more happily placed than they themselves, are gently tended as a sacred fire. In words—written or spoken—in pictures, on the stage and the films, everywhere, we find the same con-

"THE OLD AND THE NEW": THE BOURGEOISIE AND YOUNG ARTISANS

stantly repeated call to scoff at the bourgeoisie, those parasites of society and enemies of the people, who are now reaping the just reward of their deeds. It is not possible to open a newspaper without finding this call. Here is a little chat about the so-called *Sucharev* market in Moscow, the city rag-market where people, out of the middle-class, sell their last belongings to get bread—a few little trinkets, yellowing laces, some old icon, a photograph frame or a few silver spoons. The tone of the whole article is one of the most undisguised, malicious delight, as it describes, with deep scorn, these pitiful figures, their worn faces and their stony glances. "Ha, ha! just look at the old lady's dignified bearing, just notice the old gentleman's comical look of injured dignity when he is hustled down into the gutter. What incorrigible class-pride in this human rubbish!" Here is a contribution from some telephone girls. A couple of their companions at the telephone station were found to be of the middle-class, and they now ask, in indignant tones, how long they are to be forced to sit side by side with the so-called "young ladies." And here a newspaper notice of a member of the bourgeoisie who had committed suicide; the notice gives a kick to a dead dog: suicide was, it suggests, the best thing he had done in all his life.

The life of the former middle-class has become one great tragedy, of which the fate of every middle-class family forms just a little fragment. I went to look in a small Russian town for some acquaintances of earlier days, one of those thoroughly cultured, refined and lovable families in which the Russian *intelligentsia* so abounded. The father himself was a doctor. The first time I met him was many years ago in a starving village where, during a famine year, he had organized an admirable system of relief. His daughters had settled there for the winter amongst the starving peasants and fought an heroic battle with the devastating famine and all the diseases that followed in its wake. Now he and his wife were dead. After the revolution his modest pension had been taken from him, and husband and wife had literally died of starvation in the famine winter four years ago; the wooden crosses had been stolen from their graves in the churchyard, probably for firewood in the days of scarcity of fuel. The daughter was living in the utmost misery. The industrious, capable woman had, for some time, had a place in a factory, and had won there the complete confidence of the Bolshevist management, but had had to be dismissed to satisfy the demand made by the other workers. Her brother, an artist, formerly a drawing-master at a boys' school in the town, had also been dismissed; now he was living with his wife in a South Russian town, where he could sometimes get temporary work in the harbour as a dock-labourer. And their daughter, a student in Leningrad, had, in spite of the utmost privations, struggled on to the third year of her university course. But in the spring of last year, although she was amongst the first of her course, she was, as the daughter of a member of the bourgeoisie, " cleared out " of the university; in despair at this she committed suicide. This is just one specimen, taken from the fate of a single middle-class family, and such a fate is to be found in tens of thousands of cases. There is no doubt that this persecution of the bourgeoisie is of some importance as a psychic stimulant for the proletariate. They share, heart and soul, in the persecution of those who were privileged before; to be able to oppress the oppressors is almost better than to steal back stolen goods, as the phrase went at the beginning of the revolution. The unhappy fate of the bourgeoisie casts, as it were, a little glimmer of light over the proletarian worker's own misery. And the authorities, who know quite well what this means for him, are careful to see that the persecution of the bourgeoisie is continued, so that he shall not be deprived of this source of happiness.

And yet it cannot be denied that the revolutionary gain that consists in being able to witness the misfortunes of their former enemies, and to help with their own hands to add to the heavy burden, is not one of the most important items in the revolutionary credit sheet for the proletariate. There is a time limit even for hatred; after all these years the feelings of hatred have lost something of their first freshness, and the picture of their enemy lying defeated and utterly at their mercy is no longer so enjoyable. This is especially true of the Russian peasant-class. It is certainly true in great measure that the peasant has already lost this bracing stimulus because the section of the bourgeoisie that were his special enemies—the Russian landowner-class—in most cases no longer exist. But even when, in these later days, they have still survived—right up to the summer of 1925, when the Bolshevists set about their final clearance of the landowner-class, some few individuals were still existing in the villages—their downtrodden position has long since ceased to be any source of pleasure to the peasant. And the remembrance of how, eight years ago, they got their revenge for the sufferings of the peasant-class during the wrongs of centuries no longer in itself makes any peasant happy. That the landowners had to be done away with is a matter-of-course in his eyes, but his enemy's misfortune does not excite in him any vital feeling of triumph. His hatred of his former masters has lost its vehemence. The experiences of the last few years have, in part, been such as to cast a gleam of propitiation over the time of the landowners. It was certainly a time of oppression; the tyranny of the land-owning-class over the peasants during the centuries of serfdom belongs to the very darkest side of the history of old Russia. Even after an end had come to the peasants' direct slavery under the property owners, this latter class—in their capacity as the peasants' administrative guardians and their, not infrequently, very unreasonable landlords, etc.—often exercised a very hard rule over the peasants. But in spite of this, the landowners have nevertheless—it is a matter for surprise, but the observation finds continual confirmation—left a relatively good reputation behind them. This landowners' régime, in spite of much hardness and tyranny, possessed certain touches of a far-stretching, good-natured, patriarchal rule that are wanting in the Bolshevist stiff bureaucratic system. Even when the landed proprietors were terrible oppressors, they often possessed a certain personal dignity which aroused the peasants' respect in quite another way than does the irritating Bolshevist youth that now bears rule in the villages. Partly, too, the landowners and all that appertained to them have quite disappeared to the very back of their minds. It is quite striking how indifferent and uninterested the peasants are when they speak of olden times and of their former antagonists. Jakovlev narrates how he cross-questioned some seventeen or eighteen-year-old youths and found that they did not know "how it was in old times"—they made the excuse that so little had been told them; even the word "landowner," as Jakovlev states, had little meaning for them. In a village, half of which had belonged to a Count Stroganov, all the answer the young men gave to a question about him was: "We have heard there used to be a count here, but what he did we don't know."

* * *

Even if we make the very best of the revolution that has taken place in the position of the proletariate, it will yet, in the long run, be difficult to maintain that the changes for the better are very great. But what does it mean? Has not still further progress been made? Are they not, at any rate, on the royal road leading to prosperity? Ought this not to be gain enough?

A pious, childlike faith in the gospel of Bolshevism is what supports great numbers of the Russian artisan-class amidst the hardships and disappointments of the present hour. The communistic ideas themselves have taken deep root in them; years of systematic propaganda have done their work; a certain receptivity in the Russian soul for the brotherly doctrines of Communism may, too, be the more fundamental explanation. For many simple souls, Communism has become the religion to which they cling with a faith touching in its certainty, sometimes even with a purely ecstatic pentecostal religious ardour. And on this account the sufferings of the moment are less than nothing. To be allowed to suffer for the wonderful hour of human happiness that is so near at hand is, after all, a great and splendid destiny. To be, even at the price of costly sacrifices, the pioneers of a new era, the workers in a new world-mission—all this appeals as much to the fundamentally mystic vein in the Russian nature as to their proletarian self-confidence.

This is true of the artisan-class, or, to speak more correctly, of certain sections of it, but with the peasants it is otherwise. A sympathy with and an understanding of the Bolshevist ideas, deep enough to counterbalance their disappointment in the result of Bolshevism, are completely wanting in the Russian villages. The peasant is, at heart, just as ignorant of the real aims of Bolshevism now as he was eight years ago. Newspapers are very rare visitors in the villages; there are no means of buying them; in most cases the peasants cannot read them nor do they take any interest in them. Of other propagandist literature, suited to the peasants' capacity, there is an exceedingly poor supply—a striking weakness in the Bolshevist propagandist machinery, so effective elsewhere, and which, in general, really forms the highest point of Bolshevist achievement in any direction. And the oral systematic treatment, continuing without intermission day after day, week after week, to which the propaganda work in the towns has subjected the artisans, was from the very nature of things not to be thought of in the rural districts. The forces that the country itself can provide in propaganda work are insufficient and weak, and, as regards the agitation proceeding from the towns as the Bolshevist centres, it is, to begin with, of course impossible that this should embrace the whole mighty area of the rural districts. There are villages that have never seen a Bolshevist agitator—and, moreover, he is often such as to miss his mark completely. Time and again it is astonishing how Bolshevist propaganda work—so skilful elsewhere—so seldom manages to strike the right note in dealing with the peasants. The artisan-class, who are conscious that they made the revolution, and who believe that they hold the power in their hands, have a right-valiant contempt for the peasant-class, who cannot keep up with their quick pace. Some touch of this contempt cannot help peeping out when artisans are sent to carry on their propaganda in the village, even if only in an elder-brotherly tone that affronts the peasants. "Here he comes, thinking perhaps he is going to teach us!" And that is not to mention the occasions when the propaganda challenges public feelings in a much rougher way. At an open-air meeting in the market-place of one of the larger villages I heard one of those painted, bobbed, leather-jacketed, cigarette-smoking Soviet ladies, that are to be met by thousands in Moscow, preaching Bolshevism to some hundred peasant men and women. The address was not without talent, but of little gain to Bolshevism. In the crowd, listening to her with every appearance of amazement, there was a perfect hail of jovial remarks of none too refined a nature about her distinctly provocative personality. What still further stiffens the peasant's feeling against the town propaganda is his general animosity to the artisans, an animosity originating in the time when the latter came in armed expeditions to take his seed, and increased more recently when, as we have described, the peasants, with ever-increasing envy, compare their lot with the artisans'. They look askance at any artisan arriving in the village, and let him feel he is not wanted. "There came some idlers from the town over here," was how the peasants told me of the visit of some agitators.

The result of all this is that the peasants' ideas of Bolshevism are hazy in the extreme. There is ample scope for report, and hearsay tales of the wildest nature are told and believed, special credence being given to the accounts circulated of Bolshevist aggression and evil deeds. Jakovlev describes how, in village after village, he was asked if it was true that the Bolshevists would come and take the children away from their parents. This idea of Bolshevism as a child-eating Moloch is just one little sample of the peasant conception of the Bolshevists.

Although, then, to begin with, lack of knowledge of Bolshevism prevents the peasant from embracing it with any cordiality, it is also true that, in proportion as he has any real understanding of the Bolshevist ideas, these ideas, far from exercising any attractive power over him, rather act as a deterrent. The half-communistic state of things which the common possession of the land during the last decades has produced has pretty thoroughly cured him of that communistic leaning which, it is said, belongs to the Slav nature. The picture of the future that the Bolshevists paint for the peasants, viz. a welding together of rural Russia's millions of small holdings—that demand such prodigious exertions from their owners and yet barely feed them—into great collective farms conducted on communistic principles, forms a picture of the future that terrifies them. A feeling for individual rights of ownership is extraordinarily pronounced amongst them. During the universal scarcity that reigns in the villages, this has developed as never before. The contest of *meum* and *tuum* in their life is too pronounced a feature to bear witness of any ripeness for an idyllic, communistic, collective existence. A little scene, the first that met me on starting from a small Volga village on my rural expedition, has remained in my memory. Out on the village fields two peasants had flown at one another like two angry cocks and were overwhelming each other with evident torrents of abuse, that Russian abuse, coarse as the black earth itself, of which their language has such a rich assortment. They were found to be quarrelling about the boundary between their fields; one wanted it a few steps to the right, the other to the left. The whole matter perhaps meant at most a couple of sheaves of corn, but it was enough to rouse passions, as though it was a question of life itself. Long after I had driven past them I heard the wild dispute behind me, a slight manifestation of the strength of those instincts which the Bolshevists aim at conquering—a hopeless task indeed! That the task is really more difficult than is thought is acknowledged by the Bolshevists themselves. The leaders, in their speeches, refer again and again to the peasants' ineradicable antipathy to ordering their lives on a communistic basis, to their anti-social leanings, their obstinate adherence to the ideas of ownership, which are an abomination from the communistic point of view. I quote at random a few passages from a little work entitled *Sketches from the Modern Village,* by Leonid Grigorev, which is quite unimportant from a literary standpoint but very instructive in parts:

"Whilst headquarters are occupied in the great work of welding together all people into one mighty family of brothers, the instincts of the right of private ownership flourish in the village in full force. Universal brotherhood! Communistic housekeeping! Collective villages! No, these mighty passwords have not yet made their way amongst the great masses of the peasant-class. The strong iron strength in a powerful all-conquering collective body! No, this is incomprehensible for the peasant. The peasant-class have, in their great majority, set steadfastly about another work, the opposite of collectivism. One hen only! Never mind; it is mine. No more than one bucket! Yes, but if only it is my own. I am master in my own house! Then I don't care a rap for anything else!" "The peasant has yet far to go to Communism," continues the author—"oh yes, indeed, how far he has to go! Look at this, for example. In a village they join together to go out haymaking—say, in the forest, where it is difficult or impossible to divide up the ground in lots. Then the work goes something like this: one stands and smokes, leaning on his scythe; another stands, for ever whetting and sharpening his; a third gathers berries—there are, to be sure, quantities of berries in the forest; a fourth simply sits on the grass talking to a fifth, and all of them wait for someone to mow, gather together what is mown and divide it in equal portions—and that's all right. But it is quite another matter when they work on the lots apportioned to the different households. Then there is some life in our peasants, then indeed they show what they can do. Everyone hurries to work with his scythe at an incredible speed; then the peasant finishes off his allotment as quickly as possible, gathers up his grass, and it often happens, too, that he tries to get hold of some of his neighbour's as well."

The author also gives some small illustrations of the way in which the contest of Bolshevism against the peasant's anti-communistic tendencies works out in practice. One of them is worth repeating, mainly because it is not only typical of peasant psychology, but also of the way in which the Bolshevist functionaries look upon the peasants.

The chairman of the Volost Committee is complaining to the author about the peasants' unreasonableness.

"You cannot imagine any more obstinate blockheads than our idiots," he says indignantly. "You may talk to them one way and get an answer in just the opposite. Now we had proposed we should join together and buy a threshing-machine; we were to put our money together and buy one for general use. But no; our worthy folk wanted both to have a threshing-machine and at the same time were afraid to."

"What are they afraid of, Vasili Fjodorovitj?"

"The devil only understands them!" he exclaims.

"Ask them what they are afraid of—they don't know themselves."

"But, after all, I suppose they must have some reason?"

"No, it's impossible to discover any reason. One says that if we buy a threshing-machine, there is sure to be fighting about it. We shall set one another by the ears, that will be the end of it all. And the others say he is right and nod their heads: 'Yes, there'll be fighting.' I explain and prove to them that there cannot possibly be any quarrelling, that there cannot be any reason to fight, but they insist: 'We shall come to blows!' That they maintain, even if you should drive a knife into them. Ten times already we have met together and considered it, but we never get anywhere. This evening we are to have another meeting, and the point to be discussed is: Shall a threshing-machine be bought for common use or not? We shall no doubt talk and talk and break up without deciding anything."

"The chairman pauses," continues the author. "I express my astonishment at their unreasonableness, and again he bursts out wrathfully:

"'Just imagine what they say in our meetings about a collective purchase of a threshing-machine. "A threshing-machine is nice to have, but if it's to be communistic, that's a thing we are not used to. That is no good for us. What sort of thing is it: a threshing-machine with no owner? For example, I say: It is mine; and someone else says: No, it is mine. That will lead to trouble; everyone will want to have it all his own—that won't do. And the money we gave we don't get back, and the whole thing is a loss." The devil knows what's got the fine fellows. One might as well put an end to it all and send the idea to Jericho!'

"But the chairman did not give up his plan without continually calling together the peasants, and at the meetings he poured out fiery eloquence about the communistic threshing-machine at the cost of much exertion and much perturbation of spirit. When he met me he used to tell me the development of the 'job.'

"'They nag away in all kinds of tunes,' he said, 'but they are yielding.'

"'Now they are setting themselves against it again,' was his melancholy report next time.

"A few days later his face had brightened up again. 'Now they've almost consented.'

"But afterwards he was full of indignation again. 'Everything seemed to be going smoothly, when suddenly some idiot began to object. "But, good heavens! whatever will happen if we come to blows?" And all the other idiots followed him with: "There'll be fighting."'

"A day later the chairman again looked cheerful. 'It is coming right.'

"But then once more: 'Such idiots! Such snub-nosed asses!'

"I do not know," the author concludes, "if the peasants bought the threshing-machine or not, as I left the village without awaiting the final decision. But it is a hard business to move our peasants when it is a question of any collective undertaking. The peasant whose intellect is in such an anti-social condition does not understand the spirit of the times with its device: 'Universal Communism.'"

It is, however, not only the communistic principles of Bolshevism which—even though they frighten the peasants—call forth the allegiance of the principal section of the proletariate. Its ideology, even in other respects, exercises a strong power of attraction on the artisan proletariate. Its effort to plan life in general on new lines, to break with all old traditions and to clear away old prejudices, has the warm sympathy of the industrial class.

To have a hand in throwing overboard all the bourgeois ballast that, up till now, has weighed life down, to burst all the stupid bands of bourgeois convention, to create new proletarian forms for life in common amongst human beings—this both satisfies and flatters him; here, too, he feels himself a pioneer of a new time. What liberation to make short work with the religious superstitions. He carries out his icon to the rubbish-heap and breathes a sigh of relief; he deposes God in the anti-religious debate and feels like a valiant matador. He does not baptize his child but "Octobers"[1] it; he does not call it by the bourgeois names of Ivan and Maria, but Strength, Sun, International, Ninel (Lenin spelt backwards). He does away with the bourgeois ideas of morality, and realizes in this direction, too, the great proletarian freedom. There are no limits to his proletarian desire for reform with regard to the community, hampered by bourgeois ideas. "Down with modesty!" was the inscription that a number of young men carried on their shoulders when they appeared in the summer of 1925, stark naked, on the Moscow boulevards. In this case, certainly, the proletarian protest against the old narrow, bourgeois ideas was stopped by no less a person than the People's Commissary, Semasjko himself, who was heartless enough to declare that "it is a terrible mistake to think that to go about naked and to let one's hair and nails grow long is any evidence of a true revolutionary spirit."

But here, too, we find the same truth as before: what proves attractive to the artisan repels the peasants. The attempt to remodel life after a new fashion meets with their energetic opposition and exasperates them. This is, above all, true in the field of religion. Of all the mistakes that the Bolshevists have made in their policy with regard to the peasants, there is scarcely one that has been more instrumental in enraging them than the extension of their anti-religious propaganda to the villages. It is, of course, said that the Russian peasant's religious feeling, in which the world has always believed until now, is just as hollow as his much-vaunted love to his little father, the tsar, which certainly proved itself to be a meaningless phrase. It is also, no doubt, true that his religious sense does not exactly correspond with what is generally meant by the word, but that it is a mediæval mixture of real piety, gross prejudices and curious superstition. But that it exists and has a firm hold upon their hearts it would be absurd to deny. In any case, the Bolshevists have not succeeded

[1] The secular ceremony of naming a child that has taken the place of the former church baptism. It is so called from the month in which the Bolshevist revolution began.

in uprooting it. It is, of course, possible that they may be able to fight it with success by spreading light and learning in the villages, but there has been less evidence of such activity under Bolshevism than ever before. And when the Bolshevists instead now try to uproot the peasants' faith by insolent and offensive scorn of those things in religion which the latter value and hold in reverence, by defiling and forcibly closing their churches, by shooting the priests and confiscating their church funds, by burning their church books and breaking up the tombs of their saints, then all this has upon the peasants an effect the exact opposite of what is intended.

Amongst the many peasants with whom I talked I certainly found some—those who could read and were better educated—who had been really influenced by the anti-religious knowledge which had been served up for their consumption in a number of Bolshevist writings. They had themselves carried out their icons from their home and proudly declared themselves atheists. This new conviction of theirs was certainly not very deep-rooted. A peasant Communist, who for a time had been a prisoner of war in Germany, proclaimed to me, in very strong terms, his contempt for all religious belief, and, five minutes later, when we began arguing about Germany, he suddenly fell to criticizing the Protestant form of service; no, indeed, the Russian form was the only one that was any good! Another peasant poured lively contempt on a belief in God, only the next moment to assure me, with decision, that no one would ever be able to make him doubt the existence of the devil.

But it is not necessary to live long amongst the peasants to understand that the great mass of them believe both in God and the devil, and in all saints and demons as well, and that their belief has not been shaken, but strengthened, by the Bolshevist religious persecutions. In one of the gubernias that I visited during the few weeks immediately before my arrival, there had been a religious mass-demonstration of quite imposing dimensions. A miracle-working icon had been carried round the gubernia from village to village. This was a ceremony that used to be repeated from year to year, but which generally took place in no very startling form. But now it had grown into a veritable crusade. Crowds of believers had joined the procession from every direction; these crowds had then followed the icon from place to place; day after day new crowds had joined them, and at last there had been a

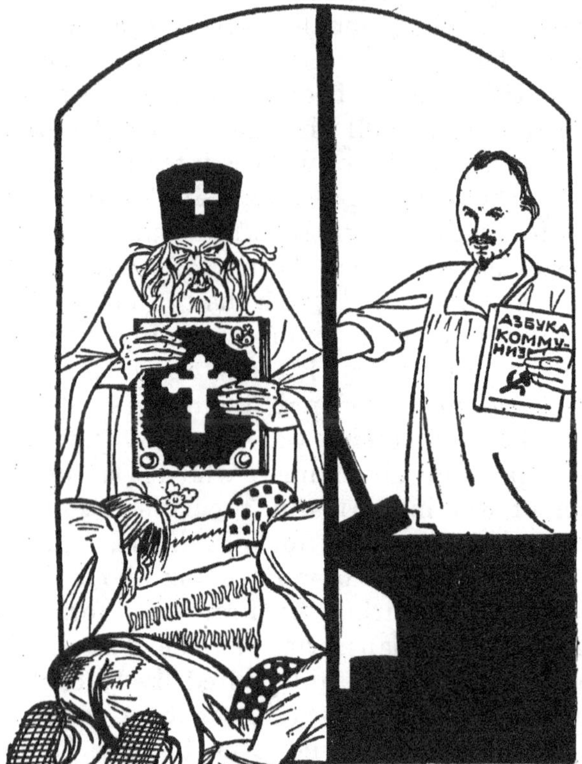

THE OLD AND THE NEW TESTAMENT
(The figure on the right hand is holding in his hand *The ABC of Communism*)

company of pilgrims numbering nearly 30,000 souls, who had left house and home and, with indescribable enthusiasm, had followed the icon on its triumphant way. Neither is it necessary to stay long among the peasants to discover that religious questions, as the result of the Bolshevist campaign, have become their main interest, to which all others are subordinated. The village population gathers in the evenings round those who can read, and they read, not the Bolshevist newspapers and propagandist literature, but the Bible, above all the Book of Revelation. They read it, read and discuss. The terminology of the Revelation is upon the lips of all; the happenings in Russia are looked at in the light of the Apocalypse, and horoscopes for the future are set up from it. And Bolshevism, that saviour of Russia and the world, takes for the peasant the place of Antichrist.

* * *

Thus, just as the Bolshevist ideas themselves have a distinct charm for the artisan-class, so the working-man feels too a certain solidarity with the Government which is endeavouring to put them into practice. So far, its promises have not been kept, yet in the eyes of many a worker it, at any rate, represents the proletariate's own attempt to order their life by their own power and in their own interest. If the sacrifices are heavy, yet, to some degree, they are felt to be self-imposed. This is particularly true of the certainly small but influential percentage of the artisan-class who have attained to membership of the Communist Party; they have the feeling (illusive, of course, but still firmly held) that they have a direct hand in the Bolshevist policy. And even the others, who cannot help seeing that they have been pushed aside, still feel some degree of solidarity with this Government; after all, it is carried on by people whom they used—even if they are widely parted from them now—to consider as one with themselves, and it has become an article of faith that this Government acts in the interests of the proletariate.

As regards the peasant-class, this bond has long since snapped, or, rather, it has never existed. The attempt to induce the peasants to recognize the Bolshevist régime as their own has been a failure from the first; the policy adopted towards them and the treatment they have experienced make this more than comprehensible. And that the new masters with whom they have to do, the communistic artisans who order them about and bully and bleed them, are people belonging to a social class very like their own, people whom they have the honour to call comrades, is but little comfort to them or, rather, it is no comfort whatever, but rather a source of greater bitterness. The oppression of the landowners was easier to understand; that an upper-class should oppress a lower-class was, so to speak, in the nature of things, and therefore also easier to bear. It is true, it was hard to have to do with their landowning master, but, after all, you see, he was a *barin*, a gentleman. This was a line of argument I often heard. But that their own comrades should "abuse" them (so they say), *that* they do think too much indeed, a fact that arouses their deepest feelings.

* * *

There is still one more thing which, in the same way, helps to maintain Bolshevist credit with the artisans, whilst leaving the peasants unmoved. If the Bolshevists have not yet given the proletariate all they expected, as regards material benefits, yet the artisan-class cling firmly to the hope that it is coming. The years of great scarcity lie immediately behind them; if they are starving now, they were starving much more then. Since that time the artisans' position has shown consistent improvement; so long as they can still maintain their hopes that this improvement will keep on, they do not quite lose heart. And I have shown how anxious the rulers are to make, at regular intervals, some very small increase to the workers' wages. Moreover, the artisans find a specially strong support for their faith in a future that becomes steadily brighter and brighter, in the prospect of a world-wide revolution. It is scarcely possible in the Western world to form any idea of what an all-important part this dream of a universal revolution plays in the national psychology. It is this revolution that is to change, at one blow, the position of the Russian proletariate. The hardships they now endure are mainly the fault of the foreign capitalists; it is their intrigues against the Soviet, their unwillingness to enter into definite relations with Russia, their stingy attitude in regard to loans, their ill-will, manifested in a thousand ways—all this it is that hinders Russian prosperity, and so still keeps the proletariate in their distress. As a matter of fact—so they say—Russia has to thank Europe for even the great famine catastrophe a few years back, since her blockade of the Russian frontiers was the really decisive factor. We continually hear and see this accusation put forward, whilst, on the other hand, there is never any allusion to the great relief work of the West during these years. Well, yes, the newspapers do mention Frithiof Nansen's name with gratitude, and his picture is stuck on the box of a superior make of cigarettes. When only the world-revolution comes, there will be an end of all their troubles; of that there is not the slightest doubt. The great majority, too, still firmly believe that the world-revolution is at the door. I cannot describe the endless sympathetic superiority with which a number of Russian workmen, to whom I was talking, listened to my assurance that the northern Governments were not faced with an immediate great social revolution. Such a poor blinded bourgeois! They knew it well enough. And how should they not know it? Does not their Press keep them supplied with information as to how the situation is ripening in country after country, and does not Zinoviev send out his notes to show that the working-class, here, there and everywhere in Europe, are standing ready to jump up on to the barricades? These notes and letters of Zinoviev's, that do not, to be sure, always meet with success in the country for which they are distributed, find a so much the more believing public at home to read them and think it can hear in the air the beating of the wings of the world-wide revolution.

Certainly there can be no denying that they sometimes begin to speculate why this longed-for event tarries so long. It not seldom happens that the principal Soviet speakers—now and again the Press reports it—at political meetings, when they have been uttering prophecies, even if somewhat hesitatingly, of the great world-wide revolution, have to accept some of those scraps of interrogation with which the Russian public at a meeting has a right to pelt the speakers: Explain, comrade, how it is that the wide-awake, highly-developed working-classes in France and

England have not risen when the Russian working-class, on such a much lower stage of civilization, have done so. Is it credible that, when they have not done so before us, they will now begin to follow our example ?—a rather hard test-question which the recipient will undoubtedly find a certain difficulty in answering. But these doubts are fought energetically and by every means. One of Russia's most celebrated scholars, one of those whose names are always used to give glory to the otherwise scanty Soviet culture, returned some time ago from a journey to Western Europe and gave utterance to a quiet unbelief as regarded the revolution's near approach. He was at once rejected as an unreliable witness. Why, the old man was plainly senile ! The world-revolution is coming, so there's no more to be said in the matter ; this is an article of faith that no one may touch.

It is, of course, unnecessary to say that, as regards the peasants, that source of comfort is completely denied them. The peasant is too ignorant of what goes on in the wide world and feels too little interest in it for any great political calculations to have the power of giving him pleasure. A single episode may be recounted as testifying to his maturity in this respect. Jakovlev's inquiry commission came, two years ago, to a village, not by any means in one of Russia's darkest corners, and was met there by the information that the peasants believed the Japanese had taken Moscow. The commission accepted this as a joke ; but no ! Inquiry proved that the peasants were really convinced of the truth of the matter Reports from the international front cannot do other than leave the peasants unmoved, even if they were more favourably disposed to it than they are.

* * *

The attitude of the Russian proletariate to Bolshevism is, as we have seen, of a particularly heterogeneous character. As regards the artisan-class, there are, in spite of all, several things that bind them to Bolshevism. When it comes, however, to the peasant-class, we look in vain for any such bonds. The feeling, therefore, to be found amongst the proletarian masses is very different in town and village.

It is not too much to say that the attitude of the peasant-class to Communism has been one great disappointment for the Bolshevists; sometimes, indeed, it is a source of very pronounced nervousness. To a certain extent, it is true, they try to hide this by assuming an appearance of forced assurance. Day after day the papers present—as though in answer to all disturbing questions—bulletins of the triumphant course of communistic ideas in Russia's rural districts—edifying tales of how peasants, hostile to Bolshevism, have had their eyes opened, pious Sunday-school stories of the conversion of whole villages, enthusiastic descriptions of how village after village has been changed into a little paradise since Bolshevism has found entrance there—tales too plainly concocted to be taken seriously by anyone, an outburst of delight reminding the hearer of the parrot who kept on calling out "All is well! all is well!" when her neck was being wrung. But now and again—it has occurred fairly often since 1923—real feelings are openly expressed. In the newspapers' leading articles, in general literature, in the speeches of the most prominent politicians, we frequently meet with unreserved avowal that the task in Russian rural districts is extraordinarily heavy and thankless, that the so-called welding together of town and village has been an utter failure, that the attitude in the villages is threatening and that strong measures are required to improve it.

Thus, even before we set a foot outside the principal cities, we understand that Bolshevist credit is at a low ebb in Russia's rural districts. But, however prepared we may be to find strong manifestations of anti-Bolshevist feeling, when we really get to these districts we are completely amazed, for what meets us surpasses all our expectations. Now I do not, of course, doubt that a traveller who confines his journey to the neighbourhood of the large towns, or visits only the more industrial parts of the country, will find signs that the Bolshevist propaganda has borne fruit. I myself lacked opportunity to verify this. But the feeling that I found in various parts of the real rural district—and which was always the same, almost without any shade of difference whatever—was this: a general dissatisfaction with the existing Government, not one of dull resignation, as in tsaristic times, but bitter, irreconcilable, uncontrolled—a dissatisfaction which they expressed freely, even to a stranger of whose views and position they were quite ignorant, without restraining themselves in any way or hesitating in their choice of forcible language.

Before I started for the rural districts I thought that, to facilitate the journey and to avoid any chance of annoyance, it might be an advantage to have some document from the authorities, and therefore applied to the Commissariat for Foreign Affairs for a paper stating that I was innocuous for the existing Government. My application was refused, although, I must say, in the most courteous manner. Such a paper was perfectly unnecessary; conditions in the rural districts were quite settled, and the permit would form a tiresome precedent, for, if it became the custom to provide foreigners with it, there would be trouble if, some fine day, a traveller should make his appearance without such a recommendation. I went my way, and never once, during the whole journey, experienced any need of the document. On the contrary, indeed, I saw that even had I had it, my most prudent course would have been never to show it. For though my journey was certainly not without a few uncomfortable experiences, these were not due to any suspicion of my hostile designs on the Soviet Government, but to the exact opposite, viz. a belief that I was in some way connected with it.

I will give two little episodes. I had come—my travelling companion being a young Russian philologist whom I had asked to take part in a journey and whose real object was to study dialects—to a peaceful little village far removed from the great highroads, and we had found accommodation—very comfortable too—in a peasant's cottage. We had jostled over about thirty versts in a somewhat exhausting tarantass, and went early to bed. I was soon awakened, although not completely, by a noise outside the cottage; in my half-sleep I heard voices talking,

talking and going on endlessly, but I was too tired to wake up quite and find out what was the cause of it. In the morning I got the explanation. Our host told us that, in the evening, he had had a couple of very strenuous hours. The whole village had, by degrees, gathered outside his cottage and desired information as to what the suspicious figures were whom he had taken into his house. He had assured tham we were harmless; but no, no doubt it was two Communists who had to see if the village was not able to pay somewhat bigger taxes. A heated discussion followed, and they had demanded that the spies should be evicted at once and sent outside the village confines that very same evening. However, his eloquence and personal influence had meantime conquered, and towards midnight the crowds dispersed. For the next few days we noticed nothing. I soon finished my work and went on, whilst my friend stayed behind with the intention of remaining two more weeks. A little time after we met in Moscow. It appeared that he had found it advisable to get away two days after me, for our case had remained under discussion, and three different opinions had been put forward about the curious strangers. A number of women had raised the question—one that, at any rate, is very typical of the feeling created in Russian rural districts by the Bolshevist anti-religious propaganda—as to whether it was not Antichrist who had come on a visit; it was not quite plain whether it was I or my companion who was identified with that celebrity. Others had suggested that we were nothing but two swindlers from Moscow, possibly escaped out of some city prison. But the majority were quite clear in their own minds: we were what was much worse than either Antichrist or Moscow rogues—viz. Communist spies. And so the peasants' attitude had become increasingly menacing, and, at last, my companion had simply not dared to show himself in the village street, and after he had found a peasant who was willing—at an astounding price—to drive him, he had left the place.

Here is another episode. After I had come to the end of my circuit through the rural district, I had sat down one summer evening at a landing-stage on the Volga, to wait for the river steamer. I was sitting on my valise, dozing in the sunshine, without taking any particular notice of the numbers of peasant men and women who were crowding round me with their bundles. Suddenly I heard a shrill voice speaking in loud, emphatic tones not far from me ; a peasant woman was pouring out, in excited tones, a full measure of abuse at Communists in general. She appeared to be talking to a little audience that had collected in front of her, but all the listeners stared fixedly at me, and it was plain that the volubility and indignation were really directed against me, and that I was again suspected of having something to do with those in power. She was soon seconded by others, and in a short time a universal loud-voiced disparagement of the Communists in general was in full swing—the Communists, who squeezed the last drop of blood out of the poor peasants and took their ease themselves in luxury ; the Communists, who filched other people's money and put it in their own pockets ; the Communists, who came nosing about in the peasants' villages ; the Communists, that they would like to throw to the bottom of the Volga, every one of them. The impromptu demonstration meeting got more and more fierce in its denunciation, so that I began to find the situation somewhat uncomfortable and felt a particularly pleasant sensation when the broad paddles of the *Third International* suddenly came splashing up the river.

Such is the feeling ; wherever one goes, there are fresh manifestations of it. And yet we must be careful not to draw too hasty conclusions from this ; it is not very probable that the discontent will end in any great collective peasant revolt. For hundreds of years the peasants suffered under tsardom ; when the revolution came it was not their doing ; and, as regards Bolshevism too, we have to reckon with their well-known inertia. It is an enormous step for the Russian, from bitter complaint over his misery to a manly effort to lift himself out of it. When, after having listened for an hour to the peasants' mighty outpourings of undying hate of the Bolshevists, I interposed a modest question as to what they thought of doing, they always slid away. "We are a patient people," was the evasive answer. In this patience Bolshevism has its best ally in the Russian rural districts.

* * *

The feeling is fundamentally different amongst the working-classes. The factors mentioned above still exercise quite considerable influence on the workers and induce the majority of them to close up their ranks round Bolshevism.

And yet it cannot be denied that the feeling is not so uniformly good as the official reports make out. This is true, to begin with, even with the picked adherents amongst the working-class, viz. the Communist Party. It would certainly be useless to deny that there are sections that flourish happily inside the Party ranks. In addition to the factors, already given, which bind the workers to Bolshevism, there is one other fact as regards the Communists, namely, the privileges that Party membership guarantees them. Even if the ordinary Communist is deprived of all the participation in power on which he had originally reckoned, and even if, in his Party service, he is under the slave-driver's whip, yet he also has, at the same time, the agreeable consciousness of belonging to the social aristocracy and of the enjoyment of a substantial material compensation for his hardships. But it does not seem possible to deny that, for the large majority, there is not any great feeling of well-being in the communistic barracks. Even the best advance-guard which, under the hypnotic influence of war, are carried on by blind and fiery enthusiasm in the moment of attack, can lose their spirits during long months of wearisome and unstimulating barrack life, under the deadening rule of iron discipline. The Communist Party is a fighting organization, adapted to a dangerous and tense conflict, originally carried on secretly. As long as Russian Communism was fighting for its life, its purely military war-discipline could be maintained; self-sacrifice at the Party's call seemed a natural thing that did not rouse any opposition. But now, when Communism has conquered and occupies the place of power, a reaction takes place; now this forcible discipline of life, as if in war-time, begins to be felt as pointless and exhausting. The demand for uninterrupted, never-slackening activity in the Party's business becomes oppressive ; it is a demand that takes very little account of the Russian temperament, with its incurable lack of energy and its veering in the directly opposite directions of energy and apathy. And the Party atmosphere in other respects—the iron control, the suppression of individual opinion, the duty of unquestioning obedience, the unceasing control by a system of spying—becomes, in the long run, simply unbearable. It is a tight-fitting coat of mail that presses hardly on the broad Russian nature, particularly now, when, after a victorious revolution, it feels it has a right to stretch its limbs a little.

To this we may add a special circumstance, viz. that the common life within the Party itself shows a continual decrease of the spirit of comradeship. It is not solely in the Party's upper ranks that they lie in wait upon one another ; even in the lower there exists a system of intrigue that poisons the relationships between the Party members. A great number of climbers and fortune-hunters have—as I showed before—crept into the Party and found there a field of operations to their liking ; now there is a mutual struggle for the Party rewards, and in this they press the Party's system of espionage into their service. And amongst those who either come off second-best in this game of intrigue or who will not condescend to take part in the place-hunting, the uncomfortable feeling of coolness becomes more and more widespread. A great deal of this discontent has a very decided objective, viz. the Jews in the Party. Rightly or wrongly—doubtless often rightly—the accusation is made that they enrich themselves at others' expense. Great numbers of Jews, with doubtful political antecedents and communistic convictions of an exceedingly problematic character, have, so we are assured, pushed into the Party ranks and elbow the others to one side, seize upon the richest morsels of the war booty, and take their ease with an arrogance that not only compromises Communism in the eyes of outsiders, but destroys comradeship within the Party itself.

Taken all in all, the Party joints are creaking. The machinery for clearing-out is continually at work; great numbers of people who cannot show the requisite energy in work or pliability of will are dismissed from the Party. It is true that no reduction in its numbers necessarily follows. So great are the attractions of the Party for those outside its ranks that new aspirants are always to be found waiting. But the quality deteriorates. Many of the best and most honourable members are amongst those that go, and the new additions are looked upon, even by the Communists themselves, with a certain mistrust; the so-called Lenin levy—of whose origin I have previously spoken—have, at any rate for the present, to be content to be considered as second-class Communists. And amongst wide circles of those who remain in the Party, the feeling is dull and depressed; they go on working, but with clenched teeth. The feeling of depression even begins to set its stamp on the whole genus. It is now a general saying in Russia that a Communist is known not only by his leather jacket and spurs, not even only by his unendurable bullying attitude, but, above all, by his soured and embittered temper. "As suspicious as a Communist" is the common expression.

The depression is so strong that sometimes, in defiance of all Party discipline, it cannot help finding expression even to a stranger. I particularly remember a Communist whom I met on a railway journey. This man, one of the most interesting and congenial Bolshevists that I had ever talked to, was certainly warmly attached to the Communist cause, and had evidently, in his responsible post down in the south of Russia, accomplished most meritorious work in the Party's service. But now he was weary and discouraged; a visit to Moscow—he was just on his return journey—had especially disturbed and embittered him. Nor did he conceal his feelings.

"There are," he exclaimed, "a great number of people in the Party who have no business to be there, nor, indeed, in this world at all."

Later on, in country places, I repeatedly met with the same bitter feeling against Moscow and its Government bureaucracy, consisting so largely of a suspicious element—especially of Jews—and against the Party rulers who suffer these Party parasites.

If the élite of the proletariate, the Communist Party, are thus beginning to lose their spirits, this is still more true of the great mass of the rank and file. In spite of everything, in spite of all the illusions which they have to cling to, in spite of their often quite sincere Bolshevist faith, one thing is certain, viz. their spirits are not high.

We do not need to undertake very deep soundings of the Russian psychology to see that the general happiness, which should exist amongst a people, who, according to the faithful communistic version, have achieved that of which all other nations dream with longing desire, is conspicuous by its entire absence. There is not the very smallest glimmer of sunshine falling upon Russian life of the present day, which, on the contrary, is indescribably overcast and grey. Decidedly the strongest impression made by new Russia—stronger even than the impression of decay and misery which otherwise strikes us—is just the fact that we meet with a general depression of spirits, a dull oppressive feeling of discomfort. The feeling may disappear for a moment. When the crowds march on under waving red flags, with revolutionary songs on their lips, when they listen to the eloquence of the chief Soviet orators, then the revolutionary hypnotism may make its reappearance. A clever Government takes care, too, that these opportunities recur as often as possible, and the Russian working-man goes—often at the expense of his regular work—from demonstration to demonstration, and from Party meeting to Party meeting. But this is an injection whose effect is but of short duration; a moment after, the old heavy, everyday feeling again prevails.

And so we no longer recognize the Russian nation, with its particularly sunny temperament, of earlier days. The difference is enormous between a summer evening on the Moscow boulevards then and now! Then, a purely carnival feeling prevailed amongst gay crowds as playful as children, shown in laughter, noise and merry jokes; now, much smaller numbers of low-voiced, serious pedestrians, wearily walking along and talking in undertones. Or take the evening atmosphere in a Russian small town. In olden days the principal street was a gay promenade in miniature; the strains of concertinas resounded from yards and alleys; down by the river there was singing and laughter. Now the streets are dark and deserted; music and songs have sunk into silence; all that is heard is the shrill notes of the "International" on some gramophone in one of the numberless beershops, and from the back streets the sounds of drunken yells.

The people are changed—brusque and unfriendly, irritable and quarrelsome. We ask a man in the street to tell us the way. In days gone by he was ready to go far out of his own road to put an inquirer in the right direction, but now we get, as a rule, even though it is only the simplest information that is wanted, a surly answer: "How should I know?" We think of having a chat as we used with our driver—in a very marked way he turns his thin back and gives his horse a savage cut with his whip. We want some information at a bank, a post- or ticket-office, and get nothing but rebuffs for answers; we want to make a purchase in a shop, and get such a reception as used to be in vogue in a public rates-office of Western Europe. And it is not, as at first we are tempted to believe, only to foreigners that they show such cross faces; a certain curiosity with regard to such individuals, still comparatively rare, contributes rather to get for the stranger something approaching a polite reception. This new tone in human intercourse is both usual and general. In this society of *tovaristji* (comrades) everyone stands suspiciously on his dignity, drawn into his shell, is on his guard against attack, and puts out his prickles at the least touch. The trifling conflicts of everyday life assume an evil complexion with extraordinary ease; purely trumpery causes give occasion for violent quarrels, in which the mutual abuse is no less thorough because the parties give each other the title of fellow-citizen, or because they often try to show that their dispute is one of principle and turn it into a discussion as to a fellow-citizen's rights and duties in any given situation. In earlier days I have travelled for weeks in a third-class railway carriage all over Russia; it was dirty, crowded and uncomfortable, but yet the journey was, after all, enjoyable. It was not a crowd of strangers who were packed together, but one big family, where everyone thought of the other, willingly lent him a hand, was ready to open his food-bag and his heart for his fellow-traveller. I used to think of those old days as I was riding in the Moscow tramcars. On they rolled, these cars, with their finely painted revolutionary phrases, full, from floor to roof, of bad temper, crammed with people, every one of whom seemed to have made it his object to render the journey as unbearable as possible for others; there were nothing but spiteful looks, angry words and hard knocks—not a tram journey without some set-to between passengers and conductor, not a stop without some dispute between passengers.

Of course, this general feeling of discomfort, of which we meet fresh evidence at every step, is not entirely, nor even chiefly, due to unhappiness under Bolshevism. Quite apart from that, the Russian people have indeed, during the last ten years, gone through suffering severe enough to destroy any national nervous system stronger than the Russian. So much is clear, however, that the advantages of living under the dictatorship of the proletariate, however boundless they are continually said to be, have not been able to help the great masses of the Russian people through the trials of the moment, to keep up their spirits or to cast a gleam of happiness over their life.

So much is clear and a little more, namely that the general, more vague depression is beginning to crystallize into acute dissatisfaction with the Government in power. If we do not take into account such sections as stand under the daily communistic control and supervision—as, for example, the factory workers themselves, who are constantly under the control of the communistic-cells in the factories—we, time after time, amongst the Russian masses, come upon evidences of an anti-Bolshevist feeling so bitter as to strike us with amazement. Listen, for instance, to the conversation of the workmen's wives whilst they wait their turn in the Co-operative shops. Starting with complaints of the Soviet's bad goods and unreasonable prices, in a second they are joining in a chorus of abuse of all Communism and Communists; they are glad to let the strange fellow-citizen hear how hard is the lot of the subordinate non-communistic workers under Communist rule. Discuss matters with the shopman behind the counter, and, in the twinkling of an eye, he begins to deal out blow after blow upon his employer, the Soviet Government. Poor goods? Yes, of course our things are poor. Do you think nowadays anything good can be made in Russia? Why, all they are good for is to kill folk! Get the snappy driver to talk—it can be managed with a little friendly sympathy—and he shoots off a terrible salvo against the Communists who oppress him and his honest calling. Talk with the boot-black or cigarette-seller in the street, with the waiter at the restaurant, with the guard on the train, they are all ready, when once the ice is broken, to give utterance to their bottled-up rage against a system that grinds them down, harasses them and condemns them to a life of misery, whilst it gives unwarrantable favours to a chosen, envied few.

And, in addition to this, there appears—and that in much increased strength—amongst the representatives of the lower ranks the same feeling upon which I touched in speaking of the feeling within the Communist Party, viz. the hatred of the Jews. One thing, plain to the mass of the people, is that it is the Jews that are in power now in the land. Some little time ago, in a circus in Moscow, the two clowns, Bim and Bom, the acknowledged favourites of the Russian people, introduced a trio, consisting of an artisan, a peasant and a Jew, and invited the public to identify them. The first two offered no difficulty. Why, it was a Russian workman and a Russian *moujik*. Then came the Jew's turn. No, that wasn't a Jew. Couldn't they see what it was? Why, the Government of the Russian artisans and peasants. The outspoken lips of both clowns could be closed, of course, by suitable means; their joke cost them a period of "isolation," but it was more difficult to master the people's opinion to which the clowns gave expression, to the huge delight of their audience.

The supreme power does not belong to the proletariate, but to the Jews, who are avenging themselves for the oppression they themselves endured in the past. We continually meet with this simplified view that the national psychology takes of what is now happening in Russia. Again and again, when we hear this subject discussed by simple men and women of the people with accusations brought against the leaders, grotesquely unreasonable, and uttered in a tone terrifying in its frenzy, we cannot help thinking of the prophecy that Bolshevism's great experiment will end with the greatest Jewish pogrom known in the world's history.

CHAPTER VIII

THE THIRD LINE OF DEFENCE

In one field the Bolshevists have known how to get quite a good reputation in the West, of which they are, in spite of their hatred and contempt for the bourgeois world, not a little proud, and this field is that of culture. That Russia now adopts an enlightened policy towards culture has, by degrees, become an article of faith, held even by those who, in other respects, are not amongst Russia's admirers. Independently of political points of view, this has been candidly recognized, and it has been felt only right to extend the right hand of fellowship to her in her work on this neutral ground; even in our northern lands organizations have been formed for cultural intercourse with Russia.

The Bolshevists, of course, have not won their fame as the friends of culture for nothing. Partly, to be sure, the fact is seen against the background of that opinion of the Bolshevists which became prevalent in the West during the first months of the revolution. Their opponents depicted them as a kind of wild horde who, in their perverted delight in destruction, demolished the whole world of culture, burnt libraries, devastated museums, and smashed works of art to atoms. When it was seen later on that this picture was wrong, and that most of such things had come through the revolution intact, the feeling that justice had not been done to the Bolshevists induced public opinion to be so much the more generous in crediting them with a more enlightened attitude. But the West has also had a number of positive facts on which to pin its faith. The Bolshevists' happy thought of putting at the very beginning of the revolution their greatest author, Gorky, as a kind of scientific figurehead and chief guardian of the world of culture was, in itself, good evidence of their zeal in that direction. Every Western visitor to

Russia has been able to certify that the condition of the museums and picture galleries, e.g. *The Hermitage*, in Leningrad is a model for all others, no matter where, and that the Moscow Kremlin and its monuments have been restored, regardless of cost and with the employment of the very best artistic help. Prominent representatives of Western culture have returned from Sovietland in raptures over the homage that has been offered to them and to the Western culture which they represent; individual Russian scientific celebrities have, with all honour, represented Russian science at the Western congresses and sometimes expressed their opinion of the favoured position of science in Russia. And a really great blow was struck in the autumn of 1925 to convince the Western world of how wonderfully scientific research flourishes under Soviet care, and the miserable slander that all representations to the contrary are, when the authorities invited Western scientists to take part in the bicentenary jubilee of the Russian Academy of Science, and in connection with this to make a great inspection of science.

The question, then, remains as to how far these goods, exposed in the Bolshevist shop windows facing Europe, are really typical of what the Bolshevist policy, with regard to culture, has to offer.

Two facts may be definitely established with regard to this policy, the first being that the Soviet interest in culture has strictly defined limits, and the second that their work in this sphere is marked, in common with Bolshevist policy in general, by a number of very serious weaknesses. These are two circumstances, each of which appreciably contributes to modify the picture of Bolshevism as the great promoter of culture.

That the Bolshevists feel themselves called to appraise with severity different cultural values is a fact which they candidly and proudly acknowledge—except when they happen to find it opportune in European society to hide their fists in kid gloves. Western idea of culture is one thing, that of the Bolshevists another.

In an article on Gorky, Trotsky draws a picture of the old and new man of culture. The old are people of Gorky's type. "When in the revolution 1917–18 the Kremlin was fired upon, when the sailors put out their cigarettes on the old tapestries"—this really did happen, even if chiefly only in the bourgeois imagination—"then Gorky was beside himself and lifted his voice in the chorus of despair over the fate of culture. Oh, what a horrible deed! what barbarism! The Bolshevists are breaking the historical vessels of every kind—painted, earthen, domestic and all the rest!" In contrast to him, Trotsky gives a more modern type: "I remember the Petersburg proletarian Vorontsov, who, immediately after the October revolution, was in Lenin's service, helping and watching over him. When we were getting ready to evacuate Petersburg, Vorontsov said to me gloomily: 'We ought to lay dynamite under Petersburg and blow it all up.' 'Don't you think Petersburg would be a loss, comrade Vorontsov?' I asked, touched and delighted with this Petersburg proletarian. 'What loss would that be? We shall come back and build a better.' Now see," adds Trotsky, "this is the right attitude to culture. There is in it not a trace of that chorus of despair. If we must ruin the fruits of past culture, let us do it without maudlin sentimentality, and then let us return to build up a new culture incomparably better." "Leninism consists in a boldly revolutionary, but at the same time a genuine and practical feeling for culture; it teaches the working-class to sift out of the gigantic stores of culture that which the workers to-day chiefly need for their social redemption and for the building up of society on fresh foundations"; it becomes in this way "the result and culmination of all earlier culture."

In the field of culture, then, the Bolshevists are only interested in such things as serve the ends of the workers, and their social scheme and all else may be sifted out as worthless. What is there, then, that, from this point of view, is worth taking care of?

To begin with, all that, from a purely practical standpoint, can be of profit to the proletariate. To determine where to draw the line of demarcation is a difficult matter and opinions have also been divided in its consideration. Many have wished to confine it within very narrow limits. "An endeavour to find a solution and a remedy for illiteracy" was how a very prominent member of the Soviet, a little time since, summed up the cultural tasks that alone were really essential; the rest one could manage without. Lunatyarsky mentions in one of his speeches that even in the Council of the People's Commissaries it was proposed to give up all other cultural policy except the care of the purely elementary education of the nation. Now, however, the leading lights in culture have induced the Bolshevists to make very substantial additions to their programme. The Soviet State needs, after all, more in several directions.

In the first place, the State has pressing need of the assistance of a number of scientific teachings in its work of rebuilding and transformation. The branches of science capable of technical application are required for the establishment and development of industry, for the care of the country's natural riches, etc.; a natural result of the great plans for the better care of public health amongst the proletariate is a consideration of the interests of medical science; for the simplification of the political and social work amongst the numbers of small nationalities included under the Soviet Government, a scientific investigation of their conditions of life and mentality is requisite. Support of scientific work in this and other fields must therefore be included in the Bolshevist policy with regard to culture, and, as a whole, nothing but good can be said of the way in which this has been done.

Interest has also been extended to several different branches of art. Dramatic art is, even if not directly essential to life, so popular that the authorities neither will nor can interfere with it; from the very first, their programme, as regards culture, has included its support in every possible way, especially in the encouragement of new, radical experiments in its domain and in providing opportunity for the proletariate to enjoy them.

Naturally they exercise great care that, as *Pravda* says, the theatre may not be utilized for any hostility to the supreme power of the people, and keep a watchful eye on the repertoire. Some extracts from the published decisions of the dramatic censorship are perhaps worth quoting: "The opera *Lohengrin,* in consideration of its mystical tendency, is replaced by the musical drama *Sigrid,* as being more suitable from an ideological point of view. In the first act of the opera *Eugen Onegin* the scene between the *barin's* wife and the peasants has been struck out as an idyll from the times of serfdom which, under present conditions, gives a false impression; the opera *Werther* is prohibited since, in our times, it is perfectly irrational to cultivate Werther sentiments; Schiller's *Maria Stuart* is prohibited as a religious and monarchical production." And in the same way the censorship, according to the report of the People's Commissariat for Education to the Soviet Congress of 1925, has forbidden the Artists' Theatre in Moscow to produce the dramatization of Dostoievsky's *The Brothers Karamasov,* "since this production, in spite of the author's talent (!), might exercise a deleterious influence."

But other branches of art as well, though less accessible to the proletariate—such as painting, sculpture, architecture—find in the Soviet Government a generous Mæcenas, a fact due less to Bolshevism than to the warm interest of individual Bolshevists in these arts, the motive-power being the æsthetically gifted People's Commissary Lunatyarsky, whose artistic interests are certainly not confined, as his slanderers aver, to ballet-dancers. Here, too, their proud aim is to try to foster a new proletarian art, upon whose achievement so far I do not venture to pronounce any judgment, whilst at the same time they, with praiseworthy piety, cherish the art inheritance from the past. That this latter course is a thorn in the flesh to many Party members is doubtless true, but, up till now, it has been possible to keep a check on these forces. Only at times has it been necessary to yield to them, as, for instance, on the occasion, mentioned earlier, when the attempt to save the imperial castle in Livadia met with failure. Art experts insisted with great emphasis that the castle was a treasure of historical art that could never be replaced. "We possess no other such monument in the range of castle-building," wrote a correspondent in *Izvestia.* "Our castle-building began with the castle of Catherine II in Tsarskoye and ended with the castle in Livadia—this was the latest stage in this line of development. Its interior is our finest specimen of art in the treatment of wood. The wood has there been transformed into a kind of marble treated in a unique manner. Russia has always been renowned for its wood, but at no time and in no place has wood been transformed into such a marvellous artistic shape as in this palace." "And at the same time," the writer points out, "the castle is of great historic interest and throws a light, unequalled anywhere else, on the life of the upper bourgeoisie in the beginning of 1900." But these points of view were completely rejected. "There is no point at all," another correspondent writes, under the heading, "Too Many Monuments to Tsardom," "poor as we are, in wasting enormous sums of money to show visitors to the Crimea the rooms and environment in which the last tsar lived. The nation would not understand us and would be perfectly right in condemning us for the maintenance of the former tsar's palace in a manner so useless to the public. The Bolshevists were, during the revolution, ruthless with regard to such useless playthings. Many people condemned them and called them barbarians. But our first and most important duty is to study the interests of the masses—of the artisans and peasants." And the Council of the People's Commissaries passed a unanimous resolution last winter to transform the castle and all its premises into a peasant sanatorium.

There are, then, a number of branches of culture whose prosperity for various reasons is considered an advantage to the State, and hence they are allowed, as a rule, not only unrestrained development, but they also enjoy the valuable protection of the Government. But if we leave these branches, which, it is true, are extensive enough to provide profitable excursions to them for European visitors, but which yet only form a very limited part of the entire field of culture, we find that the Bolshevist care for culture, in other respects, takes on quite another character, inasmuch as it only shows interest in such things as may contribute to the spread of communistic teachings. Communism is the chief flower of culture, and only that which promotes its welfare lies within the sphere of culture for the proletariate. Everything else is valueless, and not only valueless, but directly evil, and must be uprooted. Active communistic propaganda, carried on under an annexed banner of culture and, at the same time, violent destructive work in the most varied fields of culture, this, with the exceptions given above, is the policy as regards culture that is for the present adopted in Russia.

Even the most primitive forms of work in this direction, right down to the instruction of illiterates, bear the impress of these points of view. The whole of public education would be meaningless, according to Bolshevist ideas, if it was not, above all else, a means for the spread of Communism. "For us," says Lunatyarsky, "the one idea, inseparably connected with the idea of all public education, is the political propaganda and advancement of our Party. The People's Commissariat of Education, to which, as a Soviet organ, is entrusted the responsibility of the general national education, cannot fulfil its task without the dissemination of Marxian doctrines. These doctrines are an indispensable element in national education, not only important, but absolutely indispensable. We cannot imagine how any attention can be devoted to public education without imprinting on each individual brain that Marxian point of view that shall awake in his consciousness the sense of co-citizenship. We must convert all Russia, from end to end, to Marxian doctrines." "Is not," he asks in another speech, "revolutionary propaganda the truest public education and that which, in this direction, is most indispensable for the nation?"

The same view is held of all literary accomplishment. Literature must have a communistic tendency. No coquetting with any absurd ideas of art is allowed, but literary work of a good, honest, communistic type is demanded. For a moment it looked as though the revolution would produce a new literary revival: when the Russian printers got to work again, literature suddenly revived, and works that seemed to hold the fairest promise for the future were produced. But Bolshevist hands seized the new literature by the throat. Authors were not allowed to be "followers in the rear," as they termed the young guard who, although as a rule very sympathetic to Bolshevism, yet did not entirely enroll themselves amongst the ranks of the Party; they must march with the ranks and act, as one of them put it, "as drummers"; they must be, so said another, "the subordinate fingers on an iron hand that had to bend and stretch at the dictation of the first finger."

"Any idea that literary activity should be free from Party interference is wrong. We must apply class points of view, even in literary art." This was said in an interview with one of the Party leaders of culture, the chief of the Press, Comrade Kanatjikov. "The new Russia has no literature of its own," he decides; "she is only now beginning to create it. Nothing was to be expected from the old writers; we cannot demand from them any presentation of life in its new form. We must set our hopes on the new authors, and these we must educate from the artisan and peasant ranks. The contest as to how far literature ought to bear the class stamp or not is already settled for us. Literature cannot be free from class tendency; it must exist for the service of the working-class." What the result has been of this duty for literature does not indeed need telling. Literature is pining away; the orthodox communistic works that are produced in the service of their Party and times are, one and all, unparalleled in their poverty.

The case is the same with science, with the exception of certain branches touched upon above. It, too, must allow itself to be "bolshevized"—later on I will return to the demands made upon it in this regard—or else it is superfluous. Here, too, the consequences are inevitable; under this constraint, research is dying out in a number of branches of science. And such sciences as offer no possibilities of being pressed into the service of Bolshevist propaganda are cut off at once, either because they have no point of contact with politics or, still worse, because they are fundamentally opposed to the main principles of Bolshevism. There are sciences, says Trotsky, "idealistic, abstract, high-flown, deceptive from beginning to end, bound up with 'eternal truths' and such-like fancies—these we sweep aside, one and all."

Not only, then, is the Bolshevist cultural interest, thanks to its intimate association with Bolshevist policy, of an extremely one-sided character, in many directions developing into a purely hostile attitude towards culture, but there also follows the additional fact that the work really accomplished in the field of culture is often marked by the same characteristics which meet us in other departments of Bolshevist social work. There is no lack of great and new—even if sometimes extravagant—ideas and suggestions, and these are proclaimed with extraordinary self-sufficiency. But wherever these have met with opposition and difficulties they have, to a very great extent, come to a full stop—the power of organization has failed and the great reforms have been drowned in phrases and paper.

This distinctive feature of the Russian cultural policy will strike us again and again later on, as we try to examine somewhat more closely certain main sections of what the Bolshevists call "the third front," i.e. the system of primary and higher education.

* * *

"Seven years have been wasted. In seven years no such advance has been made on the third front as may safeguard us against the continual increase in barbarism; we cannot say that the people are even beginning to be able to lift themselves from the barbaric state in which they were kept by tsardom."

The quotation is not, as a Soviet enthusiast might possibly suppose, a cutting from the foreign White Army Press or a jeremiad of some old reactionary fogy of a Russian pedagogue, who has put on blinkers to escape seeing the Soviet Government's victories on the educational front; it is not one of the Soviet's enemies speaking, but one of Bolshevism's own members, and one, moreover, whose competence to express an opinion in the matter can scarcely be doubted, viz. the Minister of Public Education himself, Lunatyarsky. The passage is quoted word for word from *Izvestia's* report of one of his great speeches, delivered at the end of 1924. It is a few words from his description of what he himself calls " our collapse on the third front," " the catastrophe in public education which began after 1921, and which still continues before our eyes."

This quotation might be multiplied by others, but I will only add two more to Lunatyarsky's utterances. " The investigations in the villages, which, to a certain degree, show up their educational physiognomy," says Fru Krupskaja, Lenin's wife, who is well known as one of the most influential leaders in educational work, " disclose a somewhat dark picture. Reading-rooms are a rarity, so are libraries ; the schools are destroyed ; in a word, we must face the truth and see clearly that the educational state of the village is exceedingly disturbing." " We cannot hide from ourselves," were Rykov's own words in May, 1925, " that, as far as culture is concerned, we have not only achieved no revolution, but, generally speaking, we have done very little in comparison with what was needed on our part." The cause of the pessimism to which the leaders give such utterance was from the first to be found in the difficulties in the great campaign intended, as the phrase ran, to " liquidate " (wipe out) illiteracy.

The effort started in its time with a great flourish of trumpets. " The People's Commissary of Education and the local authorities are given the right "—so it was called —" of mobilizing the whole of the country's population who can read for the instruction of the illiterates and also to apportion to them their duty in the work. In furtherance of this wiping-out of illiteracy the Commissary for Education possesses power to use all churches, village halls, clubs, private houses, suitable premises in factories, industrial buildings and Soviet institutions." According to resolutions at various congresses, the aim must be to finish the task quickly : the " liquidation " ought to be finished by the ten-year jubilee of the Bolshevist revolution in 1927. A great bureaucratic mechanism was formed for the business, and Russia was provided—on paper—with a mighty network of "liquidation-points," and revelled in bright ideas as to how the work might be hastened and simplified. And in the pleasurable anticipation of their great triumph, they not only began but long continued to set up a veritable chorus of contempt of poor tsardom, which had never accomplished, and of the Western world which had taken centuries to accomplish, a task which Bolshevism was to settle in ten years.

I arrived in rural Russia full of keen expectations, eager to see the result of this revolutionary work of national education. Yes, quite correct! Scarcely had I driven up the street in the first village that I visited—this street bore, so the great name-plates on the little grey cottages informed us, the genteel name of the "Proletariate's Victory"—than I was welcomed by a crowd of curious peasants, even before I had thought it possible to get my first proof of the higher educational level in rural districts. We had not exchanged many words before a peasant, in very elaborate phrases, asked for "a great favour"—would it be possible to have a newspaper? I gladly emptied my pockets of all the papers I had, and they were seized by eagerly outstretched hands. But disillusion soon followed. Whilst we continued our conversation I saw peasant after peasant tear off a corner of newspaper, make a case of it and fill it with wretched native tobacco from a dirty cotton pouch produced from his belt, and light it. I had provided the village with cigarette paper for a long time to come. Afterwards I visited the village schoolmaster to get some information as to the campaign against illiteracy. It proved that a good 1,600 of the 2,000 inhabitants in the village were unable to read or write. Nothing had been done for the instruction of the adults; as far as he knew there had never been a question of any "liquidation-point," neither had he heard of any other measures—oh yes, a coloured placard, showing the charming picture of a peasant home where all the members of the family sat, each with his communistic book or paper, absorbed in reading, had been stuck up, to be of such use and influence as it might, in the Co-operative shop. Since at the same time the only school was visited—sporadically, too—by only a few children, illiteracy, instead of being wiped out, had become more firmly established in the village. And when I reminded the schoolmaster of the year 1927, he, good Communist as he was—or pretended to be—indulged in an exceedingly anti-revolutionary smile.

I afterwards pursued my inquiries as to the result of the great campaign against illiteracy in a large number of villages, but nowhere did I find any trace of it. In one or another place they had certainly had a "liquidation-point," but that had soon liquidated itself, and the peasants spoke of it with scorn: "The Communists should first see to it that the children managed to learn to read, then they could begin to teach us old folks."

It is, of course, possible, and even credible, that I was unfortunate; something, at any rate, the great organization must have set on foot. But even if we keep to the Bolshevists' own reports from the anti-illiteracy front, it is evident that the advances have been particularly insignificant.

As long as possible an endeavour was made in this, as in so many other matters, to maintain the illusion that all was going exceedingly well. At the end of 1924 there was an imposing celebration of the five years' jubilee of Lenin's manifesto—which has been already mentioned. It was, according to newspaper accounts, a jubilee celebrated with the pomp and ceremony of a triumphal feast—a theatre all in Moscow filled to its utmost limits; a frantically applauded jubilee speech by Kalinin; enthusiastic demonstrations of applause for Mme. Lenin and the chairman of the society "Away with Illiteracy," one of the many organizations formed for the great work; speeches by a number of fighters for national education, amongst them Mme. Lenin, who made the announcement—rapturously received—that 100,000 A B C books had just been given out, gratis, in the rural districts; the distribution of prizes to a number of "heroic workers on the battlefield against illiteracy," amongst whom were five old women, brought on to the platform, "who all, in spite of being already advanced in years, have voluntarily conquered (liquidated) their illiteracy," an heroic deed that brought them rewards, consisting of books, amongst others some of Lenin's writings. Such an exhibition of similar "heroic workers" who learn to read at an advanced age is an indispensable factor of all national education meetings. The communications concerning the situation on the field of action which were given, at the same time, in the papers, corresponded, however, but poorly with the fine festal arrangements. It was made known that out of Russia's 117 millions, 78 millions were still unable to read or write—this did not include a number of so-called autonomous districts, whose inclusion would have made the figures still more overwhelming. For instance, in the so-called Tchuvasshan republic 90 per cent. of the inhabitants were illiterates, in the Kirghiz republic 96 per cent. Of the town population 410 in every 1,000 could not read, and in rural districts 722 in every 1,000. In 1924, in accordance with the congress resolution, instruction ought really to have been given to 2 million illiterates—an exceedingly modest figure when compared with the sum-total of illiterates, but, according to Lunatyarsky, only 45 per cent. of even this modest achievement had been accomplished.

By degrees the authorities began to own that the whole matter was becoming a fiasco. "Have we attained the pace and the progress that Lenin pictured?" is asked in a newspaper article by the chairman of the above-mentioned society, "Away with Illiteracy." And he answers: "Of course not. The rate of work and the civic mobilization are such that they by no means correspond to the immensity of the standard proposed." The work has been "lacking in method and of varying merit," Mme. Lenin states. "The results of this year (1924) show that there are some gaps in the work; different organizations have not been able to co-ordinate their efforts, the forces at work have been divided." The society "Away with Illiteracy," Lunatyarsky continues coldly and mercilessly, "adopts excellent resolutions but achieves miserable results." The head of the society himself points out one of the causes: "As we know, the whole civic life of the Soviet State at present in process of organization, and no less too the society 'Away with Illiteracy,' is now in danger of over-bureaucracy, of being distracted by circulars, instructions, and working apparatus."

The idea of celebrating Bolshevism's ten years' jubilee by a universal knowledge of reading has now been relinquished as well. On the occasion of the six years' jubilee of Lenin's decree—which was not celebrated with imposing festivities—a revision of the programme was announced—out of the whole Russian territory fifteen gubernias had been selected for the total abolition of illiteracy by 1927, but in the rest of the land the question was postponed to some future time.

* * *

Bolshevism, in its endeavour to increase national education in general, has achieved much the same result as in the question of illiteracy. There have been plenty of proposals and ideas and a multitude of attempts have been made, but, to a very great extent, the whole thing has been on paper.

After the revolution a movement was started with many fine phrases for the care of children before school age—a crèche and kindergarten movement. Its history up to the end of 1924, as given by Lunatyarsky, is as follows: "Particularly dreadful is the ruin that has befallen all that exceedingly important education before the school stage. Before the war the number of kindergartens and crèches in Russia was 377—that is, practically speaking, such institutions did not exist in Russia. We formed more than 4,000 such establishments and began to give lessons to 213,000 children, but at the present time (the end of 1924) we have only 705 institutions in existence—that is, the whole business has practically fallen through; and it was a matter that attracted attention in other countries (!), of which we were very proud and on which we had expended much energy."

Another idea that was taken up with the same zeal was the plan of including all rural Russia in a network of reading-rooms. Not a village was to be without its reading-room; these rooms, so it was said, were to mean for the villages "windows looking out on to the Soviet world and on to the world in general." Enormous numbers of propaganda posters were distributed, showing dense crowds of peasants walking up to well-built and inviting reading-rooms that were to take the place of the churches as the centres of village life. The reality did not quite correspond to this picture. In most villages that I visited the peasants had not even heard a word of reading-rooms. After much search I at last found a village where a zealous city Communist had managed to get such an institution established. It was a reading-room where all there was to read consisted of a few revolutionary pamphlets, a couple of years of an old illustrated periodical dating from tsaristic times, three or four colporteur's novels and various numbers of the *Peasant's Paper*, this last six months old; its finances did not allow the reading-room to subscribe to a newspaper. The promoter was, however, very proud of his work—the only drawback was that the peasants did not value his efforts and that any visitor to the reading-room was quite exceptional. "In many places," thus Lunatyarsky describes the short and not particularly brilliant history of the movement, "reading-rooms have been established in a sudden access of zeal, but the people did not support them and they have had to be closed. Now these reading-rooms are bursting like soap-bubbles." "To carry out the gigantic work that reading-rooms entail when there are neither books nor papers, and often no building, or, if there is one, then it has no glass in the windows, is beyond our powers"—thus a complaint in *Pravda* in the autumn of 1925 describes the life-conditions of the reading-rooms.

The same picture is presented by another much-vaunted side of the educational policy, viz. the establishment of people's libraries. Here, too, they wallowed in grand plans, sunned themselves in self-admiration, and cast pitying glances on the lagging West. "I remember," Mme. Lenin tells in a public speech, "how struck I was when I saw in France how officials silently handed out books for which the working-men and women gave a formal receipt. Close at hand stood a gendarme—whether to stop any conversation or to guard the library from any attack on the part of the workers I do not know, but the library was a very sad spectacle." We cannot exactly emphasize the fact that Russian public libraries offer a much more edifying picture, for these institutions, whose arrangements are supposed to have reached such a much higher standard than in Western Europe, are, as a matter of fact, at the present moment non-existent. Their accomplishment has not got any farther than good intentions.

* * *

Thus the result achieved in educational work outside the schools is exceedingly insignificant. Moreover, the achievements that, after all, might perhaps be made are completely neutralized by the fact that the younger generation's school education has become more ineffectual than ever before. The public educational machinery has, according to *Izvestia's* statement at the end of last year, become something like a great sieve.

Bolshevist action as regards school-education can only be compared to a first-class pogrom. The Russian school-system lies in dust and ashes. And it is typical of Bolshevism that, when even in this department its destructive torch is being applied, it presents itself as the great light-bringer.

That the school-system inherited from tsardom was utterly worthless was their starting-point. And, indeed, we must acknowledge that it was not much to boast about, either in quantity or quality. It is, however, but just to bear witness that tsardom's particularly weak interest in public education was supplemented, to a very great extent, by civic efforts of different kinds. The network of schools which the Russian *semstvos* (rural councils) gradually brought into being—often in spite of continual conflicts with the authorities—was worthy of the greatest respect. "In tsaristic Russia a great number of localities had their own small educational departments," Lunatyarsky states in an article on the Soviet's school policy. And he records this first achievement: "We succeeded in destroying them."

After this successful beginning, they then proceeded to establish a new school. And the making of plans was again accompanied by veritable orgies of fine phrases. Instead of the bourgeois school which Western education has created and which tsardom, in all its inefficiency, tried to copy—a school where, according to Lunatyarsky, "everything is designed to give the pupils a minimum of knowledge and as much Christianity and biased history as possible, where the children are taught patriotism and attachment to rulers and masters"—instead of this there was to be established the proletariate's own school, "the working-school."

What does the Bolshevist working-school imply? This is how Lunatyarsky himself sets forth the programme.

"The bourgeoisie inherited," he writes, "their school-pedagogics from the scholastic school—a school with books, with oral instruction by teachers and oral answers from the pupils, who sit motionless on their school benches for a certain number of hours, a school with a strictly defined curriculum, a school consisting of memory-grind. We believe this school to be utterly condemned by the science of education. The best bourgeois teachers themselves have already given it up. The working-school's first principle consists in instructing the child by means of work—that is, by living, active processes. When a girl plays with her dolls she is, in this way, fitting herself to be a wife and mother; when a boy plays at soldiers, he is preparing himself to be one later; children always imagine themselves grown-up, always play at being grown-up, and by these games get practice in what they will, later on, have to do in real earnest. Play is a method of self-education. Hitherto, school-teaching has ignored this fact. It says: The child likes to jump about—keep it sitting in one place; the child likes to create for himself, to occupy himself with what he considers interesting—set him down to Latin. We adopt quite another point of view. We say: The whole work of kindergartens of different kinds and of the early school years consists in seeing that the children's play should serve some practical end. When children dance, sing, cut out, model, they are learning; their instructors ought, all the time, so to choose their games that new knowledge is acquired every day; that the children, every day, make some discovery, and that, every day, they may learn one or other little practical accomplishment. And all this must be interesting. In the primary schools the same tendency holds good, but a transition must be made from play to work in the widest meaning of the word; things must be so arranged that the child gains knowledge through games but, at the same time, works as well. Work is, as we know, a happy thing when it does not become over-exertion. The teacher must let the children divide themselves up into several groups, choose their occupations and guide them to the acquirement of certain knowledge. With a definite object in view, he must give the children materials, arranged beforehand, with which to work and to draw conclusions. The most important points in the new method of education are not instruction, not setting lessons, not questioning, but excursions, walks, drawing, modelling, and all possible kinds of work by which the child himself obtains an increase in his experience.

"Let us, for example, take geometry. You say: Look, here is a farm; divide it into separate parts. On one we must have land for the orchard, on another we must put up a building for your animals, etc. Let us do this. And then the children begin to wonder and consider how they can divide the farm properly into the necessary parts. In this way we shall show them, at any rate, the first principles of surveying, for plane geometry is land-surveying. In the same way, when you pass on to teaching stereography, then you and the children stick together cubes, pyramids, spheres. The child himself sticks them together or makes geometrical figures of wood, and so becomes intimately acquainted with them.

"Instead of teaching geography on a ready-made map, you must begin by showing them in nature what, for example, a hill, a river, or a plain really is. With the children's help you make a plateau of clay or a mountain peak. The whole class together must make such a map of their immediate surroundings, and afterwards of some other part of the republic, for instance, the Crimea. This is called instruction by work. No one can forget knowledge acquired in this way. I will take another method, the dramatic. The children should carry out by their own efforts some theatrical representation, say for a school festival. Such a piece of work, performed by united effort, is wonderfully educative. Let us assume that we are taking the barbaric period in the history of civilization. Let us live a week in summer as savages, let us betake ourselves to the forest, light our fire with a flint and prepare our own food. In the same way, let us teach the patriarchal manner of life, enacting it all, and everything will thus become a source of interest.

"We must also pay very great attention to drawing. I am not speaking here of any theoretical demand, nor of instruction in art, but of drawing as a necessary thing, as essential as speaking or writing. A man is illiterate who cannot draw. In America a teacher must be able to draw the whole of his lesson. If he is asked what an insect larva is like, he draws it for you, and every child must try to do the same. A pencil or piece of chalk in a person's hand when he is talking to a large public forms one of his organs of speech. He must be able to illustrate what he says.

"The children have been out a walk—draw the walk. There was a house—draw it. There a tree that you saw for the first time—you come home and make a drawing of it from memory. Make a sketch of the house where you live, how it is arranged, where the bed stands and where the window is—make a plan of it. Such sketches, such illustrations, are of extraordinary importance, for the power of making them is required a million times later on in life. You have given the children the task of organizing something—take a sheet of paper and draw up the plan of organization."

The principles for the Russian working-school, developed in this way, do not indeed strike us as so new as to be terribly revolutionary; most of them have been part of the ordinary equipment of Western European or of American teachers before they are now offered as original rare novelties by Bolshevism. What, however, differentiates the Russian working-school from the Western one is that all the knowledge that is to be implanted in the children in this way must have a definite communistic tendency. When the teacher has a game in the art of reading, he must at the same time play into the little brains the first principles of that political faith which alone can bring salvation. Where we, in our young days, spelt out and put together *The—good—ox—is—too—fat,* these Russian seven-year-olds begin with: *We—are—no—slaves*; and, simultaneously with their letters, they get a little lesson in the supreme power of the proletariate; they spell out: *Le—nin was the peo—ple's friend,* and, at the same time, get an idea of Lenin's life-work. And when a pen is put into the pupil's hand, he gets suitable suggestive treatment into the bargain. In school after school I saw how the children, during their first school-year, had to draw "the types in the village"—the peasant, a thin figure bowed over what is meant to represent a plough; the *kulack,* a fat monstrosity, standing with his arms crossed in his doorway; the priest, also fat and pompous, dragging along a gigantic moneybag filled with the peasants' money.

This, then, is what the Russian working-school looks like in theory: the latest ideas of modern pedagogy in the service of communistic propaganda. Even the programme itself may give us pause. However excellent the principles of the working-schools may be in themselves, yet it is, after all, questionable as to how far they are fitted to form the basis of the school educational system of an entire country. And the coupling together of pedagogy and politics, which makes the former into a lever for the latter, cannot be anything but destructive to real education. The question, however, remains: What has the Russian working-school become in practice?

It may be stated, without hesitation, that the Russian working-school has turned out the most amazing fiasco. The way in which the attempt was made to put the theories into practice made this fiasco inevitable.

Seldom has a great reform been carried out on less

strictly defined lines. A somewhat backward country, before it abolished its old educational system in order to institute an entirely new one, ought to have wished to give the latter a little careful consideration and preparation beforehand. The Government ought, if the ideas were imported from abroad—as was the case here—to have weighed well the question as to which were best suited to the conditions of their own country; they ought to have experimented with suitable types of schools, appointed with scrupulous care a teaching staff with fitting qualifications, and made certain of their power to guide the work in the desired direction; they should have ensured the supply of necessary educational apparatus and materials for the teaching, etc. In Russia they do not allow themselves to be hampered in their reforms by such sickly prudence. Here they first brought in the reform, and all the thousand questions which arose in connection with it had to be solved afterwards and by degrees.

It is not too much to say that at the moment, when they "successfully demolished" the old school and introduced the new, not a hundred persons in Russia had even a faint idea of what the matter really meant. The working-school, this latest idea in educational novelties, caught the public fancy by its name, for it was quite evidently a school that was in keeping with the workers' republic. But how the Russian working-school was to work, what it was to begin and what to end with, what measure of knowledge it was to give and in what order—to all this no one had even given a thought. In the pedagogic programme, setting forth its principles, which was issued at its inception, we look in vain for a single word of explanation; all we find there is a number of vague high-sounding phrases. "The school is to illuminate with the light of science all life around us"—its content is in such lyric style, with nothing definite to take hold of, nothing practical under one's feet. It is significant of how vague the whole matter was from the beginning, since Lunatyarsky's speech, from which the above explanation of the meaning of the working-school is quoted, was delivered to an educational audience during the third year after its introduction. Even three years after the beginning of the school its most elementary principles were still so new and strange to the company, even to those whom the reform most nearly affected, that the Commissary for the People's Education had to get up and explain the matter as simply as though they were hearing for the first time in their lives any mention of the word " working-school."

But even now, after all these years, the Russian working-school remains a somewhat misty creation of the imagination. A confused discussion is still carried on as to how these general principles may best be put into a concrete form, what the school should offer decided in detail, and how this work should be arranged—a discussion which, doubtless, testifies to pedagogic activity worthy of recognition, but which, undeniably, would have been more useful had it preceded rather than followed the school reform. Educational writings, discussing from one point of view or another the fundamental problems which ought to have been solved before the reforms began, are issued in such quantities that, in number, they almost rival the political propaganda. I returned from a visit to the People's Commissariat for Education with as large a load as a man could carry. And at the same time, wild and aimless experimentation is being carried on. Ideas are propounded by the hundred; they are accepted with delight, tried and rejected; teaching schemes are contrived and determined upon, only to be dismissed in a short time; new types of school are hammered out, exist for a little time, then vanish again; various educational ideas and methods are propounded and ordered to be put into practice, only to be shortly abolished. A young man in the People's Commissariat for Education told me about a new type of school that was to be started a few weeks later, intended to provide for millions of children in rural Russia. " There are four of us up there, the sponsors of the whole thing," he declared triumphantly—" four lads, none of us twenty-five years old yet, and we got the business carried through, though the old men opposed it."

If, then, the leading pedagogic circles are not very clear about the real physiognomy of the Russian working-school, it is comprehensible enough that those who are most nearly concerned with putting the reform into practice, namely, the rank and file of the teachers, especially those in the country districts, are completely mystified. Considering the scanty qualifications and the imperfect foundations in general possessed by these men, it is not to be expected that, unaided, they should be competent to extract anything practical from the new principles or get their bearings in the wild confusion of ideas and proposals. And since the teacher's ability to take the chief rôle in the instruction now plays a much greater part than in the old school, these teachers should be able to ask for careful guidance and detailed instructions.

Before the reform was made, the average teachers got nothing of this kind at all. All they received was an order, one fine day, to rearrange the teaching on new lines of which they had never even dreamt before. Afterwards, by degrees, "training" of the teaching staff was begun. But of what a kind!

Here is a description of these training-courses as it is given by the above-mentioned Government investigator, Jakovlev: "Last year (1923) teachers in their hundreds from every gubernia attended the gubernia and district courses. Far the greater number came on foot, since their starvation pay did not allow them to hire a conveyance. There were cases where the teachers walked 80 to 100 versts (55 to 69 miles) to attend the courses. Frequently they received no money allowance, either for travelling or food, and, during the courses, they often had to live on bread and water. And yet they listened, wrote essays and discussed. Wherever the courses did not take the form of an examination grind in the A B C of Communism—for there were many such—the national school-teachers, in these training courses, went through a school of friendly intercourse with the leaders in Party work, received some elementary instruction in educational principles and some instruction touching the Party's rural policy."

It is evident from this quotation what are the tendencies of these training courses. The main object is not the training of the teachers in education, but in politics. Even when the whole thing is not a pure and simple examination grind in the communistic catechism, the new educational teachings play a subordinate part compared with the political coaching. When the poor teachers, driven by a really touching sense of duty, make the most frightful sacrifices to be trained in the new science of education, of which they understand nothing, the opportunity is utilized to force upon them courses in Communism. The authorities are not so particular about the other training.

The same writer gives us more detailed information concerning the programme at such a course: " During the course, every teacher must give five lectures in a month: one on 'The Supreme Power of the People,' a second on 'The Military-Bureaucratic Government under Peter the Great,' a third on 'Imperialism as a New Stage of Capitalism,' a fourth on 'The Theory of Monetary Exchange,' and a fifth on 'The Fight for Naphtha.' And the poor teacher combines Bucharin and Kovalenk—the best-known political handbooks—learns it up, gives his lecture, and gets a fair report. And then he goes back to his village with a head as empty as before."

Even in his daily life at home in the village the teacher is the object of energetic "training," but carried on only in the interest of politics. For that, namely, is what is considered his chief need; it is the teachers' deficiency in the right political faith that constitutes their principal educational weakness. Jakovlev thus describes a visit to a Russian national school-teacher: " In his house there was a great icon cupboard which contained sixteen icons, not to speak of several small ones. On the wall hung the portraits of all kinds of people in authority in the good old times, in various kinds of uniform; there, too, adorned with faded flowers, hung the portraits of the former local landowner and his wife. And the teacher himself was such a slow-going old reactionary brake that, in spite of his sincere desire to work for his school, all his efforts proved fruitless after all." "The teachers are no educationists as far as regards what we require from them; they are no followers of Marx," chimes in Lunatyarsky. To remedy this undeniably fatal deficiency, the teacher is subjected to a continual and ruthless course of training; he, like the State officials, must also accept the views of the Communistic Government, and there's no more to be said about it. The local communistic-cells—or, where these do not exist, the Communistic Youth Societies—exercise, in this respect, a remarkably watchful control over him and put him through never-ending tests. One such favourite method is to compel teachers, whose views are considered suspect, to give anti-religious lectures. Jakovlev tells how the above-mentioned teacher with the icons received orders from the village Komsomol youth to deliver a series of such lectures.

The Russian national school-teacher lives, in this way, under a moral rule of terror which has set a cowed stamp on the whole class. Every national schoolmaster whom I visited met me with a nervousness that was quite painful to see, and anxiously hastened, almost from the first word, to declare his communistic views. The stranger might indeed have some connection with the Soviet Government, and it was best to be on his guard. One I particularly remember. At the very beginning of my visit he was eager to show me how his six-months-old son had learnt, at the question, "Where is our little Uncle Volodja?" to look up at Lenin's portrait on the wall; it was not until we had had a long conversation, in the course of which he noticed that his communistic phrases made no impression on me and that I did not share his small son's enthusiasm for little Uncle Volodja, that it came out, by degrees, how he suffered so much from his position that he would like to put a bullet through his head. And he gave me many intimate pictures of a Russian national schoolmaster's life under the Soviet power. One little detail I will quote. He was religious, but, of course, there could be no question of going to church, and, as a loyal official, he complied with superior orders. Now, however, his old father had just died, and he had applied for permission, on that one occasion, to be present in the church at the funeral. This had been categorically refused.

The activity, then, as regards the national school-teacher's "training" in political directions is especially energetic—unfortunately this helps him but little on the educational side of his work. He has to try to grope his way along as best he may. It is true that circulars, formulas and writings of a thousand kinds rain down upon him, but in these, contradictory and incomprehensibly expressed as they often are, he usually can find neither sense nor reason. I met schoolmasters who, with veritable despair, showed me the piles of orders and counter-orders which they had received and of which, as they candidly declared, they did not understand one word. I met others who, evidently believing all the time that I had some connection with the authorities, delivered with the monotonous repetition of a gramophone their tirades against the rotten bourgeois science of education, but who, in the continued argument, showed that they had only the most hazy, sometimes quite comically contorted, ideas of the new pedagogics.

Now it certainly must not be denied that there are schools where the teachers have succeeded in getting good results from the new methods. The very fact that the educational programme is so indefinite and incompletely thought out as to the standards it sets, enables capable teachers to get a certain freedom of action in carrying it out. Where such do exist—and Soviet-land can show quite a number—the majority, vexatiously enough, an inheritance from the discredited tsaristic schools—they have sometimes succeeded in breathing the spirit of life into the letter of the ostentatious programme and have created a kind of working-school that is both effective and interesting. Such are a number of the educational establishments in and round Moscow and other of the larger cities that are shown to foreign visitors. I can very easily understand that Western educationists, who have seen only these, may return full of ecstasy over the new Russian educational science; I imagine, too, that the Soviet, with material taken from such schools, is able to give such demonstrations in Western Europe of Russian education as grip the imagination of all interested in pedagogics.

But these schools are quite the exception; in the rural districts particularly they do not exist at all. The schools which in these parts are fairly passable are those where the teachers, in their inability to understand the new methods, have stuck to the old. The more they try to create something new, the more grotesque, in a greater or less degree, the whole thing becomes.

Lunatyarsky himself gives some amusing instances of the curious special forms of working-school which have grown up in the field of the new pedagogy.

"Sometimes," he says, "we ask the children what they have learnt during the last year. 'Very little,' they answer; 'there has been no time to learn anything.' 'What have you done, then?' 'We have done everything for ourselves, prepared the food and cleaned the fruit.' And we are told: 'Well, after all, they have learnt to work; their hands were white when they came to school, but now they are not afraid of anything; they will even carry out the refuse.'" And Lunatyarsky patiently explains that their first aim with the working-school is—an excellent thing in itself—to wean the children from their repugnance for the coarsest kinds of physical work. Or here is another choice bit. "I hear," continues Lunatyarsky, "something else as well from such working-school partisans as perhaps do not quite understand underlying principles, viz. that every factory in Russia has to be productive, therefore a school should be so as well. The children can be set to sew or to carpenter, and what they make can be sold in the market or put otherwise into circulation—then the school will by degrees cost nothing." "This shows," he says, "a complete lack of understanding that the business of a school is not to turn out goods, but well-educated human beings."

Lunatyarsky gives a third example as well. "A schoolmistress had at least understood from the working-school principles that 'rhythmical gymnastics are good, modelling and drawing are also good, but much instruction is bad.' And she therefore arranges her school so that the children have only very little work in grammar or arithmetic, but, instead, she lets them spend all their time modelling, drawing, dancing and singing."

Lunatyarsky's examples are not simply curious exceptional cases; the general rule is that the boasted Russian school reform has turned the Russian national school into nothing but a caricature. What it provides at its best is a somewhat worthless hash of unmethodical and chaotic information, served up in a badly stirred communistic sauce; the special dishes added by individual teachers baffle description. I will name only one specimen of the menu. I went to a little Volga village and, to begin with, listened to the venomously communistic teacher as, without hesitation, she recited her lesson about the miserable tsaristic and Western educational methods, and particularly the utterly absurd religious instruction. Then I followed her into the school hall to see the result of really modern and up-to-date teaching. The walls of the little room were covered with ugly old men, the pupils' work during the first school year. These pupils had, it is true, not learnt to read and write—that she granted, but she had trained them in a much more effectual way. In accordance with the new pedagogy's desire that the school should keep in touch as much as possible with practical life, and also with its recommendation of drawing as one of the best means to awaken the children's power of independent work, she had let them draw endless "portraits" of Lenin, Trotsky, Lunatyarsky and the other Bolshevist worthies.

* * *

The introduction of the working-school constitutes, however, but one side of the Soviet's school policy; there is another as well. A kindly critic may, indeed, say that the school-reform just described, after all, bears witness to a certain wakeful educational interest, even though this wakefulness is delirious to the last degree. But, unfortunately, this interest does not extend far enough to see that the Russian school, in material matters, should enjoy something approaching passable conditions. Not only is the school dosed by the Soviet educational science with patent remedies that threaten the patient's life, but the cure is supplemented by putting him on an utter starvation diet.

This is, to begin with, true as concerns the teaching staff. "The national school-teacher in our land is to be put on a higher level than he has ever before reached, or than he reaches or can reach in any bourgeois state of society; this is a truth that needs no proof," Lenin assures us. Hitherto, the proof has consisted in forcing the Russian national schoolmaster to such a proletarian existence as is unparalleled in any other country in the whole world. The Russian teacher's salary is ridiculously poor—do but listen to Lunatyarsky's own statement of the scale of payment. "In the beginning of 1924," he said in a speech at the end of 1925," a national schoolmaster's salary in the towns amounted to 14 roubles 5 kopecks a month (31s. 6d.), in the country to 10 roubles 13 kopecks (22s. 6d.). Some improvement has now taken place, and in 46 gubernias the average salary is 20 roubles 50 kopecks, but this figure does not give any right idea of his position. In the Vologda gubernia 8 roubles, in the Ryazan gubernia 6, in the Pskov gubernia 8, and in the Simbirsk gubernia 9." A few roubles have been added since that date, at least in some places, but even in August, 1925, the national schoolmasters in parts of the Ukraine, for instance, had salaries of about 10 roubles a month. In addition, moreover, these simply farcical salaries are only in exceptional cases paid at the proper time. In a letter from the Ekaterinoslav gubernia published in *Izvestia* in November, 1924, readers were informed that in one of the districts of this gubernia the teachers had not touched any salary whatever since the preceding December. Amongst the scores of schoolmasters with whom I talked in different parts of the country, there was not one who received his pauper pay until three or four months after it was due.

"They Forgot," "What Shall We Do?" "How Will It End?" "Why This?" "A Village Teacher's Cry for Help," "The Starving Teacher," are some of the titles of contributions to the Russian *Teacher's Newspaper*, collected by *Pravda* in the summer of 1925—titles that, without anything more, give a slight idea of the need that hides behind the figures we have given. These irregularly paid pittances, corresponding at their best to 33s.–45s. a month, with less purchasing power than the same sum would have in England, serve, at most, to stave off actual starvation, but do no more. Even the half-starved peasants look upon the schoolmaster and mistress as a kind of beggar proletariate, with whom—according to circumstances—they either sympathize or whom they perhaps pity or, more usually, regard with cold contempt. It is unnecessary to state that this economic need completely prevents these poor creatures from keeping themselves up to the mark intellectually. Such a thing as buying a book is, of course, absolutely out of the question, and any idea of a teacher's being able to take a paper is perfectly absurd. "When we saw the schoolmaster's children more ragged than any others that could be seen in the village, we understood that no great demands could be made on such a national school-teacher," writes Jakovlev, the Government investigator. To expect that these poor men should be able to display any particular power or keen interest is, of course, a palpable injustice, and this is the cause of the decline of the Soviet school in rural Russia, since its prosperity depends almost entirely on the teacher's personal contribution.

That the Russian teaching-staff are paid such starvation wages depends, to a certain degree, not upon the Government's, but upon the local authorities' indifference to education—an indifference that the State, owing to the ineffective administrative mechanism, cannot control. The chief authorities decide, time after time, that the teachers' salaries must be increased, but the local authorities, again and again, oppose such resolutions; it is they who, in the main, have to bear the costs, and when they have no money for such minor objects, well then, they have none. But to a certain degree it also depends upon the fact that even at headquarters there is, in reality, the feeling that it will not do any harm to keep the teaching-staff short. Even if Lunatyarsky laments a little over the indifference shown to the chief workers for education, he, at the same time, refers again and again in his writings and speeches to the fact that the teachers have quite long enough shown themselves averse to Bolshevism and are still far from friendly to Marxian doctrines—this is the crime for which they are paying the penalty. If there was the real wish at headquarters, the money too could certainly be found or means to extract it from recalcitrant local authorities. But now they wish—denial is useless—to starve the teachers into submission.

It is, however, not only the teachers that are put in this way on half-pay; speaking generally, the whole school gets a stepmotherly treatment that does not testify very favourably to Bolshevism's boasted interest in education. When we leave the palace of the People's Commissariat for Education in Moscow and the model schools of the capital and, arriving in the rural districts, are brought face to face with the educational establishments there, we are struck with amazement. The schools that are still working, as a rule, present a perfectly incredible picture. "We soon learnt," Jakovlev reports, "to distinguish the school from other houses in the village. If a house had no window-panes nor doors—then that was a school." All attempts at the maintenance or repair of the rural school-buildings—in a fairly deplorable condition even before—seem, since 1917, to have come to a full stop. With their broken windows, sagging roofs, slanting walls, they give the impression of hopeless decay. There are schools in want of everything. "In winter the schools are not heated and the children sit in their sheepskins," is a statement made by Lunatyarsky a year ago (1925); that the poor teachers have to sit in the unheated schoolrooms without sheepskins he forgot to explain. "There is one lesson-book for four children, and that an old one," Lunatyarsky goes on to say of the schools in a district of Russia. "I came to schools whose whole provision for all their pupils were one or two old worn-out lesson-books. In a little village the master complained of the difficulty he had in teaching geography. The school had, it is true, a couple of old imperfect lesson-books, published respectively in 1903 and 1910, but had nothing at all in the way of a map. Even paper and pens are lacking in some places. A teacher showed me the children's copies. They had been fortunate enough to come upon a few old account-books from some local tsaristic institution, and the pupils now wrote their letters amongst the fading figures. When the paper was all used up in this way, they turned it again and wrote the other way of the paper. Paper of the same kind was used for the drawing-lessons, in which the scanty supply of pencils possessed by the school were used by the pupils, turn and turn about."

This is the picture—if not of all, at any rate of many—of the schools that are still working; in many places the whole movement has been stopped. I visited various villages where the school lay desolate or had been adapted to another purpose; in one village the Soviet's chief representative there had installed his horse in it. Such a use of the school premises does not seem to be uncommon, either. Jakovlev reports that he had come upon a school converted, in the same way, into a stable. In that case it, at any rate, served an ecclesiastical purpose in so far as that it was the sexton who housed his horse there. In part of the country this decay of the schools has long been a general tendency. Lunatyarsky complained about it, but was powerless in the matter. "The local authorities," he explained in the autumn of 1924, "have forbidden the closing of the schools, but as they do not get any money for them from the central Government, simple prohibition is not enough. Some days ago I made a journey into the Tartar republic and saw clearly that conditions in this respect were desperate. And many gubernias are in like case." The extent of the tendency is apparent from the figures he gave. Before the war there were in Russia 62,000 primary schools; during the first revolutionary enthusiasm, when it was a question of striking the whole world with amazement at the Russian proletarian education, their number increased to 67,000, although, as he owns, a number of those newly instituted were certainly only "paper-schools." In 1924 the number was 49,000 A fifth of Russia's pre-revolution schools had gone the way of all flesh. A little later, in the end of last year, it is true that Lunatyarsky found himself in a position to state that the closing of the schools—" that wretched state of affairs "—had been stopped, but any question of the extension of school activity, as he explained, could not be entertained. On the contrary, they must concentrate their efforts on an attempt to maintain the *status quo*. Now a plan has been devised to introduce school-attendance for all in the course of ten years, but the future of this proposal is more than doubtful. Lunatyarsky acknowledges that the cost reaches a figure which has terrified the Council of the People's Commissaries.

The disorganization of the school-teaching brought about by the new pedagogy and the decay of schools as a whole, in consequence of the reduction of the money spent upon them, have together produced a result that still further contributes to reduce the importance of the school in Russian national education. It is, of course, well known that the peasants have always regarded the school with suspicion and have been most unwilling to send their children there. But the school being what it is under Bolshevism, this tendency has become more widespread than ever before. The peasants have lost all confidence in the school, to begin with, on account of its material decay. What sort of learning can it be in a school that is in want of everything, and what sort of teaching from a master in rags? " The schools," says Lunatyarsky, " are so badly equipped that the people do not believe the instruction can be effective." But, to a still greater extent, their animosity to the Bolshevist school is due to their dissatisfaction with the new school methods. " I have seen," says Lunatyarsky, " many schools and talked a great deal with the peasants about the new school. In the great majority of cases the peasants are dissatisfied with it." In Lunatyarsky's opinion the explanation is this: " The peasants feel agitated and say: 'There, you see, the icons have been carried out; the children learn no common sense; God's word has been entirely dismissed, and, instead, the children get singing and dancing all the time. It used to be better. If the children misbehaved, the schoolmistress gave them the stick, but now it has gone so far that if I want to give my boy a slap he says, "'*Pappa*, that is forbidden by the Soviet Government." The children are nothing but a scandal, and we won't be a party to it.' " Lunatyarsky's explanation of the peasant's attitude to the new system of education is most assuredly right to a certain degree. It is true that the peasant's most grievous comment on the Soviet school is that, in his opinion, the discipline is too slack and that knowledge is no longer inculcated by cuffs and blows. What kind of teaching, he asks, can it be without the rod? But this is not all. If the peasant disapproves of the working-school it is, first and foremost, because he has a very decided and very correct feeling that the instruction given in this school, as it now exists in the Russian villages, is a perfect caricature, and that school-attendance gives a terribly small return for the time spent upon it.

Thus, thanks to the peasants' boycott of the Soviet school, school instruction only reaches a minority of the growing generation. An inquiry by the People's Commissariat for Education, of which Lunatyarsky gave a report in the autumn of 1924, showed that, in certain parts of the country, only 20 per cent. of the children got any teaching at all, and that schools intended for 30 to 40 pupils were attended by 10 or 12. "There are," states a report to the Party's Central Committee in the autumn of 1925, "seldom more than 40 per cent. of the children who are taught in the schools." This phenomenon is stigmatized by Lunatyarsky as "a shame and a disgrace, for, in this respect, we are not up to the bourgeois States."

* * *

In the field of higher education, the work of destruction has been almost still more complete. The Russian public school, from an educational no less than from a political point of view, invited still more radical interference than the lower grade school—and the results of this interference have been terrific.

The tsaristic secondary boys' school, like the Western grammar-school of which the Russian was a copy, was still more of an abomination to Bolshevism than the tsaristic primary school. This was particularly true of the classical grammar-schools. It was—so people said—not education that the boys got there, but training in automatic action and a spirit of military discipline. "It was," Lunatyarsky says, "according to bureaucratic ideas, necessary for the State to have officials, and officials did not need real knowledge so much as this formal training." "Every day"—so he describes the classical public school in general—"they grind away at grammar and grammatical exceptions, and their whole attention is directed to the formal side of language. The reason given for this is that formal study is good mental training and that it is beneficial to teach the young what is tedious and of no use to him. It constitutes, so to speak, a special kind of mental gymnastics. So they cram the young brains full of grammar, grammar that they do not need and will forget, but they must submit, listen, and read what is ordered. The little grammar-school boys sit there in their uniforms, not daring to stir; they have to answer the questions put to them, but, otherwise, they are silent the whole time. But they get tasks to learn "from here to there," and they must cram into their heads what is set them; in everything a military submission is expected. They leave school with but a minimum of real knowledge. The educational monstrosity, according to Lunatyarsky, is at the same time, regarded from a political point of view, an abominable bourgeois concern. The very teaching aims chiefly at fostering bourgeois tendencies. "The bourgeoisie in these schools train their children to become capitalists or capitalist helpers, teach them the economy of private ownership, which is nothing but cannibalism, and teach them, too, a perverted attitude to the working-class," etc. The teachers are hidebound bourgeois, "a result of the tendency of the Ministry of Education to fill the teaching apparatus with their faithful adherents. In the classical public school that tsardom left behind, there was, therefore, a teaching-staff full of mental hostility to the Soviet Government." And the pupils in such a public school had been drawn from classes which the Soviet abolished;

the schools were "filled with—from a social point of view—an inferior element, viz. the children of the bourgeoisie, landowners, *intelligentsia* and business men."

How must the proletariate act with regard to this grammar-school?

Lunatyarsky reports: "In the year 1918–19 we obtained information by means of conferences and inquiries as to the feeling prevailing amongst the proletarian youth with reference to the old grammar-schools. These young people expressed, so to speak, an instinctive horror of these schools. They looked upon them as filled with children of a kind quite unfamiliar to them, and half-scornfully rejected any idea of entering and making them their own." Under the influence of this feeling, in some parts of Russia, authorities went the whole length and did away entirely with the higher school education. In the Ukraine, Lunatyarsky declares, "this type of school, thanks to the zeal displayed by the reformers, has been overwhelmed by perfect catastrophe. There, since they considered the second-grade school—this is the official name for the grammar-school, a hateful word they will not utter—diseased, they did away with the higher classes of schools and promised to open technical schools in their stead, but this, under present conditions, at an optimistic calculation, will not be possible for ten years at least.

In the rest of Russia they determined, in spite of the proletarian young people's instinctive horror of the grammar-schools, to let them live and reform them, "not as in the Ukraine, but sensibly." Not only their political character, but the educational principles that formerly dominated them were to be entirely revolutionized.

As regards education, the reform consisted in the substitution of polytechnic instruction in the schools in place of classical, and, at the same time, of the application in them, too, of the working-school principles. Lunatyarsky explains the root ideas as follows:

"We must make it our concern to see that the youth of sixteen years of age leaves school with a certain idea of what industry in general is; that he has a clear idea of the construction of a factory, an industrial undertaking, steam or dynamo engines, of the various kinds of the most important machines and of the methods of obtaining raw materials, etc. And since this second-grade school is also a working-school, such knowledge must be gained by a practical participation in the factory working processes. The pupils are to work, if only for a couple of weeks, in different departments of different factories." "The school," so Lunatyarsky continues his description, "comes to a factory, is divided into groups and distributed amongst the various workshops; in a few days the groups change places. When the children return to school, they sum up their experiences in lectures and discussions, and then the teacher gathers all into one co-ordinated picture. When they already know one factory, the next is easier for them. The teacher points out the similar and dissimilar points and explains their reason. No importance is attached to the children's becoming acquainted with a great number of such industries. It is sufficient for them to be conversant with the most important. It is desirable that boys or girls, when they leave school, should have some idea of the metal industry, the textile and the chemical, and these industries should have been shown to them."

Such a practical study of industry is, therefore, the starting-point. From this they then pass on quite naturally to all possible branches of human knowledge. "In the study of the steam engine we give an account of how it began and what existed before it; every lesson is fruitful to a high degree, thanks to the impression made on the child by his acquaintance with industry. Industry is so rich, the common meeting-ground of chemical and physical questions, of those, too, concerned with hygiene and purely economic and political questions." The school teaches the children to work, but in such a way that by means of this work, industrial work, leavened through and through by new technical science, they acquire a knowledge of the cosmic and social worlds, for all the threads of these worlds are interwoven in the factory

Even in the theoretical study, which in this way follows the practical, the aim is to spur on the pupil to independent work. "The teacher should seldom give information himself; he says to the pupil: 'Look in such-and-such a book, ask the workers themselves, find out the matter for yourself.' In this way, power of independent mental work is developed. Then come the lectures—say, for example, on the Russian textile industry, how and when it began and its present state. The pupils must prepare themselves, collect material; you must direct them to a few clues in books, give them hints whom to ask. And then they must read their essays themselves and afterwards arrange discussion. It must be so contrived that they learn nothing by heart, but find it all out for themselves."

If it is now asked how these principles were put into practice, we find the result—which indeed could have been foretold without any great educational insight—to have been as entire a fiasco as in the primary schools. It has proved practically impossible to arrange such ambulatory instruction classes in factory after factory, impossible even in towns where there are factories, and more impossible in those where no smoke from their tall chimneys is to be seen for tens of miles around. "If we consider how even model schools have solved the problem of bringing the school into touch with industry, we see," Lunatyarsky himself confesses, "that this has been done by arranging excursions to the factories, which are an estimable but very poor substitute for a school of industry." The factory atmosphere has by no means interpenetrated the school on all sides. By the proclamation of the new regulations they have only succeeded in blowing to bits the old school, such as it was, without being able to put anything new and tenable in its place. All the new public-school teaching is still in an experimental stage, where every teacher, in the absence of fixed, well-thought-out directions, gained by experience, tries to find a solution of the new problems in his own way—a way which often follows the strangest paths.

There are, of course, here, too, enough outstanding, successful teachers to inspire credulous Western visitors with naïve admiration for the advances of Russian educational science, even in this direction. But that does not prevent the Russian second-grade school, as a whole, from being in a state of complete disorganization. It has proved beyond the power of most teachers, at any rate up till now, to direct the new emancipated teaching in such a way that all the excursions and discussions of any hasty observations or experiences which the children may have chanced to make in various sides of practical life—often chosen at random—may result in something like a solid foundation of serious knowledge, and, in a land where in general the spirit of work is exceedingly bad, to induce the citizens on the school benches, now that all the "from here to there" tasks, with all the memory-grind, have been abolished, to adapt themselves to creative independent work instead of a comfortable life of lounging idleness, and by such independent work to awake in them a feeling of responsibility that makes all the old type of school discipline superfluous. I heard many parents, who in other respects were favourable to the Soviet, speak of the terrible ignorance that is the result of the modern school teaching and, with still greater horror, complain of the children's frightful tendency to take the law into their own hands, which is fostered in the new schools. The pedagogic reforms to which the new schools owed their foundation have thus, of themselves, fairly thoroughly destroyed the higher-school education in Russia. But this work of destruction has been furthered to an even greater degree by an inroad of another kind that has been made on the higher schools, for the authorities, starting from the fact that the schools hitherto have been repulsive and dangerous bourgeois institutions, have now turned them, above all else, into establishments for forcible training in communistic principles.

The higher school is to be, first and foremost, a school of Bolshevism; with that end in view they make, to begin with, a thorough cramming of communistic principles the most important branch of study in the school. In this regard the modern Russian school, without one backward glance, passes to a stage which in Western Europe we congratulate ourselves on having passed, viz. the stage when all other subjects have to yield to one only—the catechism. The only difference is that the catechism here is called *politgramota*, the political A B C. Otherwise the cases are perfectly parallel; in its arid dogmatism, in its arrangement of question and answer, the Russian catechism is an exact copy of our childhood's scourge; no doubt it is also, like that, to a great degree beyond the child's comprehension and the object of his detestation. This catechism, then, occupies the place of honour; the new educational rule that youth is not to be worried with knowledge that does not interest him is suspended in this particular without the least hesitation. In this grind, no excuse is accepted. No other knowledge whatever can weigh down the scale against poor achievement in *politgramota*. One of my acquaintances was surprised that his son, a little eleven-year-old lad in the first class of the second-grade school, failed in his examination; the boy, who was specially gifted, had, it is true, done brilliantly in other subjects, but did not possess the political knowledge required from a citizen of his age.

There is, doubtless, something worth learning, however, in the Soviet catechism; it might, after all, not be amiss if, with this new subject, other kinds of knowledge were allowed a certainly subordinate but none the less independent educational value. But the fact is that, generally speaking, the whole teaching has for its dominant note the children's political training. In whatever subject instruction is given, the political pointer is constantly in evidence. The small portion served to the young folk under the name of history is nothing but a Communist stew; the geographical excursions on the globe consist principally in finding their bearings in the seat of war of the world-revolution; every subject, no matter how ill adapted it may be for this subject, is larded, salted and flavoured with Bolshevism.

The system also naturally includes extraordinary precautions for protecting the young people from all that might cloud the communistic idea of the universe. It is a self-evident consequence that all religious instruction is forbidden; religious prejudice must be entirely rooted out of the young minds. Attendance at church is prohibited, the pupils are forced, instead, to take part in the anti-religious school entertainments which are celebrated at the time of the Christian festivals—entertainments when the children themselves take part as actors in different kinds of theatrical performances, all making frivolous fun of the Bible and religious ideas.

That all classical studies are abolished follows from what has already been said; poor Latin is considered as a purely anti-revolutionary invention. But even in subjects which, in themselves, cannot be looked upon as inimical to the Soviet State, a keen watch is kept against any bourgeois contraband. I saw with my own eyes the corrections in a Russian grammar for second-grade schools, compiled by a learned Russian expert. It might well be thought that such a lesson-book would not be fitted, in any way, to instil bourgeois poison into young minds. But the wideawake censor had discovered within its covers enough poison to stock an apothecary's shop. The book had undergone a strict scrutiny before they had ventured to put it into the young people's hands, and the red pencil had done real execution amongst the dangerous grammatical examples. "A rich merchant" was crossed out; in the new Russia it is not permissible to be either rich or a merchant. "There are many poor orphans in the world"—the sentence was crossed through, for, on paper, all orphans live comfortable lives in the Soviet's elegant Children's Homes, even though, for the present, we stumble over them in every Russian city street. As an example of a grammatical rule there was given the Russian proverb: "The slower the pace, the farther we get." The proverb was erased as tending to a reactionary attitude in a time characterized by Bolshevism's quick reforming of the world. A quotation from Pushkin, "Thou shalt be emperor of the world," was crossed out as showing plainly a directly anti-revolutionary spirit. As an example of a certain declension the word "paradise" was used. The censor had ruled out the dangerous word and substituted another which had but the one fault that it was useless for the purpose required. In the same way, the censor had crossed out the word "icon," discussed in some particular connection; since, however, its inflexion showed a special interest, the author thought of trying to save it by adding in brackets after the word the explanation: "Representation of an idol." But it is not only by teaching, suitably adapted in this way, that the school fulfils its duty in the Party service, but also in its discipline. The old discipline is, unfortunately enough, done away with, but its place is taken by a political discipline that keeps unfailing watch lest the pupils should be guilty of any political misconduct. Every tendency to heresy is denounced and inquired into. A little twelve-year-old son of my Moscow acquaintances had shirked an anti-religious Easter festival of the kind mentioned above, not in the least from any religious convictions, but simply and solely because he found these constantly repeated entertainments a bore. A few days later the boy did not come home in the evening at the usual time. Hour after hour passed, but the little fellow still did not appear. Towards midnight his father went out to look for him. The boy had been kept in at school. His teachers had felt it necessary to institute a general examination into his attitude to religion and, in connection with this, into his political views. It was not until 2 a.m., after ten hours of almost uninterrupted questioning, that he was set free. He had escaped the threatened expulsion, but had received a sharp caution for bourgeois tendencies.

It is, of course, unquestionably a very peculiar and corrupt form of educational activity that is foisted on to the school in this political supervision. Moreover, it is arranged in a way which would only occur to the new Russian pedagogy. It is not the teachers who exercise the supervision—they need to be supervised themselves—but trustworthy proletarian elements amongst the pupils themselves. A little group of future Communists, still in kilts and shorts, have been put to keep an eye on their school-fellows and to report against them to their respective Party authorities—and against the teachers as well. On the strength of these reports, attacks are made upon those guilty of political misconduct, and expulsion follows—both of pupils and teachers. Class-warfare in the classroom, that is the last word in the Russian science of education.

This method of conscientiously clearing-out the less worthy political element is then supplemented by another, viz. a resolute endeavour to provide the school with the kind of pupil as receptive as possible for communistic training. It is not the best intellects that get the benefit of the higher-school teaching, but such children as, by their parentage, are likely to become the most trustworthy Party workers—in other words, the children of the proletariate. The middle-class, whether children of the old or of the new *nep* bourgeoisie, are to be kept outside. The watchword, according to Lunatyarsky, is to be: "Proletarian young people, conquer the second-grade school!" But, it may be asked, is not one of the first and fundamental principles of the Russian school policy equal educational facilities for all? Well, yes, certainly it is. Lunatyarsky never tires of representing how Soviet Russia, in this respect, has broken with the monopoly of education for one class prevalent in Western Europe now, as it was before in tsaristic Russia. "In old Russia," he assures his hearers, "only one artisan or peasant child compared with 400 bourgeois children had any share in higher education; in Germany, France, England, in all the countries of Europe, there was no possibility of passing on from the primary to the higher school." In opposition to this (but partially true) picture of conditions in Europe, he exhibits the picture of the Russian school-system. "Since," he says, "there are no class distinctions in a socialist society, there cannot, in our land, be any distinction between a public primary school and a higher-grade school. Every boy or girl, no matter what their parentage, goes into the same first class of the one kind of first-grade school and, in the same way, each of them has the same right, after four years in the primary school, to pass on to the four years' course in the second-grade school. We have only one kind of school for all."

But then comes the reservation. In order that this common right to school education may be maintained, Russia requires many more schools. There are, of course, the old grammar-schools which have been made into schools of the second grade; but, thanks to the fact that they were only provided for the bourgeoisie, there are now too few schools of that type. For the present, until new schools can be made, therefore, it is not possible to accept all children, and a selection must be made. On the basis of class distinctions? Indeed, no such thing. "We must take our stand on the principle of passing on the most gifted to the second-grade schools." And now it comes! By passing on the proletarian children and rejecting those of the bourgeoisie we get to the really intellectual élite. "Those often seem the most gifted who are best grounded, who have the best equipped homes and who there have had more opportunity to enlarge their knowledge than peasant and artisan children. Therefore it seems to me very just to give the preference to the children of the working-class. It is a falsehood to say that, in this way, we allow the dullest and least gifted children to pass on to the second-grade school. On the contrary, amongst the mass of peasant and artisan children who, up till now, have not been able to enter the second-grade schools because they were in a worse position than children of the middle-class *intelligentsia*, there are a great number of intelligent children."

This retreat from the solemnly proclaimed principles is, of course, not elegant. But even if Lunatyarsky makes an attempt, such as it is, to save appearances, in other quarters the tactics, inherited from tsardom, of shutting out undesirable elements from education are proclaimed with open and undisguised cynicism. At the beginning of the last autumn term it was officially announced in Leningrad that in the admittance of pupils to the city second-grade schools, class principles would be strictly observed. And, in practice, this is then carried so far that the bourgeois parents, whose children are excluded from school education, are forbidden to make their own arrangements for their instruction. In a town that I visited a number of parents had joined together and set up a private school for their children who were shut out from the public schools. The result was a terrible investigation, the school was broken up, the teachers and some of the initiators sent to prison. Police guard outside the gates of education! Tsardom was not one-third as bad as this!

Forcible feeding with a warped and one-sided education of such pupils as may be considered susceptible to this non-vitalizing food, systematic mental starvation of all others, such is the Soviet Government's school policy for the furtherance of culture.

* * *

The same features that characterize the Bolshevists' policy in their attitude to school education appear again in their attitude to the university. On one side a wild desire for reform, that does not know its own objective and therefore results in a general confused upset; on the other—the only fixed point in this chaos of vague ideas—a persistent endeavour to turn the universities into Communist forcing-grounds.

Just as in the case of school education, the Soviet Government began its university policy with a grand flourish. Tsardom had been a little exclusive as regarded admission into the highest teaching centres—the entrance of the Jews, in particular, had been limited to a certain percentage of the total number of students, a limitation which, we may remark parenthetically, was never strictly observed. Bolshevism opened the university doors to their widest extent.

University education was to be accessible to all. There could be no question of requiring a certain amount of knowledge in a proletarian society, since that would, of course, mean excluding the proletariate who did not possess such knowledge. The Soviet decree stated clearly and concisely that every sixteen-year-old boy or girl had a right to be entered as a student.

For a time there was a veritable invasion by new academic citizens bursting in upon the universities, the majority being people who were not so far above illiteracy. The higher centres of education that already existed proved now totally insufficient, and therefore great numbers of new universities were created. Whether means were forthcoming to maintain them, or teachers to carry them on, was a mere trifle ; the proletariate were asking for a share in higher education and had an unqualified right to get their petition granted. One little out-of-the-way corner after another made a demand for its own university and got it. In a speech a little time back, Pokrovsky, the representative of the university board of management in the People's Commissariat for Education, recounted how application had been made to him respecting a university for Veliky Ustyug, a little backward place of no importance in the north of Russia. "Now everyone knows," he said, "that a university there is a simple farce, but a Party member of supreme authority [Lenin ?] rang me up and said that a university must be provided immediately in Veliky Ustyug. It existed," Pokrovsky concluded, "exactly one year—*how*, we will not say."

All this, of course, was very creditable evidence of the Russian proletariate's interest in education, even if, at the same time, bearing no very flattering testimony as to the amount of the authorities' sound judgment. The university conditions soon, however, became such a caricature that a retreat had to be sounded. "As might be expected, the decree had to be limited," Lunatyarsky declares quite frankly. That decrees are issued which, from the very beginning, may be expected to prove impossible evidently appears to him a most normal occurrence. And thus followed stage number two in this strange university policy: the hospitable host, who just before had invited all and sundry to come up and sit down to the higher educational banquet, now, without more ado, took the guests by the collar and bundled them out-of-doors.

It is this expulsion ceremony—for the moment being carried on with resolute energy—of which they are now as proud as they were but lately of their free-handed generosity. "Now we are going," Pokrovsky declared in his speech just quoted, after describing the rush to the universities during the early years of Bolshevism—"now we are going in the opposite direction and making most drastic reductions in the number of higher centres of education." Another member of the People's Commissariat for Education illustrates, at the same time, the work of reduction by some figures. In the year 1921–2 there were 150 higher centres and 80 so-called practical institutes, which, later, were also in reality high schools. In the school year 1923–4 there were 96 higher centres, and in 1924–5, roughly speaking, 80. In the year 1921–2 there were 190,000 students, now 100,000.

This demolishing of the higher education centres has, in certain directions, assumed the character of a perfect pogrom. It is not only universities in the style of Veliky Ustyug that are sacrificed; to be quite plain, the authorities, by preference, sweep away educational institutions with honourable traditions from the past. Amongst the towns I visited was Kasan. In former times it had been the chief centre of education in rural Russia; its university, dating back more than one hundred years, was, next to the university in the capital, the most important in the land and had numbered amongst its alumni a number of Russia's most prominent men, Leo Tolstoy being one. I went to the venerable old university building to get from the secretary's office the address of a professor, one of Russia's leading scholars in the humanistic faculty. But the young man, in sporting costume, at the head of the office coldly informed me that I had made a mistake. No professor of that name was known there, nor was there any faculty of philology—the very way in which he pronounced the word betrayed his unbounded contempt for the idea—here they had the workers' faculty. Now, since Russian workers' faculties—as we shall show shortly—in spite of their name, are by no means centres of higher education, that simply meant that the university had been done away with; as a matter of fact, the real faculties had been brought to an end, abolished as superfluous. Some of the humanistic professors—but some only—had found a place of retreat as teachers of elementary subjects in the Government so-called pedagogic institute, a teachers' seminary without the least touch of culture about it.

A similar fate has befallen a number of the principal centres of higher education in Russia; they have been closed or more or less radically mutilated. At short intervals the newspapers contain long proscription-lists of universities and high schools which have either been closed or amalgamated with others or changed into schools of a practical nature. A short ukase is issued and institutions that for generations have enjoyed the reputation of learning have ceased to exist. All this clearance, within the sphere of higher education, sometimes goes on at such a desperate speed that not even those most nearly concerned can keep abreast with it.

"Do not ask me about university conditions here in Moscow," was the answer given me by a professor there, formerly one of the principal lecturing-staff at the Moscow university. "Do not ask me—I assure you that I do not know. I must be pleased if from week to week I manage to know where I am employed myself—and pleased so long as I am employed anywhere at all." I was sitting one evening in the end of August last year (1925) at the house of another Moscow professor, when one of his colleagues came up with the *Izvestia* of that day—my host had no means himself to buy a paper—to show him a Government decree. The teaching-centre where my acquaintance was employed, after being moved during recent years from one institution to another—a teaching-centre that acted as a temporary lecture-centre in an out-of-the-way part of the city—had suddenly been closed. My host had employed the summer in working up his autumn lectures; now he was summarily dismissed, and at the beginning of the month, a few days later, he would have no salary to receive.

At the same time as great numbers of teaching-centres are closed in this way, a reduction is made in the pupils of those that are left. I will come back directly to the principles followed in this reduction; here I will only state the fact. It was but lately proclaimed that every young person over sixteen years of age had a right to participate in the higher education, but now the authorities "clear out"—so it is termed—vast numbers of those who are half-way through their education. And so far from appearing troubled and vexed at breaking faith with the young people whom they have enticed into a university career, the authorities act with cold indifference and even with cynical self-satisfaction. "We succeeded," so Lunatyarsky speaks of the great clearing-out of the universities that took place in the spring of 1924—"we succeeded, by strong pressure, in getting rid of 18,000 of the present students in attendance at a university. It cost us," he adds, "a gigantic effort"—what it cost the young people who were turned out into the streets in the very middle of their course he does not mention—"and they are still raising heaven and earth about the matter. We have still not got rid of all kinds of student delegations, various petitions, hysterical attacks, tears and threats." And he holds out the prospect of a continued clearance; the reduction that has taken place is quite too insignificant.

The university policy, as we have followed it so far, appears indeed complete folly—a meddlesome experiment with delicate and sensitive educational machinery. And yet a certain method is to be found in its madness, when university education, which, for a moment, we believe might escape unscathed, is the object of various rough attacks. When universities are closed and faculties abolished, the chief reason is that the authorities wish, in this way, to get rid of such branches of learning as cannot be tolerated or which are considered superfluous from a Communist standpoint; when enormous numbers of university students are cleared out, it is to get rid of elements that are not reliable in respect of Communism. Thus the whole movement is an outcome of the tendency that aims at the formation of a homogeneous communistic system of education; universities are to be changed from learned institutions, provided without exception for all the young people of the nation who desire education, into communistic training-establishments, the monopoly of the proletarian youth. And this is a system deserving of a little closer study.

* * *

If national education, according to Lunatyarsky's assurance, cannot, under any conditions, be considered otherwise than a powerful weapon in the hand of the proletariate for class-warfare, this is not least true of its highest form, university education. Only in so far as education of a scholarly nature follows the proletariate's behest can it be allowed to continue in a proletarian society; only in so far as scholarship enters into the service of the Communist Party will it possess domiciliary rights in the new Russia. And with this criterion before them they hold such a *tjeka* court-martial over the various university chairs and pronounce their sentence.

For some few an immediate sentence of death. This does not only fall on such as are incompatible with Marxian philosophy, as, for example, theological research, which, of course, is unthinkable in an atheistic society. All Russia's theological academies—whose standard of scholarship, we must confess, was certainly always fairly low—have been closed from the first moment of Bolshevist rule. But abolition also falls to the share of a number of chairs of knowledge which, without hesitation, are pronounced to be superfluous; amongst them classical studies. "Once upon a time," thus Lunatyarsky explains his views on the matter, "dead languages, like Latin, were very important. Once upon a time, when all Europe was Catholic, authors wrote all their books in Latin; English, Italians and Poles wrote in Latin. It was the international language at the time. Now Latin has become of no importance." And starting from this profound understanding of what it is that gives the classical languages their educational value, the authorities erase Latin from the university curriculum. Language study in general goes the same way. Modern languages are certainly still retained in the universities, but are studied in an exclusively practical way, and the texts read are, most often, foreign communistic works. But a scientific study of languages—what nonsense! The development of the poor languages follows no Marxian lines and phonetic laws have no agitation value. Even the scientific study of one's own language and language-group is included in the same judgment. In addition to the general idea of the inferiority of the science of language, there is also another motive for their persecution. The reason for that of the Slavonic group is the study of Church Slav, the old South Slav tongue which, ever since it was brought into Russia with the preaching of Christianity, has been, through the centuries, the Russian Church language. And the study of Church Slav cannot possibly be allowed in an atheistic State. The very name is odious, the ancestry of the language compromising; the old texts that exist in this tongue, chiefly Bible translations and legends of the saints, are a definite disqualification. It goes so far that when an inquiry is made in bookshops for purely scientific works in Church Slav it is met with the information that they are forbidden Again and again the chairs in Slav philology at universities are done away with, and, in a short time, they will all be abolished; only the study of present-day Russian and practical studies in other Slav languages will be allowed to continue.

Whilst the authorities in this way give short shrift to a number of less important branches of learning, the lives of others are spared But the life granted them is life in the Communist strait-jacket; they are allowed to exist upon the condition that they accommodate themselves, abjure every claim to the necessary condition for scientific existence—viz. freedom of research—and accept the views that are the only means of salvation in a Communist state of society. Amongst such studies, before all others, belongs what in Russian universities is comprised under the name of "social sciences," viz. history of the State, of literature and of culture, national economy statistics, etc., all the branches whose work, according to Lunatyarsky, is "to describe man's past, to depict his present, and to illuminate his hopes for the future."

The programme for the transformation of these studies in accordance with communistic requirements is openly shown. The starting-point is that no objective research can be found in these branches of knowledge as, up till now, they have been permeated with bourgeois theories. "The bourgeoisie gave no real freedom to sciences," says Lunatyarsky. "Capitalistic bourgeoisie has been forced to pervert science, and increasingly so as time goes on. Before their eyes has arisen the threatening growth of a well-organized enemy, challenged by themselves, viz. the proletariate, who have formed quite another picture of humanity's past, present and future and have had quite other criteria for their judgment. And when bourgeois science was compelled to fight for its life with the young proletarian science, the contest was not only concerned with ideals, but facts themselves were contorted and falsified in the interests of the ruling class and along the whole line, even right up to statistics, the 'non-party' language of figures."

It is such science more or less consciously falsified which has been, up till now, presented as objective. Sometimes the bourgeois scientists really believe that they have been promoting objective truth and have themselves not noticed how they have been entrapped by their class prejudices and have been influenced by them. "When we, the representatives of the young proletarian science, talk first with one, then with another of these grey-haired old men, who have twelve or fifteen published volumes to their credit, they are convinced, when they say that science is objective and that science is free, that they are uttering an entirely universal truth. And when we, the upholders of Marxian doctrines, talk of class-consciousness, of proletarian views regarding the universe, of proletarian scientific development, they think that is a narrow class-tendency, coloured, too, by Party ideas. Where we see white, they see black. They believe that the social science which they sucked in with their mother's milk and afterwards were fed on by professors, who have been authorities for them, is objective, whilst, from our point of view, it is infected down to its very root with thousands of prejudices, all products of bourgeois dominion that distort the very core of social processes and set them forth in a wrong light."

The proletariate now sets up its own science in opposition to this perversion. It demands that science shall, instead, be leavened with Communism: "a proletarian social science has, as its object, the dissemination of a maximum amount of its proletarian and universally human truth." If science thereby becomes biased, it does not matter.

When bourgeois science is biased, that, of course, is repulsive, for this bias is calculated to disseminate their bourgeois lies. But the "forced dissemination of communistic knowledge is a noble bias, which every bit of it promotes human development."

These demands apply, above all, to historical study; it is decreed that the indispensable condition for the continued existence of this study is that it should respect and propagate the Marxian materialistic interpretation of history. Many of Russia's foremost historians have at once been dismissed from the universities on the ground of their unwillingness to use their science in this way for the service of Communism. If the historian, when treating of the history of humanity and humanity's development, cannot turn his teaching into Communist propaganda, his instruction is worthless. A professor of the history of literature gave me instances—they sound, indeed, like imaginary tales, but are none the less facts—of the way in which this principle is upheld even when it leads to pure comedy. He had given notice of a course of lectures in the history of English literature, but had to stop them after he had given the third. The communistic clique amongst his audience—and it is this, as we will show later, which exercises an all-powerful control over a professor's teaching—decreed, namely, that they could not discover any Marxian trend in his treatment of Shakespeare.

From the historical teaching they go farther. Philosophy can only be tolerated if it teaches the favoured Marxian doctrine of "pure" materialism; all idealistic philosophy must be thrown overboard since it is in opposition to this officially protected theory of the universe. The librarian at one of the Russian university libraries described to me what a gigantic upstir there was one day when it was discovered that, on a shelf in the reference library for the use of the students, Kant's works were included as well—it nearly cost the librarian his post.

And so it continues. Natural science is allowed only if it starts from undiluted Darwinism as its one determinative foundation, only if it fulfils its duty in the Communist society. And speaking generally, "there is," Lunatyarsky declares, "no branch of knowledge, no field of science where the teaching cannot be so arranged as to contribute to the formation of a Communist theory of life. We can build a bridge to this from every science." Lunatyarsky gives an example: "Astronomy, it may seem, is an objective science, unconcerned with earthly temporal things and with questions of the day. And yet, if when you give an account of the origin of the worlds, you sow in your hearers' mind the idea of evolution, you are laying a corner-stone for their future socialistic philosophy. And if, at the same time, you expound the history of astronomy and show its evolution with special emphasis on the period in its development when religion in the Middle Ages persecuted, even to the stake, astronomy not dependent on the earth, if you dwell on the history of the martyrs of science in connection with the strife as to the truth of the universe and on the infinity of the laws ruling all in astronomy, in opposition to the narrow and rotten religious philosophies of the universe and life as a whole, then indeed you are dealing mighty blows to religious prejudices and to the representation of the past as something that only inspires feelings of reverence and devotion. I could," he adds, "take any example, any science you like, and show that nothing is easier than to bring it into union with the main stream of social propaganda."

Every science, then, that offers the least qualification for it is to become Bolshevist; this is the requirement, and the result has been the only one possible, viz. the death of scientific study in that branch. The scientific work in a number of the studies, thus degraded into tools for the communistic propaganda, has come to a complete standstill. The fruit produced by them may possibly have some value as a curiosity, but, of course, is entirely worthless from a scientific point of view.

In addition to the scientific teaching which has been completely killed or sterilized, as we have just shown, there are, however, as was pointed out in the introduction to this chapter, others that, in spite of the rich opportunities indicated by Lunatyarsky, cannot be used as Bolshevist propaganda and yet which must be tolerated. And here we come at last to branches of science hitherto left fairly intact. Physics, chemistry, medicine and other so-called applied sciences cannot, with the best will in the world, be given a Bolshevist character, and yet, for practical reasons, they are indispensable; they have had to keep their freedom of action and have even been placed under the State's occasionally very generous protection, and the consequence has been that they can maintain the high traditions of Russian science. This is a bright spot in the dark picture offered elsewhere of Russian scientific life—a bright spot on which the Bolshevists themselves try, with all their might, to concentrate Western eyes, but which should not be allowed to blind them.

These sciences are left in peace—but not entirely. If they themselves are of no value as Bolshevist propaganda, then the academic instruction in them must find a remedy for this grave defect. What cannot be asked from the science itself may, instead, be demanded from the scientists themselves. A professor of medicine, etc., must, by personal influence on his pupils, supplement what is not given in his science. After the great clearance of the universities in 1924, a workman who, as a Party representative, had taken part in the proceeding, gives in a contribution to *Pravda* some of his experiences at that time. He had been one of those appointed to sound the opinions of a number of medical students, and he owns to a little doubt, at first, of his own competence. How could he, an untutored workman, verify their stage of attainment? But he had soon found that there was a place for him to fill. It transpired, namely, that these medical students were sadly ignorant. Questioned as to the duties of a country doctor, they had shown themselves quite unacquainted with the fact that the duty of a Russian rural doctor was in the first place "to diffuse culture," i.e. to be a Bolshevist agitator. And then follows a terrific salvo against the professors of medicine who have neglected, to a pathetic degree, their teaching and who think it is enough to give their pupils instruction in writing prescriptions and in using the knife.

* * *

In order that scientific teaching-centres may become what they ought to be in a proletarian society, viz. training establishments for Communism, two things are necessary :—there must be a teaching-staff who fulfil the demands made upon them by this programme and also such pupils as possess the right qualifications for the assimilation of the new academic instruction. Zealous efforts are being made to provide both these requisites.

As regards, first of all, the metamorphosis of the academic staff in the desired direction, it has not been so easily accomplished. To compel scientists who set a high value on their science to renounce their freedom of research and to manipulate its results, so that they may become presentable from the point of view of those in power; to induce such scholars, who look upon politics in general with indifference and upon Communism with abhorrence, to become, in the first place, communistic agitators, and scientists in the second only—all this has been a matter demanding great exertions and still not successful throughout. "Ninety-five per cent. of our professors are plainly hostile to our views and approach science from a standpoint alien to us," was still Lunatyarsky's complaint but a little time ago. What, then, does the Soviet Government do to achieve its end?

The first and simplest method is, of course, to get rid of the rebellious elements. "People who are cogs in the State educational mechanism, but who do harm to the communistic propaganda or refuse to be at least passive sympathizers, must be removed remorselessly from the State apparatus." This is Lunatyarsky's verdict, formulated clearly and concisely. This method has been extensively applied; eminent scholars have been dismissed in great numbers and have been replaced by Red professors, quite mediocre folk, who have been entirely incompetent, from a scientific point of view, but, instead, so much the more deserving on the political side.

The dismissal of 99 per cent. of the academic staff and the substitution in their stead of so-called "margarine" professors has been a radical measure from which even the Bolshevists have shrunk. In the majority of cases they work away with the existing staff and endeavour, by suitable means, to compel them to submit to the communistic demands. They know they can apply very severe thumbscrews to them ; the loss of their post means, as a rule, death from starvation.

To begin with, the whole teaching of the academic staff is subject to very strict supervision, exercised—it sounds incredible, but is true—by their pupils. And this supervision leaves nothing to be desired in the way of vigilance. The authorities have been perfectly successful in impressing upon the young people that their professors are thoroughgoing old reactionaries who need a tight hand over them. "In most cases," Lunatyarsky reports with satisfaction, "the students are opposed to their teachers, have no confidence in them, and seem to say : 'You lie ; we know you ; you are nothing but a bourgeois agent.'" From this opinion of their teachers the students proceed to action. There exist in the Russian universities so-called departmental committee-meetings in which the students' delegates play first fiddle. These student representatives, who are always chosen from the Communists—heaven save the student who dared to vote for a non-Communist for this office !—administer summary justice to their teachers ; above all, they utter their criticism and dictate their demands in whatever concerns the political side of their teaching : "We are, fellow-citizen professor, very satisfied with your instruction, but in this and this you are in error" ; "your views on this point are behind the times" ; "you say, fellow-citizen, so-and-so, but Lenin has there and there shown that . . .," etc. There is no limit to the ignorant insolence which grey-haired scientists have to put up with from communistic young greenhorns. The little example given above of the literature lecturer's audience, who demanded to be supplied with Shakespeare in a communistic setting, is typical of the nature of this enlightened criticism.

In addition to this control, supervision of the university teachers' political soundness is exercised in many other ways. A spy system of varied nature surrounds them, and, at every step, they know they are watched. Time after time an expression of their opinion as regards the different questions of the day is demanded from them; again and again their names are requested on protests here, expressions of sympathy there—and woe to those who refuse! A variety of supervision in extensive use consists of inquiry-formulæ, which are constantly being sent to them to be answered. "There is a continual police-court examination of us," was the complaint made to me by a university man. And great discretion is requisite in their answers. It is not all who can treat the matter as lightly as a certain professor, one of the small minority whom they dare not touch on account of their position in the international scientific world; for this professor answered the first compulsory question of "How do you regard the Soviet rule?" shortly and to the point: "With amazement!"

In complete harmony with this control of the scientists as a kind of suspicious criminal element is the fact that, at the same time, they are kept in semi-imprisonment, viz. in as complete isolation as possible from Western Europe. The show-exhibitions of Russian science for invited guests from the West are no substitute for other frustrated intercourse. To begin with, they are debarred from the possibility of keeping up with the scientific works in Western Europe, not only because—as I shall show directly—the professors' salaries are such as to preclude all idea of buying any literature, but also because the acceptance even of a book from abroad exposes them to suspicions and annoyances. And still more completely are Russian scientists shut off from the possibility of going to Western Europe themselves. Amongst the many scholars with whom I talked there was not one who did not give utterance to an overpowering and often quite passionate longing to breathe, if only for one day, the pure air of Western intellectual liberty. But it is a longing doomed to remain unsatisfied, not only on economic grounds, but, above all, because the prison doors are inexorably closed upon them. The Russian autocracy in the days of serfdom, which, to a great extent, allowed men of learning in Russia to pine away isolated from Europe, was, in comparison with the Bolshevist rule, generous in foreign passports. There are, it is true, individual scholars to whom, out of regard for the West, the authorities do not dare to refuse permission to travel; there are well-disposed professors who are simply "commandeered" to go to Europe as witnesses of the favoured position of Russian science. It is, of course, a foregone conclusion that representatives of the sciences necessary to the Bolshevists in their social reconstruction have full liberty of movement. But the others the authorities do not let out of their sight. A number of Russians were invited to the great Slav conference of 1924 in Prague; as the economic position of the Russian professors was known, an offer was made to defray all costs of their journey. With difficulty one single Russian Slav succeeded in obtaining permission to go—the rest had to stay quietly at home. The prison régime to which the Russian scientists are condemned brings with it one thing more, viz. prison fare. As a punishment for their unwillingness to allow themselves and their science to be engaged in the service of Communist propaganda, they are put literally on bread and water—their salaries may suffice for that, but scarcely for more. In the summer of 1924 a professor's average salary consisted of 30 to 33 roubles a month—i.e. £3 7s. 6d. to £3 14s. 3d.—a sum which, at any rate in the Russian capitals, did not possess the purchasing power of its English equivalent. And from this sum deductions were made of "voluntary" contributions to the air-force and the like, or it was even paid in part in State Loan bonds which no bank would cash. In addition, the salaries were paid with the greatest inexactitude, sometimes months in arrears; at a rural university that I visited in August the May salaries had just been paid. A small addition to salaries is a monthly dole from *Tsekubu,* the institution for the benefit of science-workers of which I have already spoken. At the distribution of these subsidies, the scientists are divided into five categories; in the first, which gets most, they put professors, designated as those of "universal fame"—in 1924 these received, as a little extra to the universal fame, about 15 roubles (33s. 9d.) a month. The whole business was so scandalous that in the autumn of 1924 Lunatyarsky sounded the alarm; he did so chiefly to meet a number of attacks upon the education budget, which many fellow-citizens considered too high. He stated that a Russian scientist's salary was about one-sixth of its amount before the revolution (that means, if we take into account the purchasing power of the rouble under tsardom and under the Soviet respectively, about one-twelfth) ; he quoted as a concrete example that the director of the Pulkovo observatory, who, in olden days, received 500 roubles a month, now had 40 ; that the head of the public library in Leningrad was now paid 40 roubles a month against his former salary of 600. " There are," he said, " science-lecturers at the Moscow university who have the same pay as a *dvornik* (hostler)." (In the same week as Lunatyarsky gave these figures a Russian professor, who had been told off to Scandinavia, expatiated in the newspapers on the Russian scientists' favourable economic position, and indignantly contradicted the above-quoted figures which I had published in the Press.) The salaries have now also been raised a very little, but quite insufficiently. It is only by undertaking an abnormally increased number of lectures in several teaching-centres—if there happens to be any possibility of getting such lectures—that a professor can manage to earn anything like a decent amount. " With the present salaries," wrote the before-mentioned Professor Pokrovsky in the summer of 1925, " a university teacher in order to exist has to undertake 20 to 30 lectures per week ; I know cases where they have amounted to 40." " I believe many professors would be glad if they knew how to mend shoes," said a speaker at a congress a little time ago. It is quite certain that this occupation is in present-day Russia not only more comfortable but far more remunerative than that of a university lecturer.

However, there is undeniably one way out of this misery, viz. capitulation. If the scientist will pledge himself and his science to Communism, his economic prospects will brighten at once and numbers of possibilities are found to indemnify him. Then he is commissioned—for a substantial honorarium—to write a textbook with a communistic flavour on his own subject ; then he is commandeered to other countries with his pocket-book full of *tchervonetz*; then he is set to carry out some special investigation with generous extra pay; then he becomes, if he has any such ambition, the controller of some technical undertaking, etc.; then all troubles are at an end, and he soon forgets, too, the condition of his non-favoured colleagues. Thus indeed—if we wish to put the best interpretation on everything—we can explain the plainly untrue reports that certain Russian scientists, told off with well-lined purses to the West, leave there concerning the position of colleagues starving at home.

There certainly are some scholars who, in this way, have fallen down to worship Communism. But they are few; the majority prize their science too highly to be willing to barter it away. They accept the material starvation and the moral torture without any active resistance—which in any case would be fruitless. Sometimes with the hope that a science, which certainly is not in the Bolshevists' pay, but, on the other hand, avoids any direct defiance of them, shall one day get a maintenance right in the new Russia, they continue their faithful and honourable service for science until they go under. And go under they do. A certain number, including some of the most eminent, perished as early as the famine years, when they were pitilessly allowed to die of starvation. And those surviving are in the throes of a mortal contest with the blackest misery. What I saw in a few months of the want amongst the ranks of the scientists was revolting. The professor who sat barefooted, dressed in some kind of sacking overall, at his desk in an almost unfurnished little room, the professor who one afternoon, when I was visiting one of his colleagues, looked in to read a letter he had just received but could not make out in his own home, as the electricity had long been cut off, the professor who for want of a light sat working by the glimmer of the street-lamp outside his window—these are some instances out of a vast number.

The iron energy and the devotion to science which upholds them cannot, under such circumstances, prevent the pen from dropping, sooner or later, from their hand. Great numbers of Russian defenders of science die, and die in silence, convinced that no protest, no cry for help, can be of any avail.

"Do not write about science in Russia," said an old professor to me. "After all, it is of no good, and it will only end as it did last time. A great deal had been published about our position abroad—in France, I think—so they brought us a paper to sign, a protest against the shameless slander and an assurance that Russian science and scientists had never enjoyed such a favoured position as now. And what do you expect we should do? We, or at least many of us, signed."

* * *

Such, then, is the Russian policy of education in its relation to the present representatives of Russian science. Its attitude to the younger generation who are to enter on the scientific heritage matches it excellently. The endeavour to create a staff of lecturers without defect from a Communist point of view finds its counterpart in the attempts to train university youth into model and perfectly instructed Communists. If these attempts have not yet quite achieved their purpose, they, at any rate, give promise of great success—a success which, at the same time, implies that where the communistic training goes in, the scientific development goes out.

To begin with, the communistic kneading to which the university young people are subjected is, of course, both thorough and careful. The *politgramota*, the communistic catechism, which even in the schools is an important study, becomes, in the university, the basis of all scholarly training. The catechism course here swells to such dimensions that a student—no matter what his special course, whether mathematics or zoology, medicine or astronomy—has to devote a third of his study time to it. The drawback that a future doctor in his first year can scarcely begin his medical studies, but is set to grind at Marx, and that, later on, he has to divide his time between medicine and Communism, never strikes the authorities. It is to be hoped that his patients may some time come to feel that their doctor, even if he cannot manage much in the way of physical cure, can give them one of Lenin's words to take with them on their last journey.

The strong doses of Communism, forced in this way upon the young people, have, however, not managed to win them for Communism ; as a matter of fact, this forced feeding rather helps to sicken them with it. More effective measures are required, and so the young people are, first and foremost, put under strong communistic pressure. As everywhere else in the social fabric, each group of students has its little clique, belonging to the Communist Party, the communist-cell, which is appointed to exercise control over the non-Communists and which subjects them to a never-slackening treatment. And here, where they are dealing with those who at some time are to form the intellectual élite of society and whose political soundness is of special importance, the dominion exercised by the communistic control is particularly rigorous. The communistic-cell takes the absolute direction in every student organization ; every opposition to it is considered as a political crime of the deepest dye. It commandeers the others to political demonstrations and manifestations, dictates resolutions on questions of the day which the students as a whole are forced to adopt ; these "unanimously adopted" expressions of opinion are afterwards presented in the papers as a pleasing testimony of how the young people close up their ranks round communistic ideas. It decides the students' attitude to the teachers ; from this clique a selection is made of the delegates who, as I have already shown, are the students' spokesmen in their criticism of the professors ; only with the greatest privacy do the non-communistic students sometimes venture to communicate to the professors that they do not all support the criticism of their teaching that the Communists pronounced at the above-mentioned departmental meetings. And at the same time this communistic clique keep a never-ceasing suspicious watch over their fellow-students, organize spying, lay traps, collect gossip and give information, with the result of rustication upon rustication. The least inadvertence is enough—neglect to attend a political demonstration, an incautious word, attendance at church—this last a specially bad case. Sometimes students are expelled simply because suspected of bourgeois ideas. No one gives a single thought to the effect this system must have on the students and their studies. It is impossible to imagine—so many students assured me—the atmosphere in which the Russian students live—a poisoned air which not only contributes to moral destruction by directly fostering hypocrisy and desire for unlawful power, but which also has a very lowering effect on the studies. How can they get any desire or peace for work in the midst of all this persecution?

The weeding-out of politically undesirable elements which goes on constantly in this way has, however, proved insufficient for its object, viz. the creation of a homogeneous Communist class of university students. And so arrangements were made for a greater haul. I have already mentioned the great "clearing-out" of the universities in the spring of 1924, when, at one stroke, 18,000 men and women students were excluded. The official reason given for this measure was the overcrowding of the universities, the excessive inrush on the path of scholarship—which, as I have shown, had been brought about by the action of the authorities themselves in opening the universities without reservation to all aspirants, illiterates included. But it was also due to the fact that it got rid of all those who were not successful enough in their studies. As regards foreign countries, there has been a consistent effort to maintain the fiction that the clearance was made on this principle, and reports that other points of view were the decisive factors of the weeding-out have been indignantly denied. As a matter of fact, however—in the discussion in their own country they not only own to it but do so with pride—the aim was to make a clean sweep of political heresy. And as it was essential in a measure dealing with such a number to have a simple method of procedure, it consisted practically of excluding all those who, *à priori*, might be suspected of anti-Bolshevist tendencies, i.e. the bourgeois element. It was not those who were weak in mental achievement, not the idle and indifferent, who were cleared out, but those who suffered under a much graver accusation, viz. that they had allowed themselves to be born of bourgeois parents. "Artisans and peasants were only excluded when they displayed absolute incompetence to take advantage of the education offered," said Professor Pokrovsky some time after the clearance. There was, as a rule, no way of escape for the sons and daughters of priests, teachers, business men, etc.; it is asserted—but I would not guarantee the truth of the statement—that even the children of proletarian mothers who had bourgeois fathers sometimes had to go as well. Ability and progress, however brilliant, were not taken into account at all; several professors told me that at first they had interceded for their best pupils, but they soon desisted, as this only made their chances worse.

Thus, thousands of young men and women who, through years of sacrifice and deprivation, had fought their way along the path of study, were remorselessly sent packing; all that could be achieved by an indignation extending far beyond the universities was that students who were just going in for their final examination received, as an act of grace, permission to take it. But otherwise there was no redress. I heard numbers of heartrending descriptions of the feeling of panic prevalent in the universities during the clearing-out process and of the ghastly despair of those young people in the early twenties who suddenly stood in the streets without the possibility of continuing the career to which they had devoted themselves and without training for any other occupation. A number of them found no other way out of their desperate straits than that of suicide. Of the various cases with which I came into touch I will name one only. At a scientific institution where I was buying some books the head called my attention to a porter who was packing my parcel. The young man had been one of his university's most successful students and had showed every promise of becoming a really eminent orientalist. His father, long since dead, had, however, been a Government official, although in a very humble capacity, and for that reason his son, when he had been one year at his studies, was "cleared out." His scientific career was irrevocably closed; the institution in question, out of pure charity, had saved him from being starved to death by giving him work as a porter at a wage of 15 roubles (33s. 9d.) a month. This is how a Government, really interested in culture, looks after its best intellects.

In conjunction with this clearing-out of weeds, the authorities look round for means to keep them away in future from the well-mown lawns of the Bolshevist centres of learning. Entrance to the universities is made increasingly difficult for all those whose communistic receptivity is doubtful, for children of the old, as well as for those of the new (*nep*) bourgeoisie. If, by way of exception, they do get in, they are required—in a country where it was said all payment for instruction was abolished—to pay heavy fees; in other cases the privilege is granted in such a way as to make it purely illusive. One of my acquaintances in Moscow had got a daughter accepted for the university, but the Bolshevist sense of humour had decreed that her training should be given at the Irkutsk university. Instead, the universities are "to be," according to Lunatyarsky's phrase, "conquered by the proletariate." The method, originally applied, of transferring the workers straight from their machines to the benches of the university lecture-halls has now proved the most utter failure, and, on the other hand, the authorities do not consider they have time to wait until the second-grade schools have become entirely proletarian, thus affording an opportunity of recruiting the universities with students of a good quality socially—so they are called—for in such case, according to Lunatyarsky, there would be many years to wait before the universities became entirely proletarian. As a result of those two facts the authorities have hit upon a special method of "filling the university's veins with new blood," and have created the so-called "workers'-faculties."

These workers'-faculties are for the moment the apple of their eye for the Russian educational authorities; their pride in them knows no bounds, and they like them to be considered as something peculiar to Russia. As a matter of fact, the fine name covers nothing but very ordinary continuation schools for people with an elementary school education, who are prepared at a quick rate in them for entrance into the universities; the only new feature is that these student factories are made a kind of integral part of the universities themselves and—in many cases—take possession of the university buildings, whilst the real university courses have to find a temporary roof elsewhere. Different proletarian bodies—Party organizations, trade unions, etc.—" commandeer " suitable members for these workers'-faculties. In their choice the most important qualifications, according to Lunatyarsky, are to be " a desire for knowledge and a revolutionary disposition " ; if they have some educational grounding in addition, that will be no drawback, but, he adds, in this respect too strict a line must not be drawn nor entrance be refused to people who " beyond elementary reading have no knowledge at all." Those thus selected get for three years—during which the Government gives them free board and lodging —a certain amount of the most necessary school teaching, plus, of course, a substantial portion of *politgramota*. And when the course is completed, those who have gone through it are considered fit for study at the university, and its doors, shut for others, open automatically for them. Is it necessary to say that this new method of recruiting for the universities—which, according to *Pravda*, is the only completely reliable method of bringing young artisans and peasants into places of higher education—has given the most deplorable results and brought about an unheard-of lowering of the university standard? Even if the " commandeering " to the workers'-faculties chose the most gifted, and did not, instead, as now often happens, give the preference to those most fluent in their political creed —it goes so far that Lunatyarsky himself is compelled to state that sometimes elements are admitted who, instead of learning in a normal way, " constitute a somewhat vociferous company, who consider the workers'-faculties as an arena for political debates rather than a school "—and even if the work in these faculties was arranged on a rational basis—which is, to a great degree, prevented by the one-sided political bias of the studies—granted these two conditions, it is yet self-evident that three years' study on the top of a national-school education—defective in itself and long since forgotten—cannot give sufficient foundation for university mental work. The pupils of the workers'-faculties have, of course, after entering the universities, proved quite incompetent to follow any higher teaching. What the outcome was when they first began to try to profit by it was described by Lunatyarsky a few years ago. They had at the university met with "a wall of methods which they did not understand," and their overstrain had become "colossal, finding vent in a terrible number of cases of neurasthenia and nervous hysteria, which often ended in flight from it all, as well as in every kind of pessimism and disillusion."

And the result was—not that the workers'-faculties were rearranged so that their pupils left them better equipped, but that the university teachers received orders to come down to their level. "The professors must," so Lunatyarsky decreed, "revise their courses and adapt themselves to their audience." Thus the Russian universities have become—except when incubators for Red agitators—technical schools of the simplest kind. And Lunatyarsky celebrates the banishment of scholarship from the universities as a magnificent educational advance. It means, according to him, that they have succeeded in arranging university teaching on a better basis; it means that the professors have not been taken by their gowns and dragged down from their desks, as learned men believe, but that they have been raised out of their scholasticism to a height where they become the real teachers of the youth of the nation. And he warns the universities against opposing their promotion—if they kick against it, then an end will be put to the whole university system. "The university must understand that the workers'-faculties give to it food for the morrow, that they are its future and its hopeful sons who alone have a claim upon it. If the university desires to live it must give special facilities to its workers'-faculty."

Thus, with the exception of a few special departments, we meet the same picture everywhere throughout the

Russian educational system. Culture and scholarship are crushed by the bear's paws of Bolshevism. Sometimes these paws are lifted to deal an immediate death-blow to the victim, sometimes to clasp him to its friendly bosom—in neither case does the victim escape with his life.